OUTDOOR ADVENTURE ACTIVITIES
FOR SCHOOL
AND RECREATION PROGRAMS

Paul W. Darst
Arizona State University
George P. Armstrong

WAVELAND
PRESS, INC.
Prospect Heights, Illinois

For information about this book, write or call:

Waveland Press, Inc.
P.O. Box 400
Prospect Heights, Illinois 60070
(708) 634-0081

To Char, Linda, Heather, and Seth

contents

preface

Adventurous, outdoor, wilderness activities, which provide participants with a degree of risk, challenge, and excitement, are a timely subject in today's literature. Numerous studies point out the tremendous growth of backpacking, white-water canoeing, rock climbing, ice climbing, cycling, cross-country ski touring, and other types of adventurous recreation. Millions of men, women, and children of all ages are becoming increasingly involved with these pursuits through travel, exploration, and concern for natural environments. More and more, people are turning to programs that offer instruction and participation in outdoor adventure activities.

Unfortunately, there appears to be a general misunderstanding about the purposes as well as the benefits of adventure-oriented activities. Much of what has been written suggests a negative reaction, due to a reluctance to assume legal responsibility for those involved. The number of participants, however, continues to increase rapidly, and this growth emphasizes the need for high-quality educational programs to develop competent leaders and provide instructional services for future participants. Administrators must be convinced that proper instruction and emphasis on safety can reduce the danger of these activities by teaching people how to make intelligent and sensible judgments about the risks involved.

Educational and recreational programs that include physical education, outdoor recreation, and outdoor education need to improve their offerings with more opportunities for adventure activities. New programs can provide the knowledge, physical skills, and attitudes that are necessary for thorough enjoyment of these pursuits, to teach people how to achieve control in high-risk situations, and, ideally, to instill a healthy respect for the natural environment. Colleges and universities need to expand their facilities to develop leaders in these areas and provide in-service education programs for people who are currently in the field. Better-qualified leaders should be able to win the confidence of administrators and program directors and convince them of the increased need for expanded recreational programs.

The addition of outdoor adventure activities to recreation programs and physical education curriculums should prove to be a most significant development in this century. These pursuits will open new opportunities for people to find enjoyable movement activities that can be practiced for a lifetime during their increased leisure time. Many people have become disenchanted with traditional sports and recreation programs. They seek alternative activities that provide a challenge, a degree of risk, or an element of danger. Schools, agencies, and recreation centers must take a leadership role in providing quality services that emphasize education and safety.

This book is intended to provide a comprehensive model for implementing outdoor adventure activities within the offerings of a school or recreation program. Strong emphasis is placed on the development of program leaders. We have supplied current information on the most popular activities, with attention to equipment needs, travel arrangements, safety procedures, physical skills, teaching strategies, liability problems, and environmental concerns. Currently, no book covers all of these areas as comprehensively.

Although this book is not intended to make people expert in particular activities, it should lay the foundation for a positive attitude toward adventure activities and convince teachers and administrators that the time is right for expanding recreational services. We recommend that some of these activities be introduced at the school or recreation complex and then be further developed with overnight trips into wilderness areas. A slow, cautious approach will assure administrators that the proper instruction, training, scheduling, transporting, and emergency procedures are followed.

The first five chapters—including an introduction to outdoor adventure activities and discussions of administration in program development, program planning for outdoor expeditions, areas for outdoor adventure activities, and measurement and evaluation of outdoor adventure programs—are developed on a sound theoretical base, and many practical examples are given. Our aim has been to assist current and future leaders in planning programs in outdoor recreation, outdoor education, and physical education. The information on policies and procedures has been field tested through a nationally known program in wilderness pursuits and experiential education, Project U.S.E. M.A.I.N.E. (Urban Suburban Environments—Mountainous Activities in New England).

Chapter 6 and Chapter 7 focus on initiative games and ropes courses, which are introductory or lead-up activities. Students should be exposed to them early in the program. Initiative activities require a minimum of special equipment and can be conducted at the school or recreation center. We also recommend that a ropes course be built at the school or recreation center, where it can be used constantly as a lead-up activity to other pursuits, such as rock climbing.

Chapters 8 through 16 focus on various popular medium- and high-risk outdoor activities. Summaries of the latest equipment, physical skills, safety procedures, and environmental concerns are given in each of these chapters. This information is designed to serve as a guide for beginning participants and teachers. It should also be useful for improving the skills of people at all levels of ability. These chapters present teaching activities and techniques that have been successful in developing outdoor skills. Safety procedures are emphasized: the element of risk should always be limited to controlled situations. Backpacking and rock climbing, the two major outdoor adventure activities, are presented first, with discussions of several general topics that are important to other chapters, namely, safety, survival, first aid, and poisonous plants.

The final chapter includes predictions of the future of outdoor adventure activities and looks at some of the variables affecting the growth and development of programs in this area.

This book should be especially useful to teachers and students in physical education, recreation, and outdoor education, at all levels; to program directors and administrators of park and recreation programs; to directors and administrators of commercial programs that focus on wilderness activities; and to anyone who enjoys outdoor adventure activities.

Paul W. Darst
George P. Armstrong

one

introduction to outdoor adventure activities

GROWTH AND DEVELOPMENT

More and more people are becoming involved in adventurous, high-risk activities that make use of our earth's natural environments. The increase in the number of participants has been overwhelming during the past few years, and growth and development are likely to continue. The popularity of this type of activity presents a challenge to programs that provide outdoor recreational services.

In the late 1940s representatives from many concerned educational organizations and agencies recommended to the general educational community that camping should be a part of every child's educational experience.[1] Since then outdoor or wilderness pursuits have had an ever-growing popularity. During the last 10 years, there has been a nationwide increase in camping, hiking, canoeing, kayaking, bicycling, rock climbing, rappelling, snowshoeing, cross-country skiing, orienteering, and spelunking. Evidence of this popularity is reflected in a flock of new periodicals: *Backpacker, Back Country, Wilderness Camping, Cycling, Mountain, Nordic World, Bike World, Down River, Camping Journal, Outdoor Life, Summit, Off Belay*, and *Backpacking Journal*.

Popular and professional literature has included numerous articles about this growth. Paul Jensen points out that

> until a couple of decades ago the only people who went camping were Boy Scouts, nature buffs, prospectors, archaeologists and other odd-balls. This year tens of millions of Americans will seek the far vista without benefit of lodge or motel. Nowadays a camping vehicle may be a 30 foot luxury house trailer or a bulging backpack. Or a motor home, or van camper, converted truck or school bus, pickup truck with camper body, tent-trailer, four-wheel drive or conventional station wagon, family sedan, horse, outboard motorboat, canoe, john boat, trail bike, bicycle or sneakered feet.[2]

Diana R. Dunn and John M. Gulbis give some current statistics on the rising number of people seeking activities that make use of ice, snow, water, land, or air.

> Parachuting, mountain climbing, motorcycling, auto racing, white water canoeing, hotdogging, snowmobiling and spelunking are among the risk recreation activities which have gained

---

[1]Charles A. Bucher, *Foundations of Physical Education,* 7th ed. (St. Louis: C. V. Mosby Company, 1975), p. 480.
[2]Paul Jensen, "Ah, Wilderness! (and How to Camp Out in It)," *Saturday Review*, 24 March 1973, p. 72.

devotees during recent years. Between 1971 and 1973, the Southern California Hang Glider Association increased from 25 to 4,000 members; by 1975, an estimated 25,000 hang gliding buffs nationwide were trusting their fates to the whims of cliff and mountainside air currents. Hot air balloon pilots registered by the Balloon Federation of America increased tenfold between 1970 and 1974. Licensed glider pilots, according to the Soaring Society of America, increased from 5,000 to 15,000 between 1963 and 1973.[3]

The popularity of rock climbing has also increased. The National Park Service and the National Forest Service predicted an increase of 500 to 1,000 percent in the number of ascents of Mt. Whitney in California between 1963 and 1970.[4] The number of climbers in the Grand Teton Mountains doubled between 1963 and 1972.[5] Royal Robbins, the noted rock climber, has pointed out dramatic changes brought about by the rapidly increasing number of climbers.[6] He stresses the need to develop nondestructive methods of climbing because of the popularity of the sport; the use of chocks for protection from falls must be encouraged so that the development of clean climbing techniques can become fashionable. Brady and Skjemstad point out that the number of cross-country skiers rose from 2,000 to 500,000 between 1964 and 1974.[7] Statistics from national parks show a boom in hiking and backpacking in all parts of the country. The number of miles of bikepaths throughout the United States has grown tremendously because more and more people are cycling.

Other evidence of this enthusiasm for outdoor adventure can be cited:

1. The deterioration of many natural environments has stimulated a growing number of school systems to initiate programs in outdoor education to promote wise use of these environments.
2. Specialized books that focus on these activities are appearing more frequently.
3. Sales of equipment for these activities have boomed, and new stores are opening to meet consumer demand.
4. An increasing number of schools and programs offer experiences in wilderness activities, for example, Outward Bound programs and Project U.S.E. M.A.I.N.E.
5. More outdoor camping and recreational facilities are available.
6. Companies are beginning to recognize the value of these pursuits for their employees; for example, some corporations send their executives to Outward Bound Schools.

Colleges and universities are becoming sensitive to their students' interests in these activities.[8] Joseph Oxendine's survey of trends in basic college physical education programs shows an increase in emphasis on outdoor adventure activities.[9] The University of Utah and Ohio State University, for example, offer courses that include wilderness expeditions overnight, on weekends, and during vacation periods. Ohio State University has developed a special Program of Outdoor Pursuits (POP), which combines wilderness activities such as hiking, scuba diving, and rock climbing with studies such as biology, geology, and forestry.

According to Daryl Siedentop, college physical education programs usually set curricular trends, on the basis of the interests of society.[10] The current emphasis on outdoor adventure activities has

[3] Diana R. Dunn and John M. Gulbis, "The Risk Revolution," *Parks and Recreation* 11 (August 1976):12.
[4] "Trash Plagues Mount Whitney as Climbers Go into Thousands," *New York Times,* 30 August 1970, p. 19.
[5] J. Wilford, "Mountain Climbers Litter Trail," *New York Times,* 5 September 1972, p. 34.
[6] Royal Robbins, *Advanced Rockcraft* (Glendale, Calif.: La Siesta Press, 1973), p. 7.
[7] M. Brady and L. Skjemstad, *Ski Cross-Country* (New York: Dial Press, 1974), p. 206.
[8] Peter Donnelly, "Vertigo in America: A Social Comment," *Quest* 27 (Winter 1977):106.
[9] Joseph B. Oxendine, "Status of General Instruction Programs of Physical Education in Four-Year Colleges and Universities: 1971-72," *JOHPER* 43 (March 1972):26.
[10] Daryl Siedentop, *Physical Education: Introductory Analysis,* 2nd ed. (Dubuque, Iowa: William C. Brown Company, 1976), pp. 39-40.

slowly filtered down into secondary and elementary school programs. However, many of these programs have been limited by lack of knowledge, experience, funds, equipment, or organization.

Dunn and Gulbis point out the need for public recreation and park agencies to provide exciting high-risk activities.[11] Too many urban recreation programs could be described as dull, especially for teenagers and young adults. "New recreation forms characterized by controllable danger, excitement, or thrills are increasingly being propelled from the status of rare offerings to mainstream programs."[12]

OUTDOOR ADVENTURE ACTIVITIES DEFINED AND CLASSIFIED

Outdoor adventure activities include all pursuits that provide an inherently meaningful human experience that relates directly to a particular outdoor environment—air, wind, water, hills, mountains, rocks, woods, streams, rivers, lakes, ice, snow, or caves. A certain amount of risk, adventure, exploration, and travel are involved, depending on the skills of the participants and the nature of the activity. Competition between individuals and groups is minimal, whereas competition between people and their environment is the norm. The emphasis is not on winning or losing, but rather on facing the challenges of a natural environment.

Backpacking, camping, rock climbing, map and compass reading, cycling, skin diving, canoeing, sailing, cross-country skiing, and snowshoeing are outdoor adventure activities.

Common outdoor activities such as golf, tennis, softball, soccer, and football are not included in this category, because they do not emphasize a special outdoor environment or its exploration. In addition, they focus primarily on competition between people, while adventure activities center on cooperation among people.

It should be pointed out that most outdoor adventure activities can be adapted or arranged to provide competition between people or groups. For example, cycling, cross-country skiing, or orienteering can be organized in the form of races. It is certainly worthwhile to participate in this type of recreation for competitive purposes. We feel, however, that competition is not a necessary ingredient for rewarding experiences in natural environments.

Part of our philosophy is that people should be provided with the mental and physical skills that enable them to experience success in using, exploring, and preserving the outdoors. The challenges of nature demand a special kind of knowledge, strength, endurance, and flexibility. The magnitude of the challenge, however, should be proportional to the skill of individual participants, so that each one can experience a degree of success. Today's youth have not had sufficient opportunities for exciting encounters in the outdoors, especially in wilderness areas. A properly administered outdoor adventure is a means of introducing children to the immense rewards of being in and a part of nature.

In light of the proliferation and increasing appeal of risk-taking activities in physical education and recreational programs, it is useful to classify outdoor adventure activities according to the degree of risk involved:

1. Low-risk outdoor adventure activities.
2. Medium-risk outdoor adventure activities.
3. High-risk outdoor adventure activities.

Some activities can fall into different categories under different circumstances. For example, outdoor photography, while usually considered a low-risk activity, would certainly be considered a high-risk

---

[11] Dunn and Gulbis, pp. 12-17.
[12] *Ibid.*, p. 17.

activity if it took place on the side of El Capitan in Yosemite National Park. Some activities can be pursued by various means so that they involve different levels of risk. For example, boating might be a high-risk or a low-risk activity according to the type of boating—rowboating, speedboating, or sailboating.

Low-Risk Outdoor Adventure Activities

Low-risk outdoor adventure activities provide very little danger to the individual's life, and there is little fear of bodily harm. People who are attracted to these activities do not have to confront the immediate possibility of physical danger. Hazards in these activities arise primarily from unusual accidents. Activities in this category include fishing, picnicking, nature walks, outdoor photography, cycling, family camping, orienteering, and ice-skating.

Medium-Risk Outdoor Adventure Activities

Medium-risk outdoor adventure activities provide a moderate amount of danger to the individual's life. Since a certain degree of risk is inherent in them, it is important for participants to become aware of potential dangers. They should be able to react positively to increasing degrees of physical danger. Activities in this category include backpacking, swimming, horseback riding, cross-country skiing, snowshoeing, hunting, and boating.

High-Risk Outdoor Adventure Activities

High-risk outdoor adventure activities involve a high degree of danger and pose a potential threat to the individual's safety and well-being. Participants should be well trained. They must possess the appropriate physical skills, and they must be well prepared to react quickly and positively to high degrees of physical danger. Activities included in this category are sky diving, hang-gliding, rock climbing, mountaineering, winter camping, spelunking, white-water canoeing, tubing, kayaking, sailing, scuba diving, and skin diving.

Figure 1-1. A low-risk outdoor adventure activity: Cycling (Photo courtesy of Schwinn Bicycle Company, Chicago)

Figure 1-2. A high-risk outdoor adventure activity: Skin diving
(Photo courtesy of Zodiac of North America, Inc., Annapolis, Maryland)

Figure 1-3. A high-risk outdoor adventure activity: Kayaking (Photo courtesy
of OLD TOWN Canoe Company, Old Town, Maine)

The primary focus of this book is on outdoor adventure activities in the second and third categories of medium- and high-risk activities. Special attention is also devoted to the design of a practical model for organizing, administrating, and directing a program in outdoor adventure pursuits. Specific medium- and high-risk activities that lend themselves nicely to inclusion in public, private, and commercial recreation programs, as well as in public school programs, are discussed in some detail. Many of these activities are compatible with one another because of their common use of a similar environment. For example, many people combine backpacking with mountaineering, cross-country skiing with winter camping, or rock climbing with spelunking. Expeditions can be planned, organized, and administered to include several wilderness activities or pursuits.

REASONS FOR THE GROWTH IN POPULARITY

A variety of educational and recreational benefits can be derived from outdoor adventure activities, and several reasons can be given to account for their growing popularity. Different people have different motives for participation, but three major reasons seem consistently evident: personal, economic, and social-psychological reasons. Administrators and teachers should be aware of these motives when they formulate the objectives of an outdoor program.

Personal Reasons

1. *New experience.* Many feel that these activities provide a new and exciting experience filled with adventure, fun, and challenge. It adds a "kick" to their lives and gives them a chance to try something they have never tried before.
2. *High-risk experience.* Some individuals feel that participation in stressful activities that border on the physically dangerous will help them overcome fear, gain self-confidence, obtain emotional stability, and successfully cope with additional responsibility. They feel that they learn to become independent and self-sufficient and that they gain a new outlook on life. Although these claims may seem difficult to prove, they are real for many people.
3. *Escape.* A number of people see in these activities an escape from the complexities of modern life, a release from the tensions and anxieties of living in a sometimes dehumanized society. They say that they are able to relax, change their usual pace, slow down, and experience freedom.
4. *Success* Many people who have a limited athletic ability seem to experience a certain amount of instant success in these activities. For example, people are able to reach the top of a small mountain in a relatively short period of time without having to rely heavily on any particular physical skill. Thus, for a small investment of time and a limited amount of physical effort, a person can achieve a highly personal sense of accomplishment.
5. *Knowledge.* Some people point out that they participate in outdoor activities to learn more about the earth's environment as well as more about themselves. These activities enable people to reflect upon their goals, strengths, weaknesses, and limitations. Many feel that this knowledge enhances their feelings of personal worth.
6. *Physical fitness.* Many people participate in wilderness activities because they promote cardio-vascular-respiratory fitness. Many of these activities are quite vigorous and provide opportunities to burn calories, lose weight, and increase strength, endurance, and flexibility. This relates specifically to the nature and intensity of the participant and the activity.

Economic Reasons

1. *Minimal financial investment.* Some people claim that one of the prime reasons for their participation in these activities is the small—in some cases, negligible—financial investment required to

pursue them. For example, camping, after the initial outlay for equipment, is much less expensive than motel touring. This economic benefit is attractive to many wilderness pursuits enthusiasts and provides them with an inexpensive opportunity for an interesting and pleasant vacation.

Social-Psychological Reasons

1. *Socializing.* Because of the social opportunities presented by these activities, many people see them as a chance to meet others who have similar interests.
2. *Unity.* Some people feel that outdoor adventure activities promote unity and cohesiveness among people and groups. Families feel that these activities give them something to do together without the usual interruptions and distractions of their normal lives, for example, television, telephones, Little League, and various social responsibilities.
3. *Cooperation and trust.* Still other people feel that they participate because of the development of cooperation, trust, and appreciation of other people. A number of outdoor clubs have been developed to promote better relationships and trust among different racial groups. In addition, some feel that these activities also promote compassion and respect for others.
4. *Nature and the outdoors.* Many people feel a need to interact with or get close to the earth's environment. The reasons for this particular yearning are varied. Some point to an aesthetic appreciation for nature, while others mention the vanishing wilderness theme. This type of interaction is closely related to the personal-knowledge area discussed earlier.

OUTDOOR RECREATION, OUTDOOR EDUCATION, AND PHYSICAL EDUCATION

Some programs in outdoor recreation, outdoor education, and physical education are currently making use of outdoor adventure activities. Many programs, however, especially in physical education, have not started to teach them. Curricular change is a slow process in any area of education.

We shall briefly examine outdoor recreation, outdoor education, and physical education and clarify the goals or objectives of each particular area. It is important that teachers or administrators be able to justify the inclusion of these various activities, regardless of the particular program in which they are involved. Our justification will follow the discussion of these three areas.

Outdoor Recreation

Outdoor recreation is just one aspect of a total recreation and leisure-time program that is rapidly gaining popularity. Recreational activities are entered into voluntarily by an individual during his or her leisure time. The primary reason for participation is intrinsic enjoyment and satisfaction rather than extrinsic or material rewards. Leisure time is usually referred to as the time in which one is free from the necessities of work and the demands of one's biology (eating and sleeping, for example). Currently, Americans have more leisure time than ever. The leisure industry and leisure education are growing at a tremendous pace.

Outdoor recreation has been classified by Clayne R. Jensen as a resource-oriented form of recreation that involves the use of natural resources.[13] Resource-oriented recreation includes camping, backpacking, hunting, fishing, and similar pursuits, as opposed to activity-oriented forms of recreation such as performing or witnessing a performance in drama, art, music, or athletics. Jensen

---

[13] Clayne R. Jensen, *Outdoor Recreation in America—Trends, Problems, and Opportunities* (Minneapolis: Burgess Publishing Company, 1977), p. 8.

defines outdoor recreation as "those recreational activities which occur in an outdoor (natural) environment and which relate directly to that environment."[14]

The objectives of outdoor recreation programs obviously vary from person to person. Jensen, however, provides a nearly comprehensive list:

1. Develop appreciation for nature.
2. Enhance individual satisfaction and enjoyment.
3. Provide opportunity for diversion and relaxation.
4. Develop physiological fitness.
5. Develop desirable behavioral patterns.[15]

A brief review of outdoor recreation literature, definitions, objectives, and curriculum content makes it clear that outdoor recreation leaders are beginning to include medium- and high-risk wilderness activities in their programs. Continued growth and expansion of these activities into such programs seems to be in store for the near future.

Outdoor Education

Outdoor education is an approach to teaching and learning that utilizes the outdoors in an informal, sometimes interdisciplinary manner. Most authorities agree that this approach usually results in more meaningful and longer-lasting learning than formal, highly structured learning situations. Outdoor education is not a subject in itself and therefore has no specific subject matter of its own. Content from a variety of curriculum areas can be enhanced by being taught in the outdoors. Outdoor education makes use of the entire outdoor environment as a teaching and learning laboratory.

Learning activities in the domain of outdoor education can involve a variety of disciplines, such as science, social science, industrial arts, homemaking, art, crafts, music, health, physical education, recreation, and language arts. Although the objectives of outdoor education vary widely, they usually include several of the following:

1. Gain knowledge and appreciation of the earth's environments.
2. Develop socially through cooperative planning and living.
3. Develop knowlege, skills, and attitudes for outdoor leisure-time activities.
4. Learn more about the strengths and weaknesses of oneself and others.
5. Learn more about the concepts of responsibility, self-reliance, compassion, and leadership.

Outdoor educators try to develop all of their students' senses. They utilize learning methods of guided discovery and problem solving that involve sight, sound, touch, taste, and smell. Teachers attempt to make learning an enjoyable process so that students will want to continue it on their own time.

Physical Education

Physical education programs are concerned with the development of students' knowledge, attitudes, and motor skills in relation to competitive and expressive motor activities. Because they contribute to the general goals of education, one of which is the physical well-being of the individual,

---

[14]*Ibid.*
[15]*Ibid*, pp. 9-10.

these programs are an established part of the total school curriculum at all levels of education, from kindergarten through college. Most authorities in this area claim the following four goals of physical education programs:

1. The development of physical fitness.
2. The development of motor abilities.
3. The development of mental abilities.
4. The development of social-emotional abilities.

Throughout the years that physical education has existed in school programs, authorities have generally debated its goals. For example, some have stressed physical fitness, and others have emphasized the social-emotional goals. In general, most physical educators favor a balance of emphasis on all four objectives.

The curriculum content of physical education programs has varied according to the nature of the objectives being emphasized. Emphasis on exercise, gymnastics, marching, team sports, and games has been standard throughout the history of these programs. In recent years, the development of the Lifetime Sports Education Project of the American Alliance for Health, Physical Education, and Recreation has stimulated interest in lifetime or "carryover" activities, such as golf, tennis, bowling, and badminton. These are now included in most secondary physical education programs.

The newest and perhaps most important innovation in the curriculum of physical education programs is the addition of outdoor adventure activities. Daryl Siedentop points out that their inclusion in physical education programs is an important and healthy trend.[16] It is important for teachers in this area to start work on the development of programs that include these activities.

JUSTIFICATION OF MEDIUM- AND HIGH-RISK OUTDOOR ADVENTURE ACTIVITIES

We strongly believe that medium- and high-risk outdoor adventure activities can be a valuable addition to all types of public, private, and commercial recreation agencies as well as to outdoor education and physical education programs at all levels. Outdoor adventure pursuits are self-justifying in any program of this nature because, as a form of play, they provide people with inherently meaningful experiences; they can be considered as an end in themselves and do not have to be justified as a means to some particular end. Rock climbing, for example, does not have to be justified on the basis that it develops strength or teamwork. Daryl Siedentop makes a similar point:

> The suggestion being made here is that it is time in physical education to take play seriously; to examine the depth and breadth of the implications of play; to recognize it as the source of the meaning that we all have found in the activities of physical education; and to develop theories and programs which are consistent with the overriding human importance of an active play life. If other desirable changes occur as a result of participation in physical education, then so much the better, but we must first recognize if abilities to play are not increased but instead are held still, stunted, or thwarted, then it is unlikely that desirable changes will occur; and that most importantly, students will be left on their own to discover this important source of meaning.[17]

Many programs that include medium- and high-risk outdoor adventure activities have tried to justify themselves on the basis of a variety of benefits that supposedly occur from participation in the

---

[16] Siedentop, p. 180.
[17] *Ibid.*, p. 260.

activities and that are supposed to continue into later life: compassion, emotional security, self-confidence, cooperation, self-discovery, and human renewal. Leslie Tompkins summarizes the discussion nicely:

> Many feel that adventure programs supply the needed emotional outlets for youth who might otherwise pursue less desirable activities—that the need for self-testing can be satisfied through adventure programs. Other goals sought by adventure programs are improvement in self-awareness, self-concept, judgment, decision-making, compassion, increased potential, sensory perception, awareness of and respect for individual differences, endurance, cardiovascular improvement, strength, coordination, skills and an understanding of and cooperation with nature—a motivation to learn—in and out of the formal educational system.[18]

Although we know from experience that many of these benefits do occur from participation in outdoor adventure activities, these activities do not have to be justified on the basis of the self-improvements that may or may not occur in every case. They can be justified simply on the grounds that they are a form of play and that active play is just as important as any other part of a person's life.

In our own previous experiences in medium- and high-risk wilderness pursuits, we have experienced some feelings that are hard to define, observe, or measure—namely, compassion, cooperation, and confidence. Experiencing these feelings is important to us and to others. However, we are not sure whether these feelings have general application to other aspects of our lives. It also appears that some of our students have experienced similar feelings, but it would be very difficult to prove that such feelings arise in all participants and that they carry over into later life. Future research will undoubtedly provide some answers. In the meantime, specific definitions and observational tools need to be developed to get a sensible grasp on these behaviors.

DEVELOPMENT OF OUTDOOR ADVENTURE PROGRAMS IN VARIOUS ENVIRONMENTS

Now that a case has been built for the inclusion of selected outdoor adventure activities in various educational, commercial, and social recreation agencies, we can discuss some of the particular developments that are taking place in these areas. Programs are currently in action in all kinds of environments and at all levels of education, from elementary schools through universities. In future chapters we will discuss specific programs and describe the methods and procedures for working these programs into the daily curriculum or schedule. The following environments lend themselves to the development of outdoor adventure programs.

1. *Elementary, junior high, and senior high schools.* Many physical education programs are beginning to add adventure pursuits to their curriculums. These activities can be adapted for interdisciplinary studies and outdoor education. Some schools are even giving students release time from other classes in order to take part in outdoor expeditions.
2. *Community recreation departments.* Many recreational departments are increasing their outdoor adventure offerings. Some have added new outdoor activities, such as ropes courses and backpacking expeditions. The coordination of school and community outdoor programs offers a variety of exciting possibilities; facilities and equipment could be used jointly to improve the quality and the quantity of these programs.

---

[18] Leslie Tompkins, "As We See It," *A Newsletter for the Exchange of Ideas on Outdoor Education* 20 (Fall/Winter, 1976-77):1.

3. *Colleges and universities.* Many physical education and recreation programs at the college level have responded to the increased demands for outdoor adventure activities. Interdisciplinary programs have been developed, for example, at Ohio State University. Intramural programs have encouraged the development of outing clubs or groups for such activities, for example, at East Stroudsburg State College and Arizona State University.

4. *Scouting groups.* Groups such as the Cub Scouts, Boy Scouts, Brownies, and Girl Scouts have utilized some types of outdoor activities and programs since their origin. These activities have usually been in the low- and medium-risk categories. These groups, under the appropriate supervision, could now begin to offer additional activities in the medium- and high-risk categories.

5. *Business groups.* Some large corporations are expanding their recreational programs to include outdoor adventure activities. For example, Goodyear Tire and Rubber Company, in Akron, Ohio, offers recreational alternatives for camping, boating, fishing, scuba diving, hunting, and skiing. Such programs offer an excellent opportunity for people to develop and practice their outdoor activity skills. The possibility for expansion of these programs is unlimited and could include climbing clubs, scuba clubs, or backpacking clubs.

6. *YMCA and YWCA groups.* These programs provide another environment in which people can begin to develop outdoor adventure programs.

7. *Summer camps.* Thousands of summer camps are now available for youths of all ages. Since the primary purpose of a summer camp is to expose children to outdoor recreation, the administrative opportunities for further expansion are always present.

8. *Exceptional groups.* There appears to be some value in outdoor activities and programs for students and adults who might benefit from the opportunity for comraderie and development of self-esteem, such as alcoholics, drug addicts, delinquents, inner city youths, and handicapped individuals. Project U.S.E. M.A.I.N.E. has conducted several outdoor programs with prisoners and delinquent students in Maine. Although additional research is needed in this area to confirm the claims, there is evidence that outdoor programs can have a positive impact on the behavior of these people.

9. *Interest groups.* People with common interests in outdoor activities have begun to organize, develop, and administrate these types of programs. For example, a club in the Pittsburgh area has developed to organize weekend trips for pursuing outdoor activities.

QUESTIONS FOR REVIEW AND DISCUSSION

1. What evidence is there that outdoor adventure activities are becoming very popular in the United States?
2. How can you justify including outdoor adventure activities in the curriculum of your program?
3. Can these activities be considered a part of a physical education program? Why?
4. What is the difference between outdoor recreation, outdoor education, and physical education?
5. What types of environments lend themselves to the inclusion of outdoor activities?
6. What types of activities fall into the category of low risk? Medium risk? High risk?
7. Why should you be cautious about the claims (e.g., concerning benefits and advantages) that you make for your outdoor program?

REFERENCES

Books

Brady, M., and L. Skjemstad. *Ski Cross-Country.* New York: Dial Press, 1974.
Bucher, Charles A. *Foundations of Physical Education.* 7th ed. St. Louis: C. V. Mosby Company, 1975.

Jensen, Clayne R. *Outdoor Recreation in America—Trends, Problems and Opportunities.* Minneapolis: Burgess Publishing Company, 1977.

Robbins, Royal. *Advanced Rockcraft.* Glendale, Calif.: La Siesta Press, 1973.

Siedentop, Daryl. *Physical Education: Introductory Analysis.* 2nd ed. Dubuque, Iowa: William C. Brown Company, 1976.

Articles

Donnelly, Peter. "Vertigo in America: A Social Comment." *Quest* 27 (Winter 1977):106.

Dunn, Diana R., and John M. Gulbis. "The Risk Revolution." *Parks and Recreation* 11 (August 1976):12.

Jensen, Paul, "Ah, Wilderness! (and How to Camp Out in It)." *Saturday Review,* 24 March 1973, p. 72.

Oxendine, Joseph B. "Status of General Instruction Programs of Physical Education in Four-Year Colleges and Universities: 1971-72." *JOHPER* 43 (March 1972):26.

Tompkins, Leslie. "As We See It." *A Newsletter for the Exchange of Ideas on Outdoor Education* 20 (Fall/Winter 1976-77):1.

"Trash Plagues Mount Whitney as Climbers Go into Thousands." *New York Times,* 30 August 1970, p. 19.

Wilford, J. "Mountain Climbers Litter Trail." *New York Times,* 5 September 1972, p. 34.

SUGGESTED READINGS

Meier, J. "Leisure Today." *JOPER* 49 (April 1978):25-56.

Naylor, Jay H. "Honey and Milk Toast." *JOPER* 46 (September 1975):18-19.

Smith, Charles D., and Samuel Prather. "Group Problem Solving." *JOPER* 46 (September 1975): 20-21.

two

administration
in program development

What is administration? To explore this question, an analogy can be drawn between a cyclist taking a cycling trip and an administrator coordinating a program. The cycle might represent the frame of a program, and within this frame are the resources (brakes, tires, gears, etc.) that enable the cycle to move forward. The cyclist is the person who provides the leadership over the machine. In taking a trip, the cyclist first determines the goals of the trip, and when the goals have been determined and the resources put into action, the cyclist begins the trip. Once under way, the cyclist stops at certain checkpoints to evaluate the trip and make changes. These changes are based upon the cyclist's knowledge, experience, and goals—as well as the condition of the cycle.

Similarly, effective administration starts with a person who provides leadership to ensure that the goals of the program are achieved. Human and material resources, such as staff, budget, equipment, and facilities, are used by the administrator to run an efficient program. As the administrator moves through the program, a process of goal and resource evaluation should take place in order to keep the program—or machine—in good working order.

QUALITIES OF AN ADMINISTRATOR

In all organizations, such as schools, businesses, private agencies, or projects, one person is perched at the top. Generally chosen because of an ability to guide and influence others, as well as a knowledge of and background in administrative leadership, a good administrator has a special understanding of the ways and means by which to utilize human and material resources effectively. Intelligent leadership, generally speaking, hinges on the ability to make sensible and reasonable judgments about daily and institutional matters, and to ensure that the organization is not unmoored from its position of authority.

Kimball Wiles describes effective leadership roles as *supporting, assisting,* and *sharing* rather than directing.[1] Nondirective roles can establish an environment between administrators and resources that provide a better learning climate for student growth.

Ordway Tead, a noted authority on administration, has described the qualities of an effective administrator.

My own studies of personal <u>administrative</u> qualities stress the need for (1) sheer physical and nervous vitality and drive, (2) ability to think logically, rationally, with problem solving

---

[1] Kimball Wiles, *Supervision for Better Schools,* 3rd ed. (Englewood Cliffs, N.J.: Prentice-Hall, 1967), p. 10.

skill that "gets to the point" more quickly than average, (3) willingness to take the burdens of responsibility for executive decisions and actions, (4) ability to get along with people in a sincerely friendly affable, yet firm way, and (5) ability to communicate by voice or pen in an effective way.

Residually, then, we are talking about intellectual capacity which is in some considerable measure innate and unlearned, about high level purposiveness, about a contagious enthusiasm for goals and methods needed to achieve them, about a total glamour of personal drive that catches others up into group loyalty, persistent striving and gratification simultaneously obtained for personal desires and for those satisfactions realized through one's creative institutional contributions.[2]

In outdoor activities programs many people must take on leadership roles. Those who teach or conduct field experiences must be strong leaders. Paul Petzoldt, a foremost authority on outdoor leadership, recommends the following as essential leadership qualities: (1) knowledge of outdoors, (2) technical ability, (3) actual field experience, (4) sound judgment, (5) pragmatic realism about oneself and one's abilities, and (6) the ability to gain trust and respect from the group.[3] Of these, sound judgment must be considered the most important quality. Many years of technical experience in remote wilderness areas does not qualify a leader if he or she is going to place the students in situations that they are incapable of controlling. Poor judgment of weather conditions, students' skills, and physical conditioning can result in tragedy for participants in a wilderness experience.[4] For example, reports compiled by the American Alpine Club since 1951 indicate that a large number of mountaineering accidents can be attributed to lack of judgment or attempts by climbers to exceed their abilities.

PROGRAM DEVELOPMENT

The information presented in this section can be applied to any school program, community organization, or agency desiring to develop a program in outdoor wilderness activities. Formal outdoor activity programs are not limited to school systems. The ideal program would encompass both school and community and would serve not only students but all the people within the community.

A primary concern of an administrator in developing a program is the determination of goals based upon the interests of the students. As was pointed out in Chapter 1, our focus is on medium- and high-risk outdoor activities. There is an ever-increasing amount of evidence reflecting interest and popularity of these categories among all groups. It should also be noted that, although this text focuses on medium- and high-risk activities, the authors in no way intend to suggest that outdoor activity programs should only include activities in these categories. A complete program would include activities in all the categories: low, medium, and high.

In determining interests of the people whom the program is going to serve, an administrator could begin with interest surveys, which can be prepared and administered with a minimal amount of effort. In the survey, activities in all risk categories should be listed (see Table 2-1). Student interest could also be assessed on the basis of feedback from community programs and agencies, such as Boy Scouts, Girl Scouts, youth programs, summer playgrounds, and parks and recreation depart-

[2]Ordway Tead, *Administration: Its Purpose and Performance* (New York: Harper and Row, 1959), p. 59.
[3]Paul Petzoldt, *The Wilderness Handbook* (New York: W. W. Norton and Company, 1974), p. 146.
[4]*Ibid.,* pp. 146-147.

Table 2.1. Interest Survey in Outdoor Activities

Name_____ Sex _____ Age _____

Directions: Circle the number that indicates your level of interest in each activity.

1. High level of interest—can teach.
2. Moderate level of interest—would like more instruction.
3. Interested in learning basic skills.

Backpacking	1 2 3
Camp craft	1 2 3
Camping	1 2 3
Canoeing	1 2 3
Cross-country skiing	1 2 3
Cycling	1 2 3
Foraging for edible foods	1 2 3
Kayaking	1 2 3
Mountaineering	1 2 3
Orienteering (use of maps and compass)	1 2 3
Outdoor photography	1 2 3
Rock climbing	1 2 3
Sailing	1 2 3
Scuba diving	1 2 3
Skiing	1 2 3
Skin diving	1 2 3
Snowshoeing	1 2 3
Spelunking (caving)	1 2 3
Winter backpacking	1 2 3
Winter camping	1 2 3
Other _____	1 2 3

ments. Persons administering these programs have many opportunities to view students and other members of the community in different roles and play situations.

After the evaluation of student interest has been completed, an administrator may find it helpful to determine the answers to the following questions:

1. What expectations are reasonable and achievable for a program effort of this type?
2. What community resources, site locations, etc., are needed to begin and to maintain the effort?
3. What are the most appropriate activities?
4. What new skills may be needed and how to develop them?
5. What evaluative criteria are needed to provide guideposts for direction and changes of direction?
6. What evaluation criteria and future steps can be identified to provide linkage and reinforcement?

In resolving the answer to these questions, it is advisable to set up a planning committee. This committee should consist of various decision makers in the community, such as parents, students, faculty, administration, and community leaders.

Program models can also serve as valuable tools for developing and administering a program. Tools of this nature enable the administrator to keep in constant touch with all the facets of the program and also allow for a process by which systematic modifications can be made without total disruption of other program areas.

Figure 2-1 shows a model for designing and managing programs. The elements of the model are defined as follows:

1. *Program.* All resources, activities, goals, evaluation, and follow-up process.
2. *Ingressions.* All human and material resources needed to develop the activities. From an administrative point of view, ingressions include: (1) staff, (2) staff development, (3) staff evaluation, (4) budget, (5) equipment, (6) transportation, (7) food, (8) liability, (9) insurance, (10) public relations, and (11) construction and maintenance of facilities.
3. *Activities.* The specific pursuits designed to achieve the program goals, such as rock climbing, cycling, and canoeing.
4. *Intentions.* Formal program goals and objectives.
5. *Evaluations.* The process by which the ingressions, activities, and intentions are measured to determine the effectiveness of the program. Administrators should be concerned with evaluating: (1) staff, (2) activities, and (3) program in relationship to objectives (see Chapter 5).
6. *Follow-up.* Implementing the evaluation process.

The remainder of this chapter deals with ingressions in program development that particularly concern administrators: staff development and evaluation, budget and finance, insurance and liability, and public relations.

STAFF DEVELOPMENT AND EVALUATION

Staff training might be the most important aspect of developing an outdoor or wilderness pursuits program. In most instances, it is necessary to provide staff members and potential staff members with some type of additional training. It is a very rare situation where a ready-made staff is available. Sometimes, it becomes quite important to recruit people who are interested and enthusiastic about outdoor activities. A successful program must be able to draw upon people with a variety of competencies. A program will only be as good as its staff members. Therefore, staff development should be one of the highest priorities of the program.

The recruitment of paraprofessionals can add expertise to a full-time staff. Within a school system or community there may be interested teachers or citizens who have gained specialized skills through hobbies or professional interests which could be used to teach and lead students on actual field experiences.

The training of staff can be divided into three components: (1) content area, (2) teaching strategies or methods, and (3) evaluation.

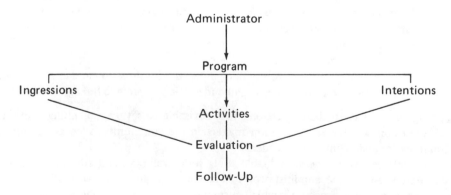

Figure 2-1. Example of a program model

Content Area

A very important area of development for staff members is the content area of outdoor activities. Content area should focus on physical skills or competencies as well as knowledge skills or competencies. Staff members should be encouraged to become certified in all areas that provide and require certification. For example, all staff members should be certified in Red Cross First Aid, American Heart Association Cardio-Pulmonary Resuscitation, Red Cross Life Saving, and Red Cross Water Safety Instructor. In addition, some staff members should obtain scuba diving certifications. These can be obtained from YMCAs, the Professional Association of Diving Instructors (PADI), or the National Association of Underwater Instructors (NAVI). In addition, other staff members should obtain certification in Red Cross Small Craft and Boating Usage.

At this time, our country does not offer certification in mountaineering. Some countries, however, such as Great Britain, do require certification, granted by the Mountain Leadership Training Board (MLTS), for rock climbing teachers in their school systems. As the popularity of mountaineering increases, there may be the need for such certification in this country. One of the greatest problems faced by outdoor enthusiasts is the untrained or inexperienced person, who is not only a danger to himself or herself but also a danger to the environment.

In the selection of staff members, certification cards should not be the only criteria. Staff members should be chosen on the basis of their skill, knowledge, desire to work effectively with students, and, most important, judgment. Remember, there is no way to certify judgment.

The new awareness of outdoor activities has created a variety of ways for developing and maintaining competencies. Most colleges and universities are offering courses, workshops, conferences, or expeditions that focus on giving people experiences in outdoor activities. There is a growing number of nationwide groups devoted to these types of activities, for example, YMCA and community recreation groups, Outward Bound, National Outdoor Leadership School, Project USE, and Project U.S.E. M.A.I.N.E. Many stores that sell outdoor equipment are also providing instructional classes in various types of activities. All of these experiences are possibilities for developing the content area of a new staff for an outdoor pursuits program. There is also a great deal of professional and popular literature on the subject available (see references in the activities chapters).

Teaching Strategies or Methods

It is our contention that all staff members should develop skills or competencies in the areas of interpersonal relations, behavioral management, planning for instruction, and execution of instruction. Development of skills in these areas should help to improve the teaching-learning environment for outdoor activities.

Interpersonal Relations. The interpersonal relations between a staff member and a student are important to learning. They play a prime role in creating the environmental atmosphere for various outdoor activities. Since students tend to repeat experiences that are pleasing to them, teachers should try to make the environment as pleasant and as enriching as possible. Developing pleasant interpersonal relations does not always just happen—staff members have to plan for it to happen. Staff members should try to focus their attention on things that their students are doing well, for example, following directions, being attentive, or helping others. This attention will increase the probability that students will repeat those particular behaviors. Staff members often pay the most attention to things that students are doing wrong and consequently create a negative learning situation for students.

Behavioral Management. The techniques of behavioral management that a staff member uses will indirectly influence the amount of learning that occurs in an outdoor environment. If students spend a great amount of time getting organized and changing activities, then obviously they are spending less time participating and practicing outdoor activity skills. Therefore, staff members must know how to devise and implement behavioral management strategies that motivate students to organize and change activities as quickly as possible, so that more time is available for instruction and participation. There are a variety of ways by which staff members can arrange contingencies in order to save time. For example, certain activities can be used to reinforce other activities, and free time can be made contingent upon completion of certain tasks. Staff members should try to reinforce only the behaviors that he or she feels are important in a given situation. In situations where certain kinds of behavior are highly undesirable, an instructor can use a form of conditioning called *extinction,* whereby the undesirable behavior is simply not recognized—and therefore not reinforced.

Planning for Instruction. The preparation for an effective teaching-learning environment is obviously of extreme importance in outdoor activities programs. Effective planning means efficient use of all available expedition time and ensures that students will be given sufficient time to practice and improve their outdoor skills. Chapter 3 will cover specific ways of planning and organization.

Execution of Instruction. Execution of instruction means different things to different people, according to their background, attitudes, and feelings. There are, however, several instructional skills that seem to have a positive effect on the learning that occurs in a given situation. It is important for staff members to become knowledgeable about these skills and to utilize them in the appropriate situations. Siedentop suggests the following:

1. Communicate as much information as possible without wasting time.
2. Decrease time spent in presentations while increasing the clarity of presentation.
3. Plan demonstrations to accomplish specific goals.
4. Increase feedback focus on what students are doing right.
5. Avoid redundant feedback.
6. Increase the information and value content of feedback.
7. Direct feedback to the target of instruction.
8. Stay with one student long enough to make feedback effective.
9. Use group-directed feedback and modeling.
10. Provide positive feedback to encourage questioning, commenting, and expression of ideas.
11. Carefully plan and execute the use of questioning as a teaching method.
12. Utilize students as teaching agents to increase the impact of your instructional system.[5]

All of these skills can be utilized at some particular time by staff members to improve the teaching-learning situation in an outdoor activities program. It is suggested that program administrators should try to encourage all staff members to gain experience in these skills through existing college courses, workshops, or conferences. Available literature in this area will be found in the reference section; works by Mosston,[6] Rushall and Siedentop,[7] and Siedentop,[8] contain excellent treatments of these skills.

Evaluation

It is extremely important that staff members are more than just competent rock climbers, backpackers, or sailors. Certainly the development of competencies in the content area is critical. In addition to content and teaching strategies, however, it is very important for all staff to become

---

[5] Daryl Siedentop, *Developing Teaching Skills in Physical Education* (Boston: Houghton Mifflin Company, 1976), pp. 223-242.

[6] Muska Mosston, *Teaching Physical Education* (Columbus, Ohio: Charles E. Merrill, 1966).

[7] Brent S. Rushall and Daryl Siedentop, *The Development and Control of Behavior in Sport and Physical Education* (Philadelphia: Lea and Febiger, 1972).

[8] Siedentop, p. 223.

knowledgeable and competent in evaluating student abilities and all aspects of the program. Evaluation is a key factor in the improvement of all aspects of the program. Chapter 5 explores various strategies and techniques for improving the evaluation competencies of all staff members.

BUDGET AND FINANCE

It is customary throughout the nation that the local board of education finance a school's instructional and extracurricular activities. In non-school programs, however, monies for operations are usually obtained from participants' fees, grants, donations, and fund-raising projects. Obligated to maintain sound fiscal management, an administrator should try to eliminate all unnecessary expenditures without cutting the quality of the program. The major budgetary items in an outdoor activities program are (1) staff, (2) equipment, (3) transportation, (4) food, (5) insurance, (6) construction of facilities, and (7) maintenance of facilities.

The following discussion is focused on the alternative methods for meeting major expenditures without having to make a dramatic increase in the original budget.

Equipment

A modern school system is generally equipped to produce some of its own equipment, especially if an interdisciplinary approach is taken. Students taking courses in industrial arts and home economics can construct specialized equipment from do-it-yourself kits now being produced by manufacturers and supply houses of wilderness equipment. Kits can be found for down jackets, down parkas, mittens, gaiters, ponchos, rain chaps, wind shells, 60-40 jackets, sleeping bags, bivouac covers, backpacks, day packs, bike packs, tents, kayaks, canoes, snowshoes, sailboats, rowboats, and other items (see Appendix). Students interested in math, science, or art can help with the technical design and construction of certain kinds of outdoor facilities. This interdisciplinary approach provides the school with many new learning experiences and projects. It could also serve as a way to develop a greater sense of unity between the various curriculums within the school. Programs and projects of this nature are not limited to the school building. Community outdoor recreation programs can be conducted in a similar manner with the involvement of parents opening their homes, workshops, or sewing rooms for designing and constructing.

Imagination and creativity are key words in developing ways of saving money. For example, a two-man wilderness tent can cost upwards of $100. An alternative to this specialized item, which also demands considerable upkeep, is sheets of 6-mil or 8-mil clear poly plastic; a large sheet of this can keep an entire group protected from the elements at a small cost. Number 10 cans with wire hangers from the school cafeteria can also serve a variety of purposes without additional cost.

The key is innovation—and imagination! Look at your needs and seek out alternatives that are readily available. Substitutions of wilderness equipment also afford students with opportunities to use their creativity, which in turn will be reflected in their daily routines. It should be noted, however, that there are limits on types of substitutions. For example, never replace items that have special safety standards—mountaineering equipment, winter sleeping bags, life jackets, and other kinds of equipment whose quality should never be compromised.

One approach that can prove to be fruitful in obtaining equipment for school or community programs is an outdoor activity demonstration. Plan a program for parents and interested citizens, involving as many students as possible, and put on a demonstration of the various aspects of your outdoor activities program. Admission to this demonstration would require the spectators to bring items that you feel would be beneficial to the equipment needs of an outdoor program. Demonstrations of this type can develop interest and unite the program within the community. Sending out invitations could also help to specify the items you might need (see Table 2-2).

Table 2-2. Sample Invitation to an Outdoor Activity Demonstration

Dear Parent and Interested Citizen:

You are invited to attend a demonstration of the outdoor activity program at _____

_____ , on _____ ,
                     (name of school or organization)   (date)

at _____ . The focus of the program is to demonstrate some of the skills we use
         (time)

in mountaineering, camping, cross-country skiing, sailing, and other activities. To gain admission to this demonstration, we ask you to look around your home and bring along any of the items listed below that you no longer use or no longer need.

We have numerous needs for equipment, and your donations would greatly help in the development of our program.

Sincerely,

List of Items

Nails	Lanterns
Lumber	Flashlights and batteries
Rope (all sizes)	Sheets of poly plastic
String and cord (all sizes)	Old, warm clothing
Old cooking pots and utensils	Rubber boots
Baskets	Gloves
Sleeping bags	Hats
Tents	Paint
Axes	Candles
Saws	Camp stoves

Transportation

If most of your programs are taking place outside the immediate area of the community, the transportation of students and equipment can be a great expense. Plan to use as many local parks, lakes, rivers, swamps, rock ledges, and wooded areas as possible. In the utilization of local areas, the use of school transportation can sometimes be avoided if hikes or cycling activities are planned within the activity schedule between the program site and the area that is going to be used for the experience. In urban communities where local pocket wilderness areas are not always available, the use of public transportation should be explored.

Food

Traditionally the board of education, family, social agency, and student fees have assumed the cost of food. Some of the cost can be deferred by means of a program garden, planted on the school site by students or by interested citizens. A vegetable garden with a variety of produce that could be dried, canned, or preserved would represent a considerable saving and would also be a good student project.

INSURANCE AND LIABILITY

Insurance

It is difficult to cite specific insurance policies for outdoor activities programs because of the variety of policies that are now available. An insurance broker can determine the type of coverage needed based on the nature of the activities, the number of students involved, and the number of days of student participation.

The program and staff should be covered for at least $1,000,000 per occurrence for physical and property liability suits. Students participating in the program should be covered for accidental death and medical indemnity under a policy provided either by the parents or guardian or by the program. The reading and understanding of insurance policies is sometimes difficult for the layperson. It is recommended that you discuss your insurance needs with the attorney for your school or organization before you enter into any agreements with an insurance company.

Legal Liability

Traditionally, on an individual base, the legal doctrine of assumption of risk has protected most high-risk activities from lawsuits. This doctrine simply states that if one participates in an activity in which there is danger that one knows to be present and this person voluntarily assents to assume the risk of this danger, then the person cannot recover in damages if he or she is injured as a result of injury in the activity.

In recent years this doctrine has been subject to many exceptions in some states, and for this reason it is recommended that the participant—whether a group leader or a group member—protect himself or herself from legal liability in the event of an accident.

Programs in which students participate in medium- and high-risk activities have the potential for bodily injuries. The administrator's first responsibility is to conduct a program that provides all the safeguards necessary to protect the students from accidents. It is difficult to eliminate all dangers that surround activities in these areas without simply eliminating the activity. Nevertheless, all safety procedures should be checked and double-checked before allowing students to participate. Administrators should have an adequate understanding of the legal liability laws within the state or states in which the program is being conducted. The staff should also be totally aware of all safety policies and procedures with regard to: (1) the nature of the activity, (2) supervision, (3) environmental factors, (4) health procedures, (5) transportation, (6) equipment standards, (7) first aid, and (8) accident reports.[9]

Negligence

The legal liability laws vary from state to state. However, Edward F. Voltmer and Arthur A. Esslinger point out that two conditions must prevail before legal action can be instituted.

1. The first of these is that negligence must be shown. Negligence is considered the failure to act as a reasonably prudent person would act under the circumstances. Courts interpret a reasonably prudent person to be one who would foresee danger of an accident. Negligence is gauged by the ability to anticipate danger. If such foresight is reasonable, failure to seek to prevent danger is negligence.

---

[9]Edward F. Voltmer and Arthur A. Esslinger, *The Organization and Administration of Physical Education*, 4th ed. (New York: Appleton-Century-Crofts, 1967), p. 479.

2. The second condition is that negligence will not arise unless there is a duty toward the person which is disregarded. The law imposes such a duty upon all teachers.

Negligence has two aspects. The first of these involves doing something that a prudent, reasonable person would not do under the circumstances because he foresees the risk of injury to others. The second aspect relates to the failure to do something that a prudent, reasonable person would foresee as necessary for the protection or assistance of another individual to whom he owes a duty.[10]

Reducing Accidents

The following are policies, procedures, and suggestions that the administrator and staff could utilize to prevent accidents and minimize the possibility of lawsuits.

1. Nature of activity
   a. Have a clear understanding of the potential danger of the particular activity.
   b. Be able to predict dangerous situations before students become involved.
2. Supervision
   a. Always be alert to the needs of students under your supervision.
   b. Always try to schedule activities in medium- and high-risk categories with two instructors for every 12 students (a 1-to-6 ratio).
   c. Never leave the class unsupervised. If you must leave, alert the other instructor of your absence.
   d. Never allow untrained students to participate in spotting or belaying duties.
   e. Always become familiar with students' abilities in relation to skill development and physical limitations.
   f. In mountaineering and certain water activities, always make sure that students wear certified hard hats.
3. Environment factor
   a. Never allow students to proceed into a wilderness area without prior knowledge of that area.
   b. Know the rules and regulations governing the wilderness area you are using.
   c. Familiarize your staff with knowledge of weather conditions, river currents, possible avalanche danger, falling rock, and other hazards before the students move into the area.
   d. Never overestimate a student's ability in planning the activities with respect to the distance of hiking, classification of rock climbing routes, and classification of white-water canoeing areas.
4. Health procedures
   a. Students participating in long wilderness expeditions or physically demanding activities should have medical examinations beforehand. (See Table 2-3.) If, for some reason, students do not want to submit to a medical examination, they should be required to submit a medical examination release form. (See Table 2-4.) This type of release is recommended only for adults over 18 years of age.
   b. Always maintain sound hygienic practices among students on wilderness expeditions.
5. Transportation
   a. Always provide safe and adequate transportation to and from activity sites.
   b. Avoid the practice of allowing students to drive their own cars to the site.
   c. Always have a supervisor along with the students while they are being transported.

[10]*Ibid.*, p. 480.

6. Equipment
   a. Never make substitutions for specialized safety equipment.
   b. Always check ropes, climbing hardware, life jackets, etc., before they are put to use.
   c. Never allow students to handle dangerous equipment without supervision.
   d. Before venturing into the wilderness, each student should be given a list of personal equipment items that are needed, and each should be checked before leaving.
7. First aid
   a. Instructors should be chosen on the basis of training in first aid, water safety, and other life-saving certification.
   b. Give only immediate and temporary care in treating an injury victim, and obtain professional medical help as soon as possible.
   c. On trips away from the community, the instructor should have the name, address, and phone number of a person who can be contacted to give permission for medical treatment; also, an alternative person should be listed in case the primary person cannot be reached.
   d. A good first aid kit should accompany the instructor on all expeditions.
8. Accident reports
   a. The administration should be notified of all accidents, their causes, and treatment.
   b. All accident reports should be kept on file in case a lawsuit is brought against the staff or organization many months after the accident occurred.
   c. Accident reports can be obtained from your insurance company or the National Safety Council.
   d. If you decide to prepare your own accident report, the following information should be included (see Table 2-5):
     (1) Name and address of student.
     (2) Nature of activity student was participating in.
     (3) Time and place of accident.
     (4) Description of accident.
     (5) Description of injury.
     (6) Treatment of injury.
     (7) Follow-up care.
   e. The accident report should be signed by the instructor in charge and the chief administrator of the program.

Acknowledgement Permission Form

The use of release forms has been a common practice for students participating in extracurricular activities. In a personal-injury lawsuit against the school or organization, release forms are meaningless. The parent or guardian who signed the form has no legal right to waive claims for personal injury to the child. It is recommended that the release form be replaced with an acknowledgment permission form, informing the parent or guardian of the exact nature of the activity. In preparing the form, be specific about the types of activities that the student will be involved in. Do not merely state that the student is going to participate in a wilderness trip or day outing in such and such an area. (See Table 2-6.)

PUBLIC RELATIONS

Because of increases in spending to support and initiate new, innovative programs, the future growth of the education process has been a growing concern of the public. When the system is supported through taxation and donations, as is the case with non-school programs, the people support-

Table 2-3. Project U.S.E. Confidential Medical History and Physical Examination Record

Instructions
1. Applicant completes Part I
2. Parent or guardian completes Part II
3. Physician completes Part III
4. Return to: R.F.D. 1, Maple Ridge Road, Harrison, Maine 04040

For Office Use Only

Date: _____

Course: _____

Approved: _____

Part I

Name _____ Male _____ Female _____

Address _____

_____ Phone _____ Age _____

Person to be notified in case of accident or injury: Name _____

Address _____ Phone _____

If not available please notify: Name _____

Address _____ Phone _____

Part II

If applicant has had any of the following conditions or is currently experiencing them, please put a check next to the number and give details below. If you have any questions about these statements please ask your physician.

1. Vision or hearing
2. Problems with teeth
3. Dizzy spells
4. Motion sickness
5. Throat infection
6. Chronic cough, bronchitis
7. Shortness of breath or asthma
8. Chest pains
9. Irregular heart beat, murmur
10. Low or high blood pressure
11. Frequent nausea
12. Jaundice or hepatitis
13. Diarrhea or blood in stools
14. Severe menstrual cramps
15. Hernia
16. Difficulty urinating
17. Kidney infection
18. Chronic pain in back, neck
19. Broken bones, serious sprains
20. Severe injury to head
21. Severe illness
22. Chronic skin problems
23. Allergy to medicines
24. Claustrophobia, acrophobia
25. Continuing use of alcohol, drugs
26. Depression, hysteria, nervousness
27. Diabetes, thyroid trouble
28. Current medication
29. Special diet

If you check any of the above items, please give details below:

_____

_____

_____

In the event that I cannot be reached in an emergency, permission is hereby given for any emergency anesthesia and/or operation which might become necessary. I have read the description of M.A.I.N.E. and understand that the program is physically and mentally demanding and is conducted in wilderness areas.

_____   _____
(date)   (signature of parent or guardian)

Source: Project U.S.E. M.A.I.N.E., Harrison, Maine. Reprinted by permission of Project U.S.E., Long Branch, N.J.

Table 2-3. (continued)

Part III—Physician's Examination

Background for the physician—M.A.I.N.E. is a year-round, outdoor educational program that conducts programs for 1 to 23 days duration in wilderness environments, in all types of weather. Conditioning and physical fitness are incorporated into all courses. Students sleep in sleeping bags and usually under tarps, parachutes or in tents during winter seminars.

Any man or woman with normal physical and mental capacity can expect to complete one of our courses. Adequate, good equipment and an ample and nutritious menu is provided. Students cook all meals, with the exception of courses which include a solo, two days and nights alone with little or no food. Students are expected to refrain from the use of tobacco, alcohol, drugs, or other stimulants or depressants during the program.

1. Birthdate: Month ————————————   Day ———   Year ———

2. Height ——————   Weight ——————   B.P. ————   P. ————

3. General appearance ————————————————————————

4. General health and nutrition

   — Skin   — Thorax and lungs   — Knees   — Hemoglobin
   — Lymph nodes   — Heart   — Peripheral vessels — Thyroid
   — Eyes   — Abdomen   — Back   — Hernia
   — Nose   — Extremities   — Genitalia   — Scars
   — Mouth and throat — Feet   — Urinalysis   — CNS
   — Neck   — Ankles

   Remarks ——————————————————————————————

   ————————————————————————————————————

   ————————————————————————————————————

5. Immunization and tests

   a. Has the applicant had a DPT series? ——————

   b. The following immunizations are required. Please indicate dates (booster shots must be up to date).

      Tetanus ——————   Typhoid——————   Polio ——————

   c. If over 21, applicant should have had a chest X-ray within the last year.

      Results: ————————————   If under 21 a TB Tine Test can be given.

   d. If over 45, applicant must have had an EKG within the last year.

6. Is applicant allergic to medicine?————————————————————

7. Is applicant allergic to bee stings or insect bites?————————————————

8. Is the applicant now under treatment of a psychologist or psychiatrist? If yes, give his or her name.   Name ————————————————————————

   Address ——————————————————————————————

Table 2-3. (continued)

9. Does the applicant use or has he used any of the following drugs: Marijuana, barbiturates, heroin, cocaine, LSD, hashish, mescaline, hallucinogens, benzedrine, amphetamines, or related drugs? If yes, give details _____

_____

10. Do you see any reason why the applicant should not attend a M.A.I.N.E. wilderness course? _____

11. Signature of examining physician: _____

Address _____

_____ Phone _____ Date _____

Table 2-4. Project U.S.E. Medical Examination Release Form

I, _____ , of _____
    (name)   (address)

_____

wish to participate in the _____
                            (name of course)

program offered by Project U.S.E. M.A.I.N.E. I have been told and, by my signature hereto, acknowledge that I have been told, by representatives of Project U.S.E. M.A.I.N.E. that the program in which I wish to participate involves strenuous physical activity. I have further been requested by representatives of Project U.S.E. M.A.I.N.E. to undergo a physical examination given by a qualified physician, so that it might be ascertained if I suffer from a condition which endangers my health and which might be aggravated by strenuous physical activity.

For reasons of my own, I do not wish to undergo such a physical examination. I realize that by refusing to do so, I preclude the possibility of discovering whether I suffer from a condition which endangers my health and which might be aggravated by strenuous physical activity.

By my signature hereto, I acknowledge the truth of the statements set forth herein and further declare that I shall hold Project U.S.E. M.A.I.N.E. harmless from any and all injuries, illnesses, disabilities, infirmities or physical disorders which may befall me while I am participating in the above-named program and which result from or are caused by a health condition which might have been discovered upon a physical examination done pursuant to Project U.S.E. M.A.I.N.E.'s request. I further declare and state that I realize that by virtue of not undergoing a physical examination, I am exposing myself to a risk of illness or injury and that I assume this risk and hold Project U.S.E. M.A.I.N.E. harmless from any such risk.

I have read this document prior to signing it.

Dated this _____ day of _____ Nineteen hundred and _____ .

_____   _____
            (witness)   (signature)

Source: Project U.S.E. M.A.I.N.E., Harrison, Maine.

Table 2-5. Project U.S.E. M.A.I.N.E. Accident Report

Date ——————————————————————

Name of Student ——————————————————————————

Course ————————————————————————————————

1. Location of accident (date, time, place)

2. General description (how the accident occurred)

3. Description of injury

4. Treatment of injury (at the site)

5. Follow-up treatment

Instructors ————————————————————

————————————————————

Source: Project U.S.E. M.A.I.N.E., Harrison, Maine.

Table 2-6. Acknowledgment Permission Form

I am familiar with the dangers, hazards, and risks involved in ——————————————

——

(specific activity or activities)

and grant my son/daughter permission to participate in the activity at ————————————

(name of location)

on ———————————————— .

(date)

Date ————————————————————   ————————————————————

(signature of parent or guardian)

ing the system have a right to know where their dollars are going. An administrator has an obligation to keep the public informed about the reliability and accountability of the program. Public relations is an essential part of the total growth and success of an education program. The citizens within a community can only formulate favorable impressions of an individual, an organization, or an idea on the basis of what they hear.[11]

Purposes of Public Relations

Public relations is a continuing process utilizing various forms of media to create favorable public support. The overall concept of public relations is to draw worthwhile publicity to the program or organization. George Butler summarizes the objectives of publicity in community recreation programs, which could also apply to school programs:

1. To give the public an accounting of the work accomplished.
2. To encourage people to participate in the activities and to use the facilities offered by the department.
3. To impress the public with the extent, variety, and accomplishments of the department's services.
4. To prepare the minds of citizens for proposed changes or exercises in the recreation system, such as the acquisition of needed areas, increased appropriations, or a new method of reserving tennis courts.
5. To interpret the significance of recreation and its importance in the life of the people.
6. To secure specific action in support of the department, such as signing a petition, speaking favorably of a measure, or voting in approval of a referendum.
7. To enlist individuals to give volunteer service in some specific form.
8. To give people information or suggestions on how to conduct recreation activities or construct facilities.
9. To stimulate appreciation of the local recreation facilities and enlist popular support of the conservation of natural resources.[12]

Methods of Building Favorable Public Relations

The single best method for creating favorable public opinion is the development of a solid, worthwhile program. It always holds true that satisfied students are your best salespeople. It is recommended that the administrator construct a program that is worth selling to students, so that they go out and sell it to the public. The students are always your first concern. Once the program is pointed in a direction of achieving its objectives, it will sell itself.

Staff should concern themselves with presenting a good public image. A loyal staff member has the opportunity to be involved with the public in many different roles. Your staff should always be informed of the intentions or new directions of the program and should be able to relate this information to the community.

Other methods include the use of television programs, radio programs, assemblies, demonstrations, bulletins, newsletters, newspaper articles, posters, brochures, and open houses. Each has its particular advantages, but no one method should take precedence over the others.

---

[11] Benjamin Fine, *Educational Publicity* (New York: Harper and Row, 1943), pp. 255-256.
[12] George Butler, *Introduction to Community Recreation* (New York: McGraw-Hill Book Company, 1967), p. 557.

The key to public relations is that it is a continuous process. Remember, when you are dealing in community services, your program is always under public scrutiny. Always build upon the strong points and try to eliminate the weaker ones.

QUESTIONS FOR REVIEW AND DISCUSSION

1. Name five qualities of an effective administrator.
2. Why should an administrator be concerned with supporting, assisting, and sharing?
3. How can administrators determine the outdoor interests of the people in their programs?
4. What are program ingressions, activities, and intentions?
5. What areas should be included in the development of a staff?
6. How can interpersonal relationships between instructors and students be improved?
7. What are some important instructional skills?
8. What are the major budget items in an outdoor program?
9. List several techniques for reducing the amount of money spent on equipment and supplies.
10. What is negligence?
11. List several guidelines for reducing accidents.
12. Why is a medical examination release form important?
13. What are the key parts of an accident report?
14. What should be included in an acknowledgment permission form?
15. Why is public relations important to program growth?

REFERENCES

Butler, George D. *Introduction to Community Recreation*. New York: McGraw-Hill Book Company, 1967.

Fine, Benjamin. *Educational Publicity*. New York: Harper and Row, 1943.

Mosston, Muska. *Teaching Physical Education*. Columbus, Ohio: Charles E. Merrill, 1966.

Petzoldt, Paul. *The Wilderness Handbook*. New York: W. W. Norton and Company, 1974.

Rushall, Brent S., and Daryl Siedentop. *The Development and Control of Behavior in Sport and Physical Education*. Philadelphia: Lea and Febiger, 1972.

Siedentop, Daryl. *Developing Teaching Skills in Physical Education*. Boston: Houghton Mifflin Company, 1976.

Tead, Ordway. *Administration: Its Purpose and Performance*. New York: Harper and Row, 1959.

Voltmer, Edward F., and Arthur A. Esslinger. *The Organization and Administration of Physical Education*. 4th ed. New York: Appleton-Century-Crofts, 1967.

Wiles, Kimball. *Supervision for Better Schools*. 3rd ed. Englewood Cliffs, N.J.: Prentice-Hall, 1967.

three

program planning
for outdoor expeditions

As we sit in our armchairs and read the adventurous tales of great explorers like Lewis and Clark, Sir Edmund Hillary, or Commander Neal Armstrong, we begin to experience a stirring of the imagination, envisioning ourselves at their side embarking upon a voyage into the unknown. Through the course of history there has always been a unique breed of people who possess the capacity to stretch their physical and mental limits in order to reach the tops of mountains, discover the source of rivers, and explore outer space. People have always been willing to journey to all corners of the earth—the depths of its seas, the frigidness of its poles, and the vastness of its skies. These journeys are generally associated with great expeditions of famous explorers and massive amounts of supplies, with departures from such places as Katmandu or Cape Canaveral.

An expedition does not always have to have the proportions just mentioned. In outdoor activity programs, they can vary in length from one class period to many days. Expeditions are journeys into the outdoor environment, which could be a schoolyard, community park, wild river, state forest, seacoast, or national recreation area. The length of time or the area is not as important as the purpose, since each journey should be designed to make discoveries or experience new feelings in a particular environment.

PROGRAM ORGANIZATION

A systematic approach to planning is essential to the total expedition program. In the development of the expedition program an initial plan should be drawn including all the "nuts and bolts" necessary to start the program moving. The components of this initial development should be the following:

1. *Staffing plan.* The recruitment of staff; staff training program; supportive staff.
2. *Scheduling of expeditions.* Activities; reconnaissance of site selections; combining activities; sequence of activities; student application form.
3. *Pre-expedition planning.* Purchase of equipment; transportation; food; final check; pre-evaluation; student equipment check-out; group equipment check-out.
4. *Post-expedition review.* Equipment check-in; evaluation of site; evaluation of activities; recommendation for improvement.

After the first six months of program operations and again after one full year, all administration and staff personnel should meet to evaluate each component and to make suggestions for improvement. Also, at this time, proposals should be initiated for three- and five-year plans. Keep in mind where the program is today and where it will be tomorrow.

Expedition Staffing Plan

In programs that are administered through a school system, the staff customarily comes from the teaching faculty or paraprofessionals within the school district. Programs administered through public or private organizations can recruit staff members through (1) advertising in camping and mountaineering magazines or journals, such as *Backpacker, Off-Belay, Wilderness Camping,* and *Mountain,* (2) friends and acquaintances of present staff, and (3) graduates of the program. In 1975, the Colorado Outward Bound School started a mailing service under the direction of the Colorado Outward Bound Jobs Clearing House.

The criteria for being on the list has been established as: anyone who has at least a minimum of a college degree and an Outward Bound course. The service is for the purpose of helping Outward Bound instructors, course directors, and other professional wilderness educators find permanent employment in the field of experiential education. Most of the jobs require Outward Bound instructor level skills, with administrative capabilities and experience. This service is also open to persons from OB-related and OB-adaptive programs. [1]

The use of this service can be beneficial to administrators in recruiting and selecting staff. In the selection of staff, however, a set of criteria must be established. The following list could be used for this selection process.

1. Ability to work with people in outdoor and stressful situations.
2. Decision-making skills.
3. Ability to communicate with people effectively.
4. At least 21 years of age.
5. Expedition experience for extended periods of time.
6. Demonstrated successful teaching experience.
7. Broad life experiences—travel, different or unique job experiences.
8. High level of skills in the activities the program is offering.
9. Leadership skills.
10. Willingness to make a strong commitment to the success of the program.

After an individual is accepted for a position, an orientation or staff training program should be held. The orientation should be designed so that the staff can become totally familiar with the philosophy, objectives, and procedures of the organization. It is also recommended that a new staff member be assigned the position of assistant instructor, before being given the responsibility of a full instructor.

Supportive staff positions, such as food packer, equipment preparer, or transportation personnel, are just as important as the instructional staff and should be filled according to similar criteria.

Scheduling

The scheduling and selection of activities and expedition sites are prime concerns of the administration in the beginning and continuing phases of the organizational process. Before a group of students is sent to participate in an activity in a specific environment, the answers to the following questions should be determined:

1. Does the staff conducting the expeditions have the technical skills to work safely within the environment?

---

[1] Colorado Outward Bound School, "Jobs Clearing House Report, 1976," unpublished (Denver: 1976).

2. Is the staff familiar with the topography of the area?
3. Can the challenges of the environment be handled with the student's skill level?
4. Is the staff familiar with the rules and regulations governing that area?
5. Does the program have the necessary equipment and safety items to conduct a program safely in this environment?

When a schedule is being constructed, there should be a constant exchange of ideas between administration and staff, and student interests, time of year, and cost should be taken into account. In school or recreational programs, it is important to remember that since the schedule is being designed for the students, they should have an active part in its construction. A review of the schedule by all the students could be very time consuming, but time could be saved if a core group of administrators, staff, and students were chosen to help finalize the schedule.

The expedition schedule can be planned to provide instruction in one specific activity or a combination or activities. In a combination schedule, it is important to remember that one activity should reinforce another. For example, if a group of students were going rock climbing, it would be beneficial for the students to have participated in ropes course activities first. The experiences of going through the ropes course or any other lead-up activity could aid the student by providing the following benefits: (1) use of known skills to engage in unknown areas, (2) application of acquired skills, and (3) management of new information and environments. (See "Objectives of Ropes Course Activities," Chapter 7.)

The daily expedition schedule should be planned around blocks of time to avoid a strict hourly schedule. Hourly schedules have a tendency to rush groups through activities, and as a result, the group is not always given the opportunity to enjoy the beauty of the environment or the opportunity to repeat an enjoyable experience.

Tables 3-1 and 3-2 are examples of expedition schedules. Table 3-1 lists the order of activities for a five-day rock climbing program, and Table 3-2 is a schedule for a combination of activities during a fourteen-day expedition.

The final procedure in determining the activity schedule is to have students complete an application form (see Table 3-3). The use of application forms can aid the staff in planning the daily activities to meet specific desires of the students.

Pre-Expedition Planning

Equipment. The specific equipment for each activity in an outdoor adventure program is described in the chapters on individual activities. A program director, however, is compelled to buy the safest and most durable equipment available. Inexpensive or poor quality equipment will generally result in a greater expense because of constant need for replacement. High-quality backpacks and sleeping bags, if properly cared for, should have a useful life of four seasons. Climbing equipment should be replaced on an annual basis or immediately if it is damaged. Almost all other items have an estimated life of one year. Table 3-4 provides an example of the number of items needed to conduct a year-round program for fourteen students participating in one particular activity at a time, and the approximate life of each item.

Transportation. The transporting of students to the expedition site can create the biggest administrative problem, because of all the logistics in moving the group from point to point. First, your state law concerning the busing of students should be reviewed carefully. Some states have very strict regulations with regard to the type of vehicles that must be used and the licensing of the driver. When it is possible, use one van or bus to transport all students, to eliminate the possibility that one part of the group might become lost en route. The driver should be completely familiar with the location of the drop-off point.

Table 3-1. Sample Program Schedule for a Five-Day Expedition

Instructor's name   Jim Howells, Denise Vcloff   **Number of students**   12   **Group**   1

Date   May 5 – May 9   **Number of days**   5

DAY	MORNING	AFTERNOON	EVENING
1 (5-5)	Students arrive at base camp, 9:00 A.M. Review of program Issuing of equipment Introduction to ropes course Begin ropes course activities	Lunch Continue ropes course activities	Dinner Night session: Introduction to Rock Climbing History Equipment Knots Safety
2 (5-6)	Breakfast Transport to climbing area, 9:00 A.M. Beginning skills Belaying Planning climbing routes	Lunch Begin bouldering; each student completes three different routes on boulder	Dinner Night session: Environment Types of climbing Climbers' responsibility to protect the environment
3 (5-7)	Breakfast Beginning climbing (single-pitch, top-roped) Split into two groups Group A routes Rising Sun Butterfield Good Night Group B routes Fire Standard Look Out Below	Lunch Rotate groups; first group completes Group B routes, second group completes Group A routes	Dinner Night session: Rappelling Anchors Types of rappels
4 (5-8)	Breakfast Rappelling; each student completes three rappels	Lunch Group works together on friction climbs	Dinner Night session: Advanced Techniques Chimney Lay back
5 (5-9)	Breakfast Multiple pitch Split into two groups Group A Morning Light Group B White Knight	Lunch Rotate groups Transport to base camp, 5:00 P.M.	Dinner Evaluation of expedition Students depart, 7:30 P.M.

Table 3-2. Sample Program Schedule for a Fourteen-Day Expedition

Instructor's name Dick Schieferstein, Bob Forney **Number of students** 12 **Group** 1

Date June 1 – June 14 **Number of days** 14

DAY	MORNING	AFTERNOON	EVENING
1 (6-1)	Students arrive at base camp, 9:00 A.M. Program orientation Issuing of equipment Introduction to initiative games and ropes course	Lunch Initiative games and ropes course activities Set up camp in the pines at base camp	Dinner Night session Review of today's activities Introduction to map and compass reading
2 (6-2)	Wake-up, 6:00 A.M. Morning run and dip Breakfast Point-to-point orienteering	Lunch Water activities Drownproofing Basic canoeing strokes Forward and backward J-stroke Steering Draw stroke	Dinner Night session Introduction to backpacking First aid
3 (6-3)	Wake-up, 6:00 A.M. Morning run and dip Breakfast Transport to Rte. 5 South Arm, 9:00 A.M. Backpacking on Appalachian Trail	Lunch Backpacking	Camp at C Pond on A Trail Night session Review of today's activities First aid (continued)
4 (6-4)	Wake-up, 6:00 A.M. Morning run and dip in C Pond Breakfast Orienteering to C Pond bluffs	Lunch Introduction to rock climbing Boulder climbing	Camp at C Pond bluff Night session Review of today's activities
5 (6-5)	Wake-up, 6:00 A.M. Morning run and dip Breakfast Rock climbing and rappelling	Lunch Rock climbing and rappelling	Camp at C Pond bluff Night session Review of today's activities
6 (6-6)	Wake-up, 6:00 A.M. Morning run and dip Breakfast Rock climbing and rappelling	Lunch Backpacking to Surplus Pond, arrive midafternoon Swimming in Surplus Pond and rest	Camp at Surplus Pond Rest for night hike Night hike, begin 12:00 midnight

Table 3-2. (continued)

DAY	MORNING	AFTERNOON	EVENING
7 (6-7)	Sunrise at top of Baldpate Mountain Breakfast Rest	Wake-up, 12:00 noon Lunch Backpacking to Grafton Notch	Camp at Grafton Notch shelter Night session Review of night hike and today's activities
8 (6-8)	Wake-up, 6:00 A.M. Morning run and dip Breakfast Hike and Tyrolean traverse on Old Speck Mountain	Lunch Hiking	Camp at Grafton Notch shelter Night session Review of today's activities Canoeing
9 (6-9)	Wake-up, 6:00 A.M. Morning run and dip Breakfast Meet van and canoes at Rte. 26 Repack equipment for canoes	Transport to Wilson's Mills Lunch in van Canoeing on Andro- scoggin River	Camp at base of Aziscohos Mountains Night session Review of today's activities Portaging
10 (6-10)	Wake-up, 6:00 A.M. Morning run and dip Breakfast Portage at Aziscohos Mountain Lake	Lunch Canoe across Aziscohos Mountain Lake	Camp at mouth of Aziscohos Mountain River Night session Review of today's activities
11 (6-11)	Wake-up, 6:00 A.M. Morning run and dip Breakfast Canoe into Umboggog Lake	Lunch Canoeing	Camp at southwest shore of Umboggog Lake
12 (6-12)	Wake-up, 6:00 A.M. Morning run and dip Breakfast Canoe to Big Island, in center of southern sector of lake	Lunch Begin solo on island	Solo
13 (6-13)	Solo	Solo	Pick-up from solo Dinner Night session Review of solo
14 (6-14)	Wake-up, 6:00 A.M. Morning run and dip Breakfast Canoeing to Rte. B	Lunch Pick-up and transport to base camp Pack equipment for storage	Dinner Final evaluation Students depart

Table 3-3. Student Application Form

Name _____ Age _____

Course date _____

1. My reasons for wanting to participate in _____
   are: (name of activity)

2. My previous experience in this field is:

3. I would like to learn the following skills as they relate to _____ :
                                                              (name of activity)

4. I could teach the following skills:

Table 3-4. Equipment Inventory

TYPE OF EQUIPMENT	NUMBER OF ITEMS	APPROXIMATE LIFE
Backpacking		
1. Ensolite pads	14	2 seasons
2. Summer sleeping bags	14	4 seasons
3. Winter sleeping bags	14	4 seasons
4. Backpacks	14	4 seasons
5. Tents	7	4 seasons
Rock Climbing		
1. Perlon ropes (150 ft × 11 mm)	7	1 season
2. Climbing helmets	14	3 seasons
3. Ice axes	14	Replace only if damaged

Table 3-4. (continued)

TYPE OF EQUIPMENT	NUMBER OF ITEMS	APPROXIMATE LIFE
Rock Climbing (continued)		
4. Ice hammer	14	Replace only if damaged
5. Rock hammer	2	Replace only if damaged
6. Nylon slings	250 ft	1 season
7. Carabiners	40	2 seasons
8. Figure 8's descender	4	2 seasons
9. Stoppers and chocks	All sizes	Replace only if damaged
10. Crampons	14 pr	Replace only if damaged
11. Ice screws	All sizes	Replace only if damaged
12. Jumar ascenders	3 pr	Replace only if damaged
Canoeing		
1. Canoe	7	Replace only if damaged
2. Life vests	16	2 seasons
3. Canoe paddles	16	2 seasons
4. Canoe bag (watertight)	14	2 seasons
5. Canoe trailer	1	Replace only if damaged
Snowshoeing		
1. Snowshoes	14 pr	Replace only if damaged
2. Snowshoe bindings	14 pr	Replace only if damaged
Cross-Country Skiing		
1. Skis	14 pr	Replace only if damaged
2. Ski bindings	14 pr	Replace only if damaged
3. Ski poles	14 pr	Replace only if damaged
Miscellaneous *		
1. Cooking pots	6	
2. Frying pans	4	
3. Camp grills	5	
4. Cups	14	
5. Spoons	14	
6. Canteens	28	
7. Can openers	4	
8. Water jugs (collapsible)	4	
9. Stoves	5	
10. One-quart fuel bottles	5	
11. Compasses	7	
12. Maps	Covering all terrain to be explored on expeditions	

*The approximate life of miscellaneous items is based on wear; items should be replaced as the need arises.

Table 3-5. Sample Transportation Sheet

Instructor's name   D. Schieferstein, B. Forney   **Number of students**   12   **Group**   1

DATE	ITEMS OR ADDITIONAL EQUIPMENT NEEDED	PICK-UP POINT AND TIME	TRANS-PORT
5 June 1980	Rock climbing equipment and food— boxes 2 and 3	Rte. 5, Andover, 3:00 P.M.	Ragged Jack Mountain
8 June 1980	Canoeing equipment and food— boxes 4 and 5	Ragged Jack Mountain, 12:00 noon	Errol, N.H.
10 June 1980	No equipment or food needed	Bethel, Me., 5:00 P.M.	Base camp

When the group is going to be dropped off at one point and picked up at another point, it is recommended that a transportation sheet be developed, similar to the one shown in Table 3-5.

Food. The energy required for participation in outdoor adventure activities is far greater than the energy expenditure of daily living. In ordinary activities, an average person expends about 1100 calories per 100 pounds of body weight per day. In an outdoor pursuits program, the average person requires between 4,200 and 6,000 calories per day to maintain the high level of energy necessary. In winter activity, it is extremely important to expend between 5,000 and 6,000 calories per day for energy and body heat.

All food consists of three major components: protein, carbohydrates, and fat. Proteins, found in milk, cheese, eggs, and meat, are broken down into amino acids by the digestive system. The principal functions of amino acids in the body are the building of new tissues, the upkeep of tissues, and the maintenance of energy. Carbohydrates are sugars or starches formed from a combination of many sugar groups; sugars are the principal source of energy in the body. Fats are formed by the combination of fatty acids with a glycerol or glycerin compound. Good sources of fat in the diet are meat, butter, margarine, cheese, egg yolks, and nuts. Fats are valuable as a concentrated source of body fuel.

For winter activities, the diet should consist of the following food groups in this order of importance: (1) fat, (2) carbohydrates, and (3) protein. In warmer weather, the order is (1) carbohydrates, (2) fats, (3) protein. Fats and carbohydrates are of prime importance for both warm-weather and cold-weather activities for the energy and concentrated body fat properties.

Food supplies for an expedition can be purchased in bulk from a retail food store, which adds considerable weight and requires repacking. Dried foods weigh less but cost a great deal more than food purchased from a retail grocery. The most common dried foods are called *freeze-dried*, but actually dried foods are produced by several methods, namely, freeze drying, puff drying, and vacuum drying. The type of process can affect the flavor, and water-soluble nutrients, including vitamin C, will also be lost. Another drying process is dehydration, which involves evaporating the water rather than refining. In the preparation of dried food, great care should be taken when water is added to rehydrate the food; it is important to follow the manufacturer's directions carefully.

In planning a menu, it is recommended that you experiment with the different types of drying processes to determine which one meets your program's needs in relationship to cost, preparation, and nutrient values. Table 3-6 is a sample menu using dried food and foods purchased from a store. This combination is beneficial in keeping the cost down and providing the highest possible nutrient

Table 3-6. Sample Food List

Instructor's name _____ J. Howells, D. Veloff _____ Number of Students ___12___

Date _____ May 5 – May 9 _____ Number of days __5__

DAY	BREAKFAST	LUNCH	DINNER
1 (5-5)	None	Tuna on Triscuits Fruit drink	Spaghetti with sauce Vienna sausage Lettuce and tomato salad with dressing Fruit drink or tea
2 (5-6)	Bacon (canned) and eggs (powdered) Bread Fruit drink Cocoa or tea	Salami and cheese Bread Dried fruit Fruit drink	Beef stroganoff (freeze dried) Biscuits (powder mix) Fruit drink or tea
3 (5-7)	Oatmeal with raisins and honey Fruit drink or tea	Peanut butter on jelly on graham crackers Fruit drink	Chicken and gravy Rice Vegetable (canned) Applesauce (freeze dried) Fruit drink or tea
4 (5-8)	Pancakes with honey or jelly Bacon (canned) Fruit drink or tea	Deviled ham on Triscuits Gorp Dried fruit Fruit drink	Chow mein with noodles (freeze dried) Fudge Fruit drink or tea
5 (5-9)	Cream of wheat with raisins and honey Fruit drink or tea	Hard bread with cheese and honey Candy bar Fruit drink	Beef stew Biscuit (powder mix) Fresh fruit Fruit drink or tea

Extras:
Hard candy	Salt and pepper
Energy bars	Seasoned salt
Butter	Cinnamon
Brown sugar	Powdered milk

values. For additional information and recipes for outdoor meals, the authors recommend the following books for supplementary reading: *The Wilderness Handbook, Food for Knapsackers,* and *The Freedom of the Hills.* Complete references are found in the suggested readings section at the end of this chapter.

Final Checks. Once the daily expedition schedule, menu list, and transportation schedule have been completed, the instructor should compile the final checks: (1) pre-evaluation check, (2) student equipment list, and (3) group equipment sign-out. Tables 3-7, 3-8, and 3-9 are forms used by the Ohio

Table 3-7. Pre-Evaluation Check

Instructor: _____   Asst. Instructor: _____

Course: _____   _____

Time and Place of Departure: Supervisors: _____

_____   _____

Time and Place of Arrival: _____

_____   _____

Time and Place of Return:

_____

1. Emergency Procedures (please list).
   A. During the trip—transportation.
   B. While the trip is in progress—first aid procedures.
   C. Emergency contacts—phone number, location of nearest medical facilities.
   D. University contact—name and number.

2. Estimated trip location (include major points of location during travel).

3. Check the following items: *Yes*   *No*   *Explanation and Comments*

   A. Emergency addresses.   _____ _____ _____

   B. All members insured.   _____ _____ _____

   C. First aid kit.   _____ _____ _____

   D. Equipment cleared.   _____ _____ _____

   E. Transportation cleared vehicle check. _____ _____ _____

   F. Health ratings listed on all students. _____ _____ _____

   G. Pre-training complete.   _____ _____ _____

   H. All students properly registered.   _____ _____ _____

   I. Safety and first aid procedures covered _____ _____ _____
      with students prior to trip.

   J. Food and personal equipment checked. _____ _____ _____

   K. All instructors and supervisors have _____ _____ _____
      liability insurance.

4. Transportation:
   A. Types of vehicles—   B. License numbers—
   C. Drivers' names and numbers on license—

5. General course progression and objectives (continue on back if necessary)—

6. Student deviations from trip—

         Signature of Instructor and Date _____

Source: *Instructors Manual,* Program in Outdoor Pursuits, Ohio State University. Reprinted by permission of the Program in Outdoor Pursuits.

Table 3-8. Project U.S.E. M.A.I.N.E. Student Equipment List

Name _____ Date _____ Course _____

Instructor's name _____

Backpack and frame _____	Cross-country skis _____
Summer sleeping bag _____	Ski poles _____
Winter sleeping bag _____	Snowshoes _____
Ensolite pad _____	Climbing helmet _____
Canteen _____	Adjustable crampons _____
Cup _____	Ice axe _____
Spoon _____	Life vest _____
Snowshoes _____	Canoe bag _____

Other _____

I have received the above items and found them in good condition. At the completion of my course I will return all items checked and pay for any damage which is above normal use.

_____
(student signature)

_____
(date)

Source: Project U.S.E. M.A.I.N.E., Harrison, Maine.

State University POP (Program in Outdoor Pursuits) and Project U.S.E. M.A.I.N.E. to obtain resources needed to start the expedition.

A pre-training session should be held with the students as part of the final checks. A session of this type should provide the following information:

1. The nature of the expedition and the reasons for going.
2. Departure and return times.
3. A description of skills to be used in a controlled environment, e.g., knots, belay techniques, land canoeing skills, and packing the backpack.
4. A review of the safety rules and policies to be followed during the expeditions.
5. A review of the daily schedule, with a final opportunity to change it.

Post-Expedition Review

Upon completion of the expedition the instructor should file a post-expedition report with the administrator. (See Table 3-10.)

Table 3-9. Equipment Sign-Out Sheet

Instructor: ——————————————

Course: ————————————————

Departure: ———————————————— Return: ————————————————

I.	Departmental Equipment Needed	Out	In	Signature of Instructor
	A.			
	B.			
	C.			
	D.			
	E.			

II.	P.O.P. Equipment	Out	In	Signature of Instructor
	A.			
	B.			
	C.			
	D.			
	E.			

III.	Books, A.V. Aids being used	Out	In	Signature of Instructor
	A.			
	B.			
	C.			
	D.			
	E.			

IV. Equipment Required of Students
    A.
    B.
    C.
    D.
    E.

Instructor's Signature ——————————————————

Administrative Head ——————————————————

Source: *Instructors Manual,* Program in Outdoor Pursuits, Ohio State University. Reprinted by permission of the Program in Outdoor Pursuits.

QUESTIONS FOR REVIEW AND DISCUSSION

1. What constitutes an outdoor expedition?
2. What are the initial components of program planning for expeditions?
3. How can staff members be recruited?
4. Name five or six criteria for the selection of a new staff member.
5. In determining a program schedule, what factors should be considered?
6. Why should hourly blocks of time be avoided in the scheduling process?
7. Prepare a three-day schedule for a course that includes rock climbing, backpacking, and canoeing.
8. What factors should be considered in transportation?
9. What types of foods are important for winter and summer expeditions? Why?

Table 3-10. Post-Evaluation Form

Instructor or Supervisor: _____

Course: _____

1. Transportation details:

   A. Mileage covered—

   B. Vehicle problems—

   C. Future suggestions—

2. Evaluation of location.

3. Brief summary of trip—course content—evaluation.

4. Any emergency problems.

5. Equipment check—practicality and needs.

6. Suggestions and recommendations for future trips—be specific.

7. Personnel analysis (include use of outside people and agencies).

Signature of Instructor _____

Date _____

Source: *Instructors Manual,* Program in Outdoor Pursuits, Ohio State University. Reprinted by permission of the Program in Outdoor Pursuits.

REFERENCES

Colorado Outward Bound School. "Jobs Clearing House Report, 1976." Unpublished. Denver: 1976.

SUGGESTED READINGS

Bunnelle, Hasse. *Food for Knapsackers.* San Francisco: Sierra Club Books, 1974.
Petzoldt, Paul. *The Wilderness Handbook.* New York: W. W. Norton and Company, 1974.
Climbing Committee of the Mountaineers. *Mountaineering: The Freedom of the Hills.* Seattle, Wash.: The Mountaineers, 1974.

four

areas for outdoor adventure activities

For a person to actually learn an outdoor adventure activity, it becomes important to have access to a special section of our earth's environment, such as a river, lake, mountain, rock face, or cave. Few, if any, schools or recreation agencies have these types of environments on their immediate grounds. Travel will be necessary to nearby lands which may be owned privately or by the state or federal government. The availability of these nearby lands is slowly becoming a problem because of the rapid growth in the number of outdoor activity enthusiasts and the gradual reduction of our earth's natural playgrounds.

This chapter will explore several available options for environments that can be used for outdoor pursuits, including:

1. Privately owned land.
2. State-owned land.
3. National forests.
4. National parks.

In addition, we will briefly examine national legislation directed at preserving lands for the use of outdoor activities. These include:

1. The National Wilderness Act.
2. The National Wild and Scenic Rivers Act.
3. The National Trail Act.

In conclusion, we shall also make some recommendations for increasing environmental awareness and for formulating strategies to maintain and preserve the wilderness areas that you and your groups will be using for the selected outdoor activities.

PRIVATE LAND

Privately owned land in your local area should be available for many outdoor activities. You may have to spend some time searching and asking questions in order to find out the most appropriate areas. We suggest that you first explore the areas within close proximity of the school or recreation center. There may be some suitable areas within walking distance. Many times, these areas can be adapted for ropes courses, hiking trails, cross-country skiing trails, or initiative games. The majority of these activities can be introduced at the school or recreation complex and then developed in a specific wilderness area appropriate for the activity.

The unimproved land throughout the United States totals approximately 1.4 billion acres, of which about 50 percent is suitable for use in outdoor adventure activities. These areas, which include both water and land, are usually owned by individuals or companies. These areas are currently used mostly by hunters and fishermen; however, many areas, such as northern Maine or Minnesota, can provide a rich resource of land and water for all types of outdoor activities. This land, which is privately owned by several large paper companies, can be available to participants under a certain set of prescribed conditions which are set up by the owner.

In using privately owned land, a good relationship should be developed between the participant and the landowner. This can only occur when all of the conditions are followed carefully. Participants need to remember that the use of private land is a privilege and should be treated as such. Before activities are conducted on any type of land or water body, the owner should be consulted for permission. In requesting permission for use, the participant should state the reasons for using the area, the nature of the activity, the number of days for use, and the effect of the activity on the environment.

At times, it may be difficult to identify the owner of a particular area. This information can generally be obtained through tax records within the township where the land is located, through local mailmen, or through owners of the adjoining land. We have found that most landowners give permission if they can be reassured that the land is to be used for a worthwhile activity and that no harm will come to the land as a result of the activity. As the growth of these medium- and high-risk activities continues, the use of private land will become more and more essential. It is the responsibility of all individuals to protect the rights of the landowner so that the land will be available for generations to come.

STATE-OWNED LANDS

Since many schools and recreation programs do not have adequate environments for specialized programs of outdoor activities, they are turning to state-owned lands or state parks. These lands are of vital importance because of the recent desire of commercial land developers to capitalize on the growth of outdoor adventure activities, such as cross-country ski touring, downhill skiing, and rock climbing. Since the acquisition and preservation of state lands for outdoor activities will be vital as the growth of these activities continues, program participants should actively support state governments in acquiring and preserving new land facilities.

The Constitution of the United States, by the Tenth Amendment (concerning states rights), gives each individual state the right to provide facilities and programs for recreational use for the people. The state parks system, which is the result of this specific amendment, can provide you with a convenient area for many outdoor activities. These lands are located in a variety of geographic settings. Information on available environments in your state parks can be obtained through your State Forest Service.

NATIONAL FORESTS

The first national forest in the United States was the Shoshone National Forest in Wyoming, originally known as Yellowstone Park Timber Land Reserve. This land space resulted from an act passed in 1891, which gave the president of the United States the right to reserve land for public domain. The act resolved

> That the President of the United States may from time to time set apart and reserve, in any State or Territory having public lands, wholly or in part covered with timber or undergrowth, whether of commercial value or not, as public reservations, and the President shall, by public proclamation, declare the establishment of such reservations and the limits thereof.[1]

---

[1] As cited in Clayne R. Jensen, *Outdoor Recreation in America: Trends, Problems, and Opportunities,* 3rd ed. (Minneapolis: Burgess Publishing Company, 1977), p. 64.

Figure 4-1. The National Forest System of the U.S. Forest Service
(Reprinted from U.S. Department of Agriculture, Forest Service)

Presently, the U.S. Forest Service contains about 187 million acres of land within 124 different national forests (see Figure 4-1). The bulk of these forests are found in the western United States. The Forest Service has made a commitment to using this land in a manner that will preserve our earth's natural resources. In 1960, Congress passed the Multiple Purpose Act, which has served as the basis for the preservation of the national forests for multiple uses, that is, for outdoor recreation as well as for timber, range, watersheds, and wildlife preserves. The act states that multiple use means

> The management of all the various renewable surface resources of the national forests so that they are utilized in the combination that will best meet the needs of the American people; making the most judicious use of the land for some or all of these resources or related services over areas large enough to provide sufficient latitude for periodic adjustments in use to conform to changing needs and conditions; that some land will be used for less than all of the resources; and harmonious and coordinated management of the various resources, each with the other, without impairment of the productivity of the land, with consideration being given to the relative values of the various resources, and not necessarily the combination of uses that will give the greatest dollar return or the greatest unit output.[2]

In compliance with the Multiple Purpose Act of 1960, the U.S. Forest Service has developed many meaningful educational and recreational outdoor activity programs. A significant effort of the Forest Service is the development and administration of the Operation Outdoor Project. This project is a five-year program charged with developing adequate facilities to meet the growth and demand of outdoor activities.

NATIONAL PARKS

The National Park Services governs a total of 31 million acres, including nearly 300 parks in 49 states, the District of Columbia, Puerto Rico, and the Virgin Islands. It maintains parks, monuments, battlefields, cemeteries, historical sites, seashores, lakesides, and preserves. Of the total acreage, about 24,887,024 acres can be used for outdoor activity programs.

NATIONAL LEGISLATION SUPPORTING OUTDOOR ACTIVITY PROGRAMS

This country has always been privileged to have individuals like John Muir, Henry David Thoreau, and Theodore Roosevelt, who had the determination and foresight to protect our natural resources. Recently, groups such as the Sierra Club, the Appalachian Mountain Club, the Appalachian Trail Conference, and the American Alpine Club have helped to lobby for greater expansion of the natural resources. The following federal legislation is the result of efforts of these individuals and groups.

National Wilderness Act

The National Wilderness Act, which became public law on September 3, 1964, has become a cornerstone in the preservation of our natural environment. The purpose of the act is "to establish a National Wilderness Preservation System for the permanent good of the whole people, and for other purposes." The passing of the act gave the National Forest and Parks Services the legal right to protect more than 36 million acres of land. Since that time numerous additional acreage has been

---

[2] As cited in *ibid.*, p. 67.

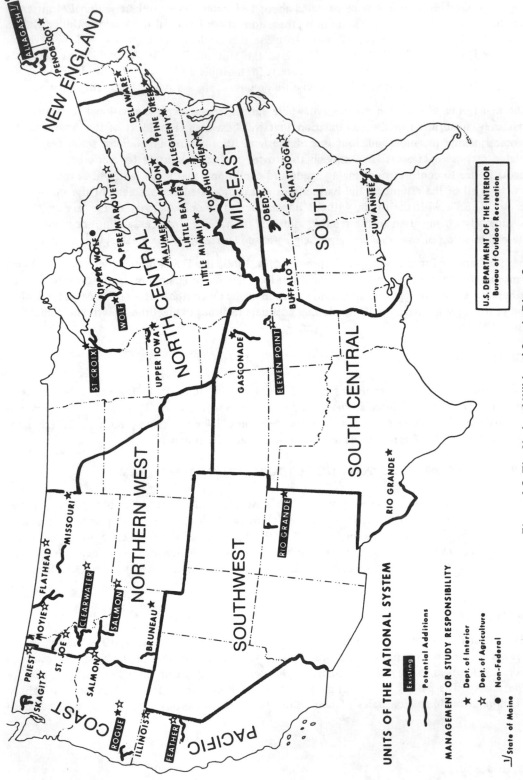

Figure 4-2. The National Wild and Scenic Rivers System
(Reprinted from U.S. Department of the Interior, Bureau of Outdoor Recreation)

UNITS OF THE NATIONAL SYSTEM

Existing

Potential Additions

MANAGEMENT OR STUDY RESPONSIBILITY

★ Dept. of Interior

☆ Dept. of Agriculture

● Non-Federal

1/ State of Maine

U.S. DEPARTMENT OF THE INTERIOR
Bureau of Outdoor Recreation

set aside to create the National Wilderness Systems. One of the major objectives of the act is the following:

National Forest Wilderness shall be so administered as to meet the public purposes of recreational, scenic, scientific, educational, conservation, and historical uses; and it shall also be administered for such other purposes for which it may have been established in such a manner as to preserve and protect its wilderness character. In carrying out such purposes, National Forest Wilderness resources shall be managed to promote, perpetuate, and, where necessary, restore the wilderness character of the land and its specific values of solitude, physical and mental challenge, scientific study, inspiration, and primitive recreation.[3]

National Wild and Scenic Rivers Act

On October 2, 1968 the United States Congress passed Public Law 90-542, authorizing the U.S. Department of the Interior and the U.S. Department of Agriculture to establish the National Wild and Scenic Rivers System. The rivers and adjacent land initially designated to develop the system were the Clearwater, Middle Fork (Idaho); the Eleven Point (Missouri); the Feather (California); the Rio Grande (New Mexico); the Rogue (Oregon); the Saint Croix (Minnesota and Wisconsin); the Salmon, Middle Fork (Idaho); the Wold (Wisconsin); the Lower Saint Croix (Minnesota and Wisconsin); the Chattooga (North Carolina, South Carolina, and Georgia); the Rapid (Idaho); and the Snake (Idaho and Oregon). Under the act, rivers are divided into three categories: (1) wild river areas, (2) scenic river areas, and (3) recreational river areas. The criteria for each category are as follows:

Wild River Areas. Those rivers or sections of rivers that are free of impoundments and generally inaccessible except by trail, with watersheds or shorelines essentially primitive and water unpolluted. These represent vestiges of primitive America.
Scenic River Areas. Those rivers or sections of rivers that are free of impoundments, with shoreline or watersheds still largely primitive and shoreline largely undeveloped, but accessible in places by roads.
Recreational River Areas. Those rivers or sections of rivers that are readily accessible by road or railroad, that may have some development along their shorelines, and that may have undergone some impoundment or diversion in the past.[4]

Other rivers that are under study but are currently not included in the system include:

1. *New York.* Hudson's Adirondack headwaters.
2. *Connecticut.* Housatonic.
3. *Tennessee.* Nolichucky.
4. *Alaska.* Aniakchak, Alagnak, Kanektok, Andreafsty, Unalaklect, Salmon, Noatak, Killik, Alatna, Tinayguk, Nowitna, Beaver, North Fork Koyakuk, Wind, Ivishak, Porcupine, Sheenjek, Birch, Charley, Fortymile, and Bremner.

National Trails System Act

The National Trails System Act was passed into public law on October 2, 1968. This act (Public Law 90-453) states:

---

[3]*A Handbook on the Wilderness Act,* The Wilderness Society, 729 15th Street N.W., Washington, D.C.
[4]*Wild and Scenic Rivers Act,* U.S. Department of the Interior, U.S. Government Printing Office, Washington, D.C., 1975.

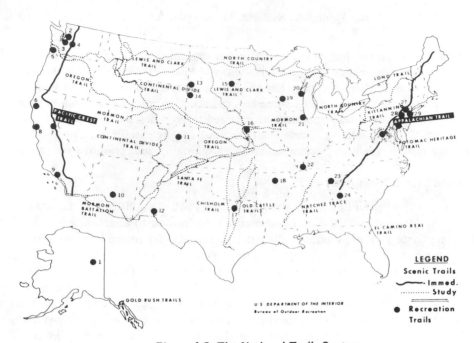

Figure 4-3. The National Trails System
(Reprinted from U.S. Department of the Interior, Bureau of Outdoor Recreation)

In order to provide for the ever-increasing outdoor recreation needs of an expanding population and in order to promote public access to, travel within, and enjoyment and appreciation of the open-air, outdoor areas of the Nation, trails should be established (1) primarily, near the urban areas of the Nation and (2) secondarily, within established scenic areas more remotely located.

The National Scenic Trails are designed for the use of hiking, backpacking, and camping, while all motorized equipment is prohibited on these trails. The initial trails set aside in this act were the Appalachian Trail and the Pacific Crest Trail. In the same public law, Congress designated fourteen additional trails for study and possible inclusion into the National Trails System (see Figure 4-3). Table 4-1 lists the National Scenic Trails, the total distance of each, and their locations.

ENVIRONMENT AWARENESS

The result of the growth and popularity of medium- and high-risk outdoor activities across the country is having a detrimental effect on some areas of our natural environment from overuse and misuse. A condition now exists, for example, that requires that proper steps be taken to preserve the wilderness areas that still exist. At one time the McKinley National Park in Alaska was considered a true wilderness park, but in the summer climbing season of 1976, between 70 and 80 climbers stood on North America's highest point in a single day.[5] Mount McKinley is now sometimes referred to as "Garbage Mountain," which is a sad and striking statement; in 1975, a ton of trash left behind from climbing parties was removed from her slopes.[6]

[5] Robert Gerhard, "Denali Dilemma," *American Alpine Journal* (1977), p. 96.
[6] Price Zimmermann, "Crisis on Denali—Another Look," *American Alpine News,* no. 137 (June 1976), p. 7.

Table 4-1. National Scenic Trails

TRAIL	DISTANCE (IN MILES)	LOCATION
Continental Divide	3,100	From the Mexican border in New Mexico, northward along the Continental Divide to the Canadian border; ends in Glacier National Park
Potomac Heritage	825	From the mouth of the Potomac River to its sources in Pennsylvania and West Virginia; includes the 170-mile Chesapeake and Ohio Canal towpath
Old Cattle	800	From the vicinity of San Antonio, Texas, through Oklahoma to Abilene, Kansas
Lewis and Clark	—	From Wood River, Illinois to the Pacific Ocean, following both the outbound and the inbound routes of the Lewis and Clark expedition
Natchez Trace	600	From Nashville, Tennessee to Natchez, Mississippi
North Country	3,200	From the Appalachian Trail in Vermont, through New York state, Pennsylvania, Ohio, Michigan, Wisconsin, and Minnesota to the Lewis and Clark Trail in North Dakota
Kittanning	—	From Shirleysburg, Pennsylvania to Kittanning, Pennsylvania
Oregon	2,000	From Independence, Missouri to Fort Vancouver, Washington
Santa Fe	800	From Independence, Missouri to Santa Fe, New Mexico
Long	255	From the Massachusetts border northward through Vermont to the Canadian border
Mormon	—	From Nauvoo, Illinois to Salt Lake City, Utah
Gold Rush	—	Alaska
Mormon Battalion	2,000	From Mount Pisgah, Iowa through Kansas, Colorado, New Mexico, and Arizona to Los Angeles, California
El Camino Real	30	From St. Augustine to Fort Caroline National Memorial, Florida, along the southern boundary of the St. Johns River

Source: *National Scenic and Recreational Trails,* U.S. Department of the Interior, U.S. Government Printing Office, Washington, D.C., 1975.

To protect our nation's remaining wilderness areas from further deterioration, it is imperative that instructors of outdoor activities teach not only technical skills but also an awareness of the environment and man's relationship within it. It is the responsibility of outdoor instructors to help their students make intelligent decisions related to the effective use and preservation of the outdoors.

The process of becoming an environmentally aware and concerned individual must begin with a living experience. All individuals should view themselves as a part of a total environment and not separate from it. Activities and experiences conducted in an outdoor area can facilitate this process by showing individuals the role they can play to maintain the nation's natural environments.

Each individual participating in a wilderness expedition has a responsibility to protect the environment, and the following rules should always be observed.

1. Only travel on established trails and footpaths.
2. Only camp in established campsites.
3. Avoid wearing lug-soled boots on footpaths. Lug-soled boots are designed for rocky terrain and will actually bulldoze a path on a dry trail. On dry trails and footpaths a good walking shoe is less destructive.
4. Never wash or bathe with soap in a stream or lake, even if the soap is biodegradable.
5. Never wash cooking pots in a lake or stream; the best practice is to gather water and wash on the bank.
6. Carry out all trash.
7. Backpacking or camp stoves are better than open fires, which leave behind a fire ring of scorched earth.
8. Never pick or cut any type of plant or tree; leave the wildflowers for all the people to see. Take pictures but leave everything else behind.
9. Never deface anything with your initials, name, or sayings; the outdoor community does not need this type of immortality.
10. Pay close attention to all trail signs and markers for specific rules and regulations for that area.

QUESTIONS FOR REVIEW AND DISCUSSION

1. What information do private landowners need to have about people using their land for outdoor activities?
2. How would you go about locating the owner of some land where you wanted to take a group camping?
3. What procedures would you follow to preserve the land of a private owner?
4. Why are state and federal lands becoming important to outdoor activity enthusiasts?
5. What is the Multiple Purpose Act?
6. Name two federal acts supporting land use.
7. What are the categories of rivers in the National Wild and Scenic Rivers Act?
8. What were the two original trails in the National Trails System Act?
9. List five rules that you should follow during wilderness activities in order to preserve the environment.

REFERENCES

Book

Jensen, Clayne R. *Outdoor Recreation in America: Trends, Problems, and Opportunities.* 3rd ed. Minneapolis: Burgess Publishing Company, 1977.

Articles

Gerhard, Robert. "Denali Dilemma." *American Alpine Journal* (1977), p. 96.
Zimmermann, Price. "Crisis on Denali—Another Look." *American Alpine News*, no. 137 (June 1976), p. 7.

Pamphlets

A Handbook on the Wilderness Act. The Wilderness Society, 729 15th Street N.W., Washington, D.C.
Wild and Scenic Rivers Act. U.S. Department of the Interior, U.S. Government Printing Office, Washington, D.C., 1975.

SUGGESTED READINGS

Books

Gray, William R. *The Pacific Crest Trail.* Washington, D.C.: National Geographic Society, 1975.
Fisher, Ronald M. *The Appalachian Trail.* Washington, D.C.: National Geographic Society, 1972.
Melham, Tom. *John Muir's Wild America.* Washington, D.C.: National Geographic Society.

Pamphlets

Establishing Trails on Rights-of-way. U.S. Department of the Interior, U.S. Government Printing Office, Washington, D.C.
National Recreation Trails. U.S. Department of the Interior, U.S. Government Printing Office, Washington, D.C.
National Recreation Trails, Information and Application Procedure. U.S. Department of the Interior, U.S. Government Printing Office, Washington, D.C., 1975.
Proceedings: National Symposium on Trails, 1971. U.S. Department of the Interior, U.S. Government Printing Office, Washington, D.C., 1971.

five

measurement
and evaluation of
outdoor adventure programs

Measurement and evaluation are an integral part of any outdoor adventure program, just as they are important to any other type of educational or recreational program. It is impossible to ascertain what progress a program has made without measurement and evaluation. Administrators and directors of outdoor programs need to understand and use modern techniques of measurement and evaluation.

EVALUATION AND MEASUREMENT

Evaluation is primarily a subjective process that utilizes the results of a variety of measurements to arrive at a value judgment—an appraisal made according to a set of values. Evaluation should be a means of determining the extent to which the objectives of a program are being accomplished. Therefore, to evaluate a program effectively, one must know exactly what is to be evaluated. Specific program objectives must be established and then evaluated. An overall evaluation procedure should be designed and utilized to examine the strengths and weaknesses of the program and its objectives. The process should provide a continuous check on where the program is and where it is going. Evaluation should not be an end in itself.

Measurement is an important part of evaluation, which uses specific tools and techniques to quantify what is to be evaluated. A variety of techniques, devices, and instruments are available for the evaluation of outdoor adventure programs: eyeballing (subjective observation), checklists, anecdotal records, questionnaires, interviews, self-appraisals, rating scales, and objective observation scales.

Measurement focuses on the current status of a program in terms of its proposed objectives, and it can indicate the best techniques for achieving them. Measurement provides a current check on students' knowledge, attitudes, and skills in relation to what the program purports to be accomplishing. This monitoring of a program helps clarify its objectives, methodologies, and techniques.

EVALUATIVE PROCESS

All aspects of an outdoor adventure program should be evaluated continually, both formally and informally. It is advantageous to consult with an expert or a team of experts, if possible, every other year for a thorough evaluation. It seems that the best way to evaluate a total program is to start with the students involved in it and then to analyze aspects of the program that have an effect on them. The most important part of a program is its effect on students' lives. It is also important to be able to show others exactly how the program affects the students who are involved.

In addition to evaluation of the students who participate in the program, there should be an evaluation of:

1. Instructors.
2. Objectives of the program.
3. Content of the program.
4. Learning opportunities.
5. Environment.
6. Equipment.

EVALUATION OF STUDENTS

The evaluation of students should depend upon the goals or objectives of the program. For example, if the focus is the development of a person's self-concept, a definition of *self-concept* should be developed and then an evaluation procedure should be established to see whether the program did indeed affect it. If the program is focused on developing physical skills, for example, rappelling techniques, knot tying, or canoeing strokes, then measurement and evaluation should focus on these particular skills. It is imperative, therefore, for administrators and program developers to establish goals or objectives in advance of the development of measurement and evaluation procedures.

Most programs purport to develop the ability to perform certain physical skills, such as knot tying, rock climbing, map and compass reading, first aid, canoeing, cooking, cycling, or cross-country skiing. An effective procedure for evaluating the acquisition of physical skills is to administer a battery of tests that focus exactly on those skills. This battery of tests could be given in a pre-test and post-test format, to insure a degree of scientific procedure. Tests should be developed and selected on the basis of reliability and validity. Reliability refers to the consistency of measurement for a given test; that is, a test should yield similar results when it is administered to the same students at a later date. Validity refers to the ability of a test to measure what it purports to measure. For example, a test on canoeing strokes should measure these strokes and not some other variable, such as strength or power. It is also important to make sure that testing procedures do not take too much time.

There are no standardized tests that focus on the physical skills associated with common outdoor activities. Therefore, program directors must become skilled at developing tests that meet the needs of their program.

Another method for evaluating the acquisition of physical skills is to make use of a list of specific behavioral or performance objectives. Behavioral objectives are instructional aids in the form of specific statements of the intended outcomes of a particular activity. A properly constructed behavioral objective should describe (1) the specific behavior as an observable, measurable activity, (2) the conditions or setting for the behavior, and (3) the criterion for accomplishment. Teachers can modify the conditions and the criteria to set up a progressive learning sequence.

Performance objectives can be administered in several different ways. Students could be given the objectives on the first day of the course, so that they would know exactly what is expected of them in terms of skill development. Then, each following day could be organized so that students would have a certain amount of time to practice the skills. This method would enable students to proceed at their own rate of development; the performance objectives would serve as a motivational device. In addition, outside people would know exactly what physical skills are developed in the program, and this could help in the selling of the program.

Table 5-1 includes a list of behavioral or performance objectives that were used with seventh- and eighth-grade students in a skin-diving instructional unit on the use of the face mask. These objectives

Table 5-1. Behavioral or Performance Objectives for Using the Face Mask in Skin Diving

Write the date when each performance objective is met.

_____   1. Adjust the face mask strap to your head size.

_____   2. *Fog preventative.* Apply saliva to the face mask—rub all around the face plate. *Do not rinse.*

_____   3. *Vertical tilt.* Fill the mask with water and hold it to the face without the strap. In chest-deep water, go under in a vertical position and, by tilting the head backwards from the chest, push against the upper edge of the mask and exhale gently. Completely clear the mask in three out of five attempts.

_____   4. *Horizontal roll.* Fill the mask with water and hold it to the face without the strap. While in a horizontal position, roll on the left shoulder, pushing gently with the right hand against the side of the mask, and exhale gently. Completely clear the mask in three out of five attempts.

_____   5. Repeat step 3 with the strap attached to the back of the head.

_____   6. Repeat step 4 with the strap attached to the back of the head.

_____   7. In six feet of water, submerge to the bottom of the pool and by pinching the nostrils, gently exhale into the mask until you feel the pressure equalize in your ears. Successfully equalize the pressure in four out of five attempts.

_____   8. Repeat step 7 in nine feet of water.

_____   9. Repeat step 3 in deep water.

_____   10. Repeat step 4 in deep water.

_____   11. Throw the mask into shallow water, submerge, and put the mask on. Complete a vertical tilt and clear the mask in one breath in four out of five attempts.

_____   12. Throw the mask into shallow water, submerge, and put the mask on. Complete a horizontal roll and clear the mask in one breath in four out of five attempts.

_____   13. Repeat step 11 in six feet of water.

_____   14. Repeat step 11 in nine feet of water.

_____   15. Repeat step 12 in six feet of water.

_____   16. Repeat step 12 in nine feet of water.

could be modified and adapted for use in other outdoor activities programs involving different age levels.

Most outdoor programs have a cognitive component, that is, they require the acquisition of knowledge, for example, of belaying techniques, canoeing strokes, parts of a sailboat, map symbols, and first aid procedures. Obviously, the evaluation of this phase of a program could be completed with some test of knowledge. Cognitive tests are usually classified as either standardized or teacher-made. Since each outdoor program is unique in some way, it is virtually impossible to develop a standardized cognitive test. Therefore, directors of outdoor programs must learn to construct such tests themselves. Donald K. Mathews suggests the following procedures:

1. The important aspects of the subject matter should be covered in the same proportion that they were covered in the instructional unit.
2. Directions should be explicit and succinct.
3. Ambiguity should be avoided.
4. A large number of items should be included.
5. The instructor should be aware of stereotypes determiners, such as all, never, nothing, always, and no.
6. Statements should be brief; if possible, not more than twenty-five words should be used.
7. The distribution of scores for the examination should approximate the normal curve.
8. Trivial items should not be included.[1]

The most difficult aspect of student evaluation in an outdoor program is that of affective learning. This type of learning focuses on feelings, attitudes, and values. The elusive nature of the affective domain makes it difficult to show causal relationships between an outdoor program and changes in a student's attitude. Research in this area is continuing and should provide some new insights.

A common technique for measuring a person's attitude or opinion is to use some form of the Likert Scale. The first step in this technique is to develop a number of statements that describe an attitude toward some aspect of a program, for example,

1. Rock climbing helps you recognize the strengths and weaknesses of other people.
2. Initiative tests force some people to exhibit leadership behavior.
3. Rappelling teaches you about fear.

Next, a scale is designed to indicate a person's attitude toward the statements. The following scale is commonly used:

SA—Strongly agree
 A—Agree
 U—Undecided or neutral
 D—Disagree
SD—Strongly disagree

Students are then asked to react to every statement; the scoring procedure usually involves assigning five points to the most favorable attitude and one point to the least favorable. The highest score then represents the most favorable attitude toward the program. The obvious problem with an attitude scale is that the person might not indicate his or her true feelings because of negative consequences that might result from revealing a particular attitude. Table 5-2 and Table 5-3 are attitude scales that were developed by Project U.S.E. M.A.I.N.E. in several of its wilderness programs.

Another method for uncovering attitudes or opinions is the personal interview. The interviewer should direct the same questions to each person and should remain in a value-free position. Again, there is a problem with validity, because the subject might answer differently from how he or she really feels.

---

[1] Donald K. Mathews, *Measurement in Physical Education,* 4th ed. (Philadelphia: W. B. Saunders, 1973), pp. 361-362.

Open-ended questions are another technique for obtaining information by allowing students to express their attitudes and opinions about various issues. (See Table 5-4.) They can respond orally or in writing, whichever seems to best suit their needs and interests. The following types of questions could be used:

1. What does leadership mean to you?
2. What people in your group exhibited leadership behaviors?
3. Did you learn anything about leadership from the other members of your group?
4. Which activities will you continue to participate in?

Although the affective domain can be difficult to observe and measure scientifically, it is nonetheless important in any outdoor adventure program. It should not be neglected on the grounds that it does not lend itself nicely to scientific inquiry. The limited research literature on adventure programs indicates that they do have a positive effect on the attitudes and feelings of participants.

Another measurement and evelation strategy that merits attention is the use of objective behavioral observation systems, which can be designed to collect objective information on students' behaviors in an outdoor environment. This objective information can be valuable in improving the program and strengthening the impact that it has on students. Too many times, programs are changed on the basis of subjectively collected information. To collect objective information on student behavior, evaluators need to become skilled in the use of the following observation and recording techniques:

1. *Event recording.* A tally is made of every predefined, observable behavior as it occurs, according to a set of reliable definitions for certain categories of behavior. This technique records the number of behaviors shown during a given block of time. This output, converted to a rate per minute, can then be used to make comparisons.
2. *Duration recording.* The total elapsed time of a specific behavior during a certain observation period is recorded. A stopwatch is needed to measure the duration of each interval.

Table 5-2. Attitude Scale for Project U.S.E. M.A.I.N.E. ("Impact" Program)

Scale

SA—Strongly agree
 A—Agree
 U—Undecided or neutral
 D—Disagree
SD—Strongly disagree

1. An individual can gain greater knowledge of himself or herself through a direct encounter with stress.
2. Close involvement with others through the interaction of the group provides you with an effective means of dealing with a variety of different behaviors.
3. Excitement and challenge should be as much a part of human experience as routine and ritual.
4. Rock climbing helps you realize the strengths and weaknesses of other people.
5. Group problem-solving tasks force some people to exhibit leadership behavior.
6. Rappelling provides you with information about fear.

Source: Project U.S.E. M.A.I.N.E., Harrison, Maine.

Table 5-3. Attitude Scale for Project U.S.E. M.A.I.N.E. ("Pay" Program)

In the following section there are sets of descriptive phrases. Place an *X* on the line which indicates where you feel you are in terms of those statements after taking part in the Project U.S.E. program.

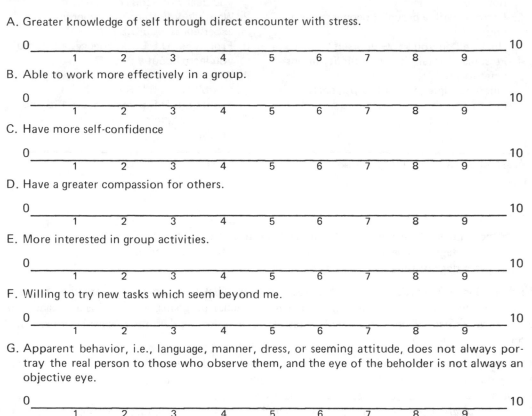

A. Greater knowledge of self through direct encounter with stress.

0 _____ 10
    1   2   3   4   5   6   7   8   9

B. Able to work more effectively in a group.

0 _____ 10
    1   2   3   4   5   6   7   8   9

C. Have more self-confidence

0 _____ 10
    1   2   3   4   5   6   7   8   9

D. Have a greater compassion for others.

0 _____ 10
    1   2   3   4   5   6   7   8   9

E. More interested in group activities.

0 _____ 10
    1   2   3   4   5   6   7   8   9

F. Willing to try new tasks which seem beyond me.

0 _____ 10
    1   2   3   4   5   6   7   8   9

G. Apparent behavior, i.e., language, manner, dress, or seeming attitude, does not always portray the real person to those who observe them, and the eye of the beholder is not always an objective eye.

0 _____ 10
    1   2   3   4   5   6   7   8   9

Source: Project U.S.E. M.A.I.N.E., Harrison, Maine.

3. *Placheck recording.* An observer scans a group of students from left to right and counts the number of pupils engaged in a predefined behavior. This number can be converted to a percentage of the total class. Scans should be made on a predetermined schedule throughout the observation period.

4. *Time sampling.* The specific behavior of one person is observed at a designated time during a session.

5. *Interval recording.* The behavior of a person that categorizes an interval of time is observed according to a predetermined set of behavioral definitions.

These observation and recording techniques can be used to gather information about various student behaviors. The following are some possibilities:

1. The number and level of skills acquired per unit of time.
2. The percentage of time spent on task or off task.

Table 5-4. Open-Ended Questions for Project U.S.E. M.A.I.N.E. Program

PRE-COURSE QUESTIONS	POST-COURSE QUESTIONS
1. I tend to deal with stress or painful situations by . . .	1. From your U.S.E. experiences, how did you deal with stress or pain?
2. Learning with a group of people means to you . . .	2. What did you learn from your group experiences with U.S.E.?
3. How well do you know yourself?	3. From your U.S.E. experiences, what did you learn about yourself?
4. Personal adaptability or flexibility means what to you?	4. What did you learn about adaptability or flexibility from U.S.E.?
5. What are some of your key personal needs?	5. From your U.S.E. experiences, did you find out anything about your personal needs?

Source: Project U.S.E. M.A.I.N.E., Harrison, Maine.

3. The percentage of time in which the student is active or inactive.
4. The percentage of time in which the student is productive or unproductive.
5. The percentage of time spent getting organized.

The definitions of behaviors should obviously vary somewhat from program to program. Evaluators define the behaviors that are important to their particular programs. Table 5-5 is an example of a coding format focused on five student behaviors. The following definitions have been used in this system:

1. *Appropriate behavior.* Any behavior that contributes to the educational environment, e.g., carrying out directions, maintaining eye contact with the teacher during a demonstration, helping a classmate with a skill, or cheering a classmate's performance.
2. *Inappropriate behavior.* Any behavior that detracts from the educational environment, e.g., talking during a demonstration, failure to carry out directions, or pushing a classmate while standing in line.
3. *Active learning.* Actual physical involvement in the planned activity for the class, e.g., swimming, hiking, tying knots, paddling a canoe, or plotting a map courrse.
4. *Inactive learning.* Any learning behavior that does not involve the person physically, e.g., waiting in line, listening to a lecture, or watching someone else perform.
5. *Managerial time.* Time required to get organized for a class activity, to change from one activity to another, or to end a final activity, for example, time spent rotating from station to station, time spent checking attendance, or time spent lining up for an activity.

Sections 1 and 2 of the sample coding format are placheck recordings, which focus on the behavior of the entire group. The recorder scans the group and counts the number of students engaged in the selected behavior. This number is then recorded in the appropriate box. At the end of the observation session, a mean percentage of students engaged in the selected behavior can be obtained; for example, 90 percent of the class was appropriate while 75 percent was actively involved. Section 3 is a time sampling procedure for two students selected from the class, who are observed at predetermined times to obtain information on how they spend their time in the class. A percentage of observation instances is obtained; for example, 50 percent of the observations found the student

Table 5-5. Objective Coding Format for Student Behavior

Teacher _____ Date _____

Time _____ Observer _____

Number in Class _____ Activities _____

		1	2	3	4	5	6	7	8	9	10	11	12	13	14	Total
1. *Placheck* Appropriate/ inappropriate behavior																
2. *Placheck* Active/ inactive behavior																
3. *Time Sample* Appropriate	Student A															
Inappropriate	Student B															

4. *Duration* Managerial time	1	2	3	4	5	6	7	Total
Specific episode	8	9	10	11	12	13	14	

behaving inappropriately. The fourth category of student behavior, recorded in section 4, is the duration of time spent in management episodes, measured by a stopwatch. A percentage of class time spent in managerial activities can be obtained with this strategy. All this information has implications for planning and improving a program. For example, if students are spending inordinate amounts of time getting organized or managing, the teachers need to become aware of this situation so that appropriate adjustments can be made.

EVALUATION OF INSTRUCTORS

The evaluation of instructors continues to be a critical problem for a number of reasons. The complexity of the teaching-learning process and the variety of opinions on exactly what constitutes good teaching are additional difficulties.

A scientific approach to evaluation and, consequently, improvement of teaching skills should be utilized. This has been referred to as a "tools of the trade" approach by N. L. Gage and Daryl Siedentop.[2] This approach assumes that there are a number of teaching skills that a person can learn and develop through practice. It also assumes that such learning should take place in a systematic, data-based fashion rather than on a trial-and-error or hit-and-miss basis.

Traditional methods for evaluating teaching are unsystematic and are usually based on few objective data. The three most common techniques are what Siedentop calls eyeballing, anecdotal records, and rating scales or checklists.[3] Eyeballing uses few objective data and relies instead on the perceptions of the evaluator. Anecdotal records are notes on what takes place in an environment, which are kept for discussion later. Checklists or rating scales make use of statements or lists of characteristics related to teaching or teachers. Evaluators make a value judgment about the statements or characteristics and then discuss the ratings with the teacher. Obviously, each of these methods is limited in different ways, depending on the values of the evaluator.

Systematic observation and recording of teaching behaviors require the use of the aforementioned techniques of event recording, duration recording, time sampling, and interval recording. Teaching behaviors that should be considered include:

1. Percentage of time spent verbalizing.
2. Percentage of attention given to on-task or off-task behavior.
3. Percentage of attention given to students at various levels of ability.
4. Rate of praising.
5. Rate of scolding.
6. Variety of reinforcers.
7. Rate of positive information feedback.
8. Rate of corrective information feedback.
9. Rate of managerial cues.
10. Incidence of use of students' first names.
11. Rate of modeling behaviors.

We shall examine several systems that have been used in physical education and outdoor teaching environments.

---

[2] N. L. Gage, *Teacher Effectiveness and Teacher Education: The Search for a Scientific Basis* (Palo Alto, Calif.: Pacific Books, 1972), p. 195; Daryl Siedentop, *Developing Teaching Skills in Physical Education* (Boston: Houghton Mifflin Company, 1976), p. viii.

[3] Siedentop, pp. 23-27.

Teacher Reaction Scale

Teacher reactions seem to have an important effect upon the behavior of students in the program. The Teacher Reaction Scale (Table 5-6) includes four categories of teacher reaction behavior, each of which is dichotomized according to general and specific behaviors. Student teachers in physical education have used this scale to modify their teaching behaviors, with positive results.

The Ohio State University Teacher Behavior Scale

The Ohio State University Teacher Behavior Scale (Table 5-7) has also been used with student teachers and various research projects in physical education at Ohio State University. Eight teaching behaviors should be systematically observed by event recording. This scale, in conjunction with several intervention strategies, such as modeling and directed information feedback, has been effective in modifying selected teacher behaviors.

These observation scales should be selected to fulfill the needs of a particular program. They can be very simple or quite sophisticated. It is important to select and utilize a scale that you thoroughly understand and that will provide reliable data. Make sure that the data obtained are used in a non-threatening manner and for the purpose of improving the teaching skills of those who are being evaluated. It is also important to keep a proper perspective on the scope of the instrument. What constitutes good teaching is still very much a debatable issue with a thin research base to draw upon for guidance. It should be pointed out that these systems and observation techniques are mere tools, and what is important is *how* they are used and what specific teaching-learning behaviors they are focused upon.

It is beyond the scope of this book to delve into the theoretical and philosophical bases of teacher behavior and its effect on students, but it is certainly important for all staff members and administrators to become familiar with the effects that might be brought about. Group discussion among staff members should focus on such topics as teacher-student interactions, teachers' instructional or demonstration behaviors, information feedback behaviors (positive, negative, and corrective), use of first names, nonverbal interactions, management behaviors, students' productive and non-productive behaviors, students' active and inactive behaviors, and students' appropriate and inappropriate behaviors.

All these behaviors can be defined, observed, measured, analyzed, and evaluated with some form of objective observation scale. Efforts should be made to involve all staff members in the development of behavioral definitions and the selection of observation scales. Baseline rates of behavior should be established and goals should be set according to the specific situation. With the aid of sound evaluation, teachers can gradually progress towards the specific goals established and then maintain them over a period of time.

The scientific approach to the study and improvement of teaching has been gaining popularity in the past 10 years. Professional literature and conferences have devoted much space and time to this approach. Eyeballing, or subjective examination of the teaching-learning environment, is being reduced or almost eliminated. The scientific approach is obviously important to staff development in an outdoor activities program. The references cited at the end of this chapter are recommended for further treatments of evaluation.

EVALUATION OF PROGRAM OBJECTIVES

It is impossible to evaluate a program without examining its specific objectives. Therefore, a considerable amount of time should be spent in the development, examination, and evaluation of

Table 5-6. Teacher Reaction Scale

Categories

Skill-Positive—Positive verbal or non-verbal reaction after a skill attempt.
Skill-Negative—Negative or corrective verbal or non-verbal reaction after a skill attempt.
Behavior-Positive—Verbal or non-verbal reaction to appropriate student behavior.
Behavior-Negative—Verbal or non-verbal reaction to inappropriate student behavior.
(Each category may be subdivided to record whether the teacher reaction included specific information related to the skill or behavior or whether it was a general reaction.)

Teacher _____ Class _____ Date _____

Length of recording interval	Skill-Positive		Skill-Negative		Behavior-Positive		Behavior-Negative	
	specific	general	specific	general	specific	general	specific	general

Summary: Rate per minute _____ Ratio of positive to negative _____

Source: D. Siedentop, "Teacher Reaction Scale," unpublished (Ohio State University, School of Health, Physical Education, and Recreation, 1973). Reprinted by permission of the author.

Table 5-7. The Ohio State University Teacher Behavior Rating Scale

BEHAVIOR CATEGORY	BEHAVIORAL PARAMETERS
1. Input teaching acts	Includes all teacher behaviors that provide a discriminate stimulus function directly related to learning. This includes questioning (teacher asks a question), explaining (teacher elaborates or summarizes previous material or clarifies a problem for better understanding), informing (answering a question), and providing guidance (including verbal guidance, demonstration, forced-responding, and physical restriction) (Rushall and Siedentop, 1972).
2. Managerial	Refers to teacher behaviors that provide a discriminative stimulus function indirectly related to learning. This includes establishing and maintaining order, directing equipment, etc. Also includes roll taking, marking down performance scores, and other forms of record keeping directly related to current behavior of students. These behaviors are primarily teacher initiated (discriminative function) and are not teacher reactions to student disturbances (consequential function).
3. Monitoring	Refers to watching the class as a whole, a subset of the class, or an individual student. No verbal or non-verbal interaction occurs.
4. No activity	Refers to all teacher behaviors in which visual contact is broken and no verbal or non-verbal interaction occurs. Includes looking out the window, being out of the room, talking to another teacher, and record keeping not directly related to immediate behavior of students.
5. Skill attempt Positive IF	Refers to all positive verbal and nonverbal teacher reactions to an appropriate skill attempt by a student.
6. Skill attempt Negative IF	Refers to all negative verbal and nonverbal teacher reactions to an appropriate skill attempt by a student, including corrective feedback. Does not necessarily imply a punishing or menacing tone.
7. Positive reaction to on-task behavior	Refers to all positive verbal and nonverbal teacher reactions to on-task student behaviors other than skill attempts.
8. Negative reaction to off-task behavior	Refers to all negative verbal and nonverbal teacher reaction to off-task student behavior.

Source: D. Siedentop and C. Hughley, "O.S.U. Teacher Behavior Rating Scale," *JOPER* 46 (February 1975):45. Reprinted by permission of the publisher.

program objectives. In setting up objectives, teachers and administrators should consider the following influences:

1. The interests, characteristics, and attitudes of prospective students.
2. The interests, problems, and conditions of the community or society in general.
3. The recommendations of outdoor program specialists.
4. The content of existing outdoor programs.
5. The values of the school district or community.

Remember that the objectives that are formulated should be ones whose accomplishment can be clearly demonstrated by solid evidence. Be careful not to base objectives solely on what you think might be accomplished.

Objectives should be specific and stated in terms of behaviors sought in the learner. They should cover a wide range of knowledge, attitudes, and physical skills that are consistent with the overall school or program objectives.

EVALUATION OF PROGRAM CONTENT AND LEARNING OPPORTUNITIES

Content and learning opportunities should be examined to see whether they do indeed accomplish the program's objectives. Experimentation with new and old activities will enable you to arrange the best possible learning opportunities for your students. New and innovative activities should be considered to see whether they can improve the program; content and learning opportunities should be up-to-date. It is also important that they be appropriate for the students' level of maturity. Learning opportunities should be examined to see whether students are receiving enough feedback and enough actual practice time for them to achieve the stated objectives.

The motivational aspects of content and learning opportunities should also be evaluated. Are the students receiving positive reinforcement from (or experiencing success in) the particular activity or learning opportunity?

In addition, content and learning opportunities should be examined in relation to the diversity of students' abilities. Is there any allowance for individual differences?

Finally, the economics of the content and learning opportunities should be considered. Obviously, some activities require greater expenditures for equipment and travel. You must be sure that they are providing exactly what you are trying to provide.

EVALUATION OF ENVIRONMENT AND EQUIPMENT

An outdoor adventure program should make optimal use of all outdoor environments that are reasonably close to the base of operations. Students should become familiar with different environments and with environmental problems that concern mountains, rivers, caves, beaches, oceans, lakes, rain, snow, and wind. Program leaders need to make themselves aware of outdoor sites in the immediate area through reading, exploring, asking questions, checking with a National Park Services office, checking with local dealers of outdoor equipment, and checking with local scouting groups. The possibility of transportation to gain access to different environments should be considered by program administrators. Traveling for a few hours might bring you into various different environments. Judgments about where to conduct your activities should refer to the program's objectives and commitments. The competencies and skills of instructors can also be a factor in determining which environments are suitable for your program. However, it is best that all available possibilities in the community be explored and utilized.

Other components of the physical environment that require evaluation include class size, facilities, and equipment. Class size is difficult to evaluate: one is always faced with the dilemma of whether to limit the size of the group so that special attention can be given to each individual or whether to increase the size of the group so that more people can enjoy the experience. Obviously, there are many factors to consider before a decision is made, for example, the age and background of the students, the objectives of the program, and the availability of equipment.

The safety of facilities and equipment is of paramount interest for any evaluation. In addition to its safety, equipment should be considered for its effectiveness, practicality, and durability. Equipment and facilities should be evaluated in accordance with the course or program objectives.

Besides evaluation of the physical environment, evaluation of a program's mental or emotional environment should also be conducted. Many of the activities of an outdoor program involve some risk, and situations of danger generally affect the emotional environment. It is important for program organizers to be aware of such situations and to be able to deal with them effectively. The interpersonal relationships between teacher and students, students and students, and teachers and teachers are critical to the overall mental atmosphere of the program. Interpersonal relations can be defined in observable, measurable terms and then can be evaluated by the number and types that occur in a given observation period. The recording and observation techniques discussed previously in this chapter can be used for this purpose.

QUESTIONS FOR REVIEW AND DISCUSSION

1. What is the difference between measurement and evaluation?
2. What is meant by a data-based approach to measurement and evaluation?
3. What types of student learning needs to be evaluated?
4. How can performance objectives be used to evaluate student learning?
5. Which type of student learning is difficult to evaluate?
6. Why is teaching a hard area to evaluate?
7. Explain the difference between event recording, duration recording, placheck, time sample, and interval recording.
8. What is a disadvantage of eyeballing and anecdotal records as evaluation techniques?
9. Besides teaching and learning, what other aspects of an outdoor program should be evaluated?

REFERENCES

Gage, N. L. *Teacher Effectiveness and Teacher Education: The Search for a Scientific Basis*. Palo Alto, Calif.: Pacific Books, 1972.

Mathews, Donald K. *Measurement in Physical Education*. 4th ed. Philadelphia: W. B. Saunders Company, 1973.

Siedentop, Daryl. *Developing Teaching Skills in Physical Education*. Boston: Houghton Mifflin Company, 1976.

six

initiative games

Many decisions must be made before and during wilderness trips, and all group members must work together to overcome obstacles encountered along the way. One person's reluctance or inability to work within the group can place all the others in danger. Groups adventuring into the wilderness are comprised of different personalities who have many reasons for participating. The process of uniting these individuals' characteristics into a cooperating group is not something that just happens. Just as it is important for individuals to have an understanding of the environment, it is also important that individuals taking a wilderness trip with a group have an understanding of themselves and their relationship with other members of the group.

Initiative games provide one method for integrating individual personalities within a group. An initiative game is a group problem-solving task. Benjy Simpson, director of Encounter Four, an outdoor educational program at Butler County Community College, in Butler, Pennsylvania, gives this definition:

> An initiative game is usually a clearly defined physical and/or mental task which a group is required to do. The initiative game is so designed as to challenge the physical and mental abilities of the participants within a group. In most instances, the initiative game requires the joint efforts of the members of the group if the task is to be completed. It is a lesson in determination, teamwork and planning. Initiative games may take place either outdoors or indoors. Some initiative games require special props and/or settings, while others do not and can be done almost anywhere.
>
> The initiative game activity is a problem-oriented approach where a question is presented and no answer given. How are you going to do it? What is your plan? These questions must be answered. The group must find the solution; and does so through planning, trying, initial failures, and finally achieving. The initiative game activity supports the idea of learning by doing rather than by talking about it.[1]

OBJECTIVES FOR INITIATIVE GAMES

The objectives of initiative games vary according to the people who are involved. These games can be used to accomplish a variety of goals or objectives; it all depends upon which games are used, and how they are administered. The following objectives can be built into an initiative game, depending upon the organization and administration of the game:

---

[1] Benjy Simpson, *Initiative Games* (Butler, Pa.: Encounter Four, Butler Community College, 1974), pp. 1-2.

I. *Cognitive Objectives (Knowledge)*
  A. The students will gain knowledge about themselves, e.g., strength, endurance, leadership behaviors, decision-making behaviors, and cooperation behaviors.
  B. The students will gain knowledge about other people, e.g., strength, endurance, leadership behaviors, decision-making behaviors, and cooperation behaviors.
II. *Affective Objectives (Attitudes or Feelings)*
  A. The students will trust other people in the group, e.g., falling backwards into the arms of others.
  B. The students will make decisions based upon group consensus.
  C. The students will cooperate with other members of the group in completing the games.
  D. The students will communicate with other members of the group in completing the games.
III. *Psychomotor Objectives (Physical Skills)*
  A. The students will develop a variety of motor skills, e.g., strength, flexibility, agility, balance, coordination, and endurance.
IV. *Experience Objectives*
  A. The students may experience high risk, success, failure, disappointment, fun, or enjoyment of the games.

INTRODUCTION OF INITIATIVE GAMES

In presenting the initiative game, the instructor must first give the group members reasons why they are going to participate in the activities. For most groups, initiative games are a totally new experience, and some prior justification is needed so that the games become more meaningful to the individual participants.

Once this basic information has been presented, the group can move to a particular game. The instructor should state the task and the parameters in which the group may work. No solutions should be given by the instructor. (*Example:* The Stump—the instructor states that each member must stand on the stump without any outside aid.) It is also recommended that a story be introduced along with the description of the game. (*Examples:* The group must get everyone over the boiling peanut butter; you are about to cross a 10-billion-volt electric fence. . . .)

After the task and its parameters have been explained, the group begins to determine a solution and then the application of their plan to complete the task. If the group is not successful the first time, the whole process is repeated. There is no one set way to complete the task as long as the solution abides by the stated rules. If the group is having repeated difficulty, the instructor can move to another task or stop the process and discuss reasons for failure through open-ended questions.

The instructor should never choose an initiative game that is beyond the group's ability. It is best to follow a progression: start with a simple task and move to a more difficult one, but always stay within the physical and mental capacity of the group.

DESCRIPTION OF INITIATIVE GAMES

The following activities are a collection of initiative games used in outdoor programs across the nation. They are by no means the only ones; the possibilities are limited only by one's imagination and creativity.

People Pass

Description. The participants sit on the ground, one in front of the other, with legs spread out in front. They should sit as close as possible. The first member stands and is passed over the heads of the group. Each member is passed until all have returned to their original places.

Figure 6-1. People Pass

Ring Trust Exercise

Description. The group forms a small circle around one person, who stands with arms at sides and then leans back in any direction as far as possible. The group is responsible for keeping that person in an upright position. Each member of the group takes a turn in the center and leans back six or eight times.

Mr. Machine

Description. The group forms a large circle. One person goes to the center of the circle and moves and makes sounds to represent a machine part. Then a second person joins the first person in the center and attaches himself or herself to the machine. The machine is complete when all members are in the center.

Artist-Clay-Model

Description. Divide the class into groups of three people. One member of each small group, the artist, is blindfolded. A second member poses as a model. The third member is the clay. The artist must mold the clay into the position assumed by the model.[2]

Backward Trust Fall

Description. One member stands on a platform five or six feet off the ground in front of the others in the group, who form two parallel lines and lock hands. With his or her back to the group, the person on the platform falls backward into the arms of the other group members.

[2]*Ibid.*, p. 12.

Figure 6-2. Ring Trust Exercise

Figure 6-3. Backward Trust Fall

Safety Procedures. Participants should remove all jewelry (watches, rings, bracelets) and interlock their wrists. The person falling backward should be instructed to keep the body straight and arms at the sides.

Height Alignment

Description. Each member is blindfolded. The group is then instructed to align themselves according to height, without talking.

Search and Rescue

Description. Each member is blindfolded. The instructor then takes one member and places him or her in a spot away from the group. The group must then organize a search to find the missing person. The missing person may not talk or signal in any way. A large open area is needed for this game.

People Tree

Description. Select a big tree with large, low-hanging limbs. The group is instructed to get everyone into the tree as quickly and as efficiently as possible.

Safety Procedures. Each person must spot another until the whole group is in the tree. Spotting is also a necessity on the way down.

The Stump

Description. The entire group must stand on a stump or platform about two feet off the ground, with no outside help.

Figure 6-4. The Stump

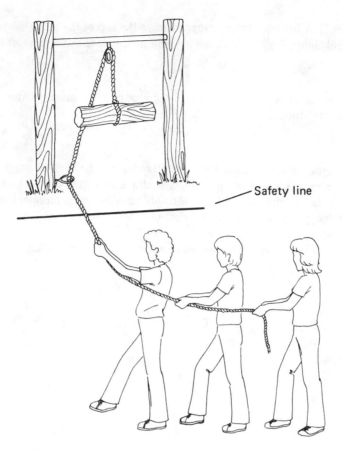

Safety line

Figure 6-5. Log Pull

The Cave

Description. Two 36-inch drainage pipes are placed end to end. One member of the group enters at one opening, and another member enters at the other opening; upon meeting in the middle, they must go over or under each other and come out at the opening opposite from the one that they entered.

Carabiner Walk

Description. Select a steep incline or a thickly wooded area. Each individual ties wrist loops around his or her wrist with heavy string or small-diameter rope. Then, with carabiners, attach each member to another through their wristloops to form a circle. The group must then move up the incline or through the woods.

Log Pull

Description. The group pulls the log up to the pulley (see Figure 6-5) and lowers it again, as many times as possible in two minutes.

Safety Procedures. The log may not be dropped from the top of the pulley. A safety area should be drawn on the ground about five feet from the log, and no one is allowed to enter that area.

Cocoon

Description. A rope circle is placed in front of the group. They must get the entire group into the circle and then raise the rope over their heads.

Ship Hull

Description. The group imagines that they are stranded in the hull of a sinking ship and that water from a broken pipe is pouring in on them. The ship's hull can be represented by a side of a building. About 20 feet above the ground is the shut-off valve, which is represented by a spot on the wall. One member of the group must get to the shut-off valve with no outside aids in order to stop the inward flow of water.

Safety Procedures. Select a wall with no windows or objects protruding from it, and enforce spotting techniques.

Figure 6-6. Ship Hull

Figure 6-7. The Wall

Monster Race

Description. Divide the group into two small groups of equal size. Each group is instructed that they are to create a monster by attaching their bodies to one another. The monster must make a sound and move from point *A* to point *B*, a distance of 50 yards, with only so many feet and hands on the ground; for example, a group of twelve may have only five feet and five hands on the ground. Both groups start at the same time and are given about five minutes to create monsters and move to the finish line.

The Wall

Description. Get the entire group over a high wall as quickly and as efficiently as possible without outside aids.

Construction. The wall, from 12 feet to 14 feet high, is built between two trees with 1 × 8 or 1 × 10 tongue-and-groove lumber. The middle support should be a 4 × 4. It is helpful to construct a platform on the back, so that participants can stand to help the others climb up.

Rules. The group may not use the trees to help in climbing. Once one person is over the wall, he or she may help only in spotting or by pulling a person up from the top of the wall.

Here to There

Description. The group stands on two 10-foot wooden planks supported by seven bricks. By successively moving the bricks and placing one plank in front of the other, the group must cross a distance of about 30 feet. Only the bricks may touch the ground. If any one person touches the ground, the entire group must return to the beginning. No bricks or planks may be left behind.

The Beam

Description. The entire group must climb over a beam as quickly as possible without any aids.

Construction. Select a strong, round log whose radius is from four to six inches. The log should be spiked and lashed between two trees about eight feet from the ground.

Safety Procedures. Remove all rocks, sharp sticks, and stumps from the area about 10 feet on either side of the beam.

Rules. The supportive trees may not be used for climbing. Only four people are allowed on the beam at one time. Once a participant is over the beam, he or she can only spot. At no time can a person's head be lower than his or her feet.

Stretcher Problem

Description. One member of the group is tied to a litter or stretcher. The others carry the victim to a suspended cargo net. They must get the victim into the net and over the other side.

Construction. Suspend a strong cargo net between four trees about seven or eight feet off the ground.

Safety Procedure. The ground around the net should be cleared (remove all rocks, sticks, and stumps).

Figure 6-8. The Beam

Figure 6-9. Stretcher Problem

Rules. Only four participants are allowed in the net at one time. Once a participant has gotten into and out of the net, he or she may not come around to help. No outside aids are allowed for lifting the victim into or out of the net.

Platform

Description. The group stands on the first of three platforms placed 14 feet apart in a straight line. The first and the last platforms should be of equal size; the middle platform should be smaller. The group is given a 12-foot board and a 4-foot board to use as aids in crossing from one platform to the next. The task is completed when the entire group is standing on the last platform.

Rules. If any member of the group or either of the boards touches the ground, the entire group starts over from the first platform.

Flash Flood

Description. Participants imagine that a flash flood is approaching the group. With the materials provided, they must construct something to get the entire group at least two feet off the ground within 10 minutes.

Materials. Three logs about 4 inches in diameter and about 8 feet long; one section of ¼-inch rope about 20 feet long; and one section of ½-inch or ¾-inch manila rope about 30 feet long.

Nitro Crossing

Description. The group is given a container that is three-fourths full of "nitro" (water), which they must transport between two "trip wires."[3]

---

[3]*Ibid.,* p. 41.

Figure 6-10. Platform

Figure 6-11. Nitro Crossing

Figure 6-12. Electric Fence

Construction. Place four wooden stakes in the ground with at least 10 inches above ground level. On top of the stakes place a rigid wooden crosspiece to represent the cross "trip wires." Between two supports, attach a length of ½-inch cable and in the center of the cable attach a 1-inch manila rope about 25 feet long with a monkey's fist knot at the end. Use two U-bolts to keep the swing rope in place.

Rules. No knots are to be tied in the swing rope except for the monkey's fist knot at the bottom. No participants are allowed to step between the "trip wires." If any water is spilled, the group must start over again and the container must be refilled.

At the start, participants may not step into the area between the "trip wires" to obtain the swing rope; they may use only their bodies and their clothing.

Electric Fence

Description. The objective is to get the entire group over the "electric fence" without touching it. The group's only aid is a 4 × 4 beam about eight feet long.

Construction. Stretch a piece of ¼-inch rope between two supportive trees five feet off the ground.

Safety Procedure. Enforce the need for good spotting.

Rules. The supportive trees may not be used for climbing over or crossing the rope. No participants may reach under the rope to help the next participant.

If someone touches the rope, the entire group must start over, or that person is considered electrocuted and his or her body must be passed over the rope.

Figure 6-13. Boardwalk

Boardwalk

Description. Walking on the tops of two 2 × 4 boards laid out flat (see Figure 6-13), the group must move from point *A* to point *B,* a distance of about 30 yards. If a participant steps off the two boards, the entire group must return to the starting point.

QUESTIONS FOR REVIEW AND DISCUSSION

1. What is an initiative game?
2. What are the goals or purposes of initiative games?
3. State two cognitive objectives, two affective objectives, and two psychomotor objectives for initiative games.
4. How should an instructor introduce an initiative game to the students?
5. What safety procedures should be followed in initiative games?
6. Describe the Electric Fence initiative game.

REFERENCES

Simpson, Benjy. *Initiative Games.* Butler, Pa.: Encounter Four, Butler County Community College, 1974.

SUGGESTED READINGS

Rohnke, Karl. *Cowstails and Cobras.* Hamilton, Mass.: Project Adventure, 1977.

seven

ropes course

Challenge and adventure are an essential part of the total human experience. Modern living conditions, however, have virtually eliminated the sense of challenge in our daily lives, so that there is a definite need for opportunities to experience challenge as part of the total educational process.

A ropes course is a series of obstacles designed to present a challenge with a degree of controlled risk. The obstacles are made from a variety of ropes, cables, trees, ladders, cargo nets, swings, tires, and rings, on which participants climb, balance, swing, jump, crawl, and fall. Beneath the obstacles are water, mud, trees, or cargo nets. The course can be designed so that each task is linked to another or so that each task is attempted separately.

The learner proceeding through the course experiences a wide range of unique bodily movements and human feelings. Ropes course activities have the following objectives:

1. Experience success in solving a variety of problems involving balance, coordination, and agility and in overcoming situations that might produce fear as a result of the height at which the activity must be performed.
2. Place demands on the muscular system and increase the functioning abilities of these systems.
3. Place demands on the muscular system and increase levels of strength and flexibility.
4. Experience a sense of belonging to a group and helping or being helped by others.
5. Experience personal feelings about fear, risk, height, balance, speed, fun, and adventure.

A ropes course also functions as a lead-up activity to rock climbing and other outdoor pursuits. The experiences of moving on unfamiliar surfaces (e.g., ropes, tires, and logs) at various heights will help the student meet challenges in other environments.

PRESENTING THE CHALLENGE

The primary concern of the instructor in presenting ropes course activities is to provide basic motivation so that the students will accept the challenge and complete the task. To prepare them both physically and mentally, a series of preconditioning activities should precede the actual experience on the ropes course. A review of the components of teaching strategies and methods discussed in Chapter 2 is recommended before a ropes course activity is conducted.

In the physical realm, a presentation of warm-up activities is recommended. The activities should include: (1) stretching and flexibility exercises, (2) tumbling and rolling exercises, and (3) spotting and belaying techniques.

The instructor should prepare students psychologically to meet the challenges. To overcome their initial fears, the instructor should present the activity in a manner that enables them to feel secure.

One way to accomplish this objective is to utilize more experienced students to demonstrate each challenge. In addition, information should be presented so that students will feel confident in completing the task. Avoid the practice of demonstrating the activity and then allowing students to participate without pre-instruction. Remember that some students will be very fearful of these challenges; overwhelming fear can prevent a student from completing the task. The instructor should develop teaching strategies that convey the message that the activity is safe and that students have the ability to meet the challenges.

CONSTRUCTING A ROPES COURSE

Many factors should be considered in the planning stage before construction of a ropes course actually begins. The first consideration is the selection of the site. A good site contains many large trees (preferably of hardwoods) on a level surface. The type and degree of challenges built into the course depends on the age group for which the course is built. We recommend a progression, starting with obstacles close to the ground and a low degree of difficulty and then moving to higher degrees of difficulty. A course designed with a good progression will enhance the development of the students' self-confidence as they take on each obstacle.

The amount of funds available has a direct relationship to the number of challenges that can be placed within a course. With imagination and creativity, the cost of constructing a ropes course can

Figure 7-1. An example of a sequence of obstacles in a ropes course

range from a few hundred to thousands of dollars. It is important to remember that creativity should never be substituted for safety.

It is also highly recommended that you seek the advice of outside advisors (e.g., Project U.S.E. M.A.I.N.E.) who have experience in designing and constructing ropes courses. They can help you save money and eliminate hidden dangers to ensure greater safety. The Project Adventure program at Hamilton-Wenham Regional High School in Hamilton, Massachusetts, has published a helpful text on ropes course activities and construction.[1]

The following tools and hardware are needed to construct a ropes course. Quantities vary according to the size of the course.

Tools	*Ropes*
Adjustable hand drill	2-inch manila (hawser)
Auger bits, ½-inch and ⅜-inch	1-inch manila
Axe	¾-inch manila
Block and tackle	½-inch manila
Bolt cutter	¼-inch manila
Chain saw	$\frac{7}{16}$-inch nylon
Come-along	*Hardware*
Crescent wrenches	Duck tape
Hacksaw	8-penny nails
Hammer	10-penny nails
Handsaw	16-penny nails
Measuring tape	40-penny nails
Posthole digger	½-inch cable clips
Pulleys	¾-inch cable clips
Shovel	1½-inch horseshoe spikes
Sledgehammer	
Cable Wire	
½-inch cable	
⅜-inch cable	

ACTIVITY STATIONS

There are generally no blueprints available for constructing a ropes course. It is a matter of selecting a site and then studying that area to determine a sequence of individual activities that will fit into a logical and safe arrangement of tasks. There is no set order in which the activities should be placed.

Although they can be placed in any sequence, each activity has a specific objective. Certain tasks lend themselves more to the development of strength; others are designed for increasing balance, flexibility, and agility. Arrange them to include a combination of these, but alternate the types of tasks. For example, avoid a sequence that places two strength tasks back-to-back.

The following activities can be conducted on a ropes course. No attempt has been made to arrange them in sequence.

Commando Crawl

Description. The student moves across a 2-inch manila hawser rope by laying his or her chest on the rope, passing it under the pelvic area, and hooking the top of the foot over the rope. The

---

[1] *Project Adventure* (Hamilton, Mass.: Project Adventure, 1974).

Figure 7-2. Commando Crawl

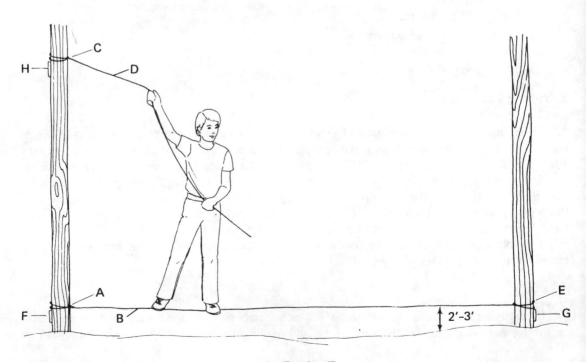

Figure 7-3. Tension Traverse

opposite leg hangs free for balance. The student pulls with his or her arms and pushes with the back foot, in a "caterpillar" movement.

Construction

A. Secure the rope to the tree with a bowline knot.

B. Use a 2-inch manila hawser rope. The length of the rope used depends on the span between the two trees; 25 or 35 feet is recommended.

C. To secure the opposite side of the hawser rope to the tree, wrap it one and a half times around the tree. Then tie it off with two half hitches. A come-along should be used to pull the ropes semitaut.[2]

D-E. Wood blocks should be secured to the tree to prevent the rope from slipping down.

Safety Procedures. The person who is crawling should be spotted on both sides of the rope. The spotters should move along side-by-side with that person to make sure that no falls occur.

Tension Traverse

Description. The student stands on a rope secured between two trees and uses a support rope to cross from one end to the other. The student should stand sideways on the secured rope and hold the support rope with both hands, with one hand at his or her waist and the other over his or her head. The student is instructed to keep tension on the support rope and lean away from the tree to which the support rope is secured.

Construction

A-B. The traverse rope is ¾-inch or 1-inch manila, secured to the tree by a bowline. The length of the traverse depends on the distance between the two trees; 25 or 35 feet is generally recommended.

C-D. The support rope is ½-inch or ¼-inch manila, secured to a tree with a bowline. It should be secured at a length equal to the length of the traverse rope. To determine the length of the support, add the length of the traverse rope and the length of the securing point (e.g., traverse, 20 feet; length of securing point, 20 feet; total length of support rope, 40 feet).

E. To secure the opposite end of the traverse rope, pass it around the tree one and a half times and then tie off with two half hitches. A come-along is needed to pull the traverse rope taut. The traverse should always be taut.

F-G-H. Wood blocks should be secured to prevent both ropes from slipping.

Safety Procedures. Instruct the students that, if they should lose balance and cannot regain it, they should let go of the support rope before jumping to the ground. Holding on to the support will cause the student to swing back into the tree, to the point where the support rope is secured.

Triangle Tension Traverse

Description. A triangle tension traverse is formed by the addition of two more sides to a tension traverse. The student starts at one intersection of the support ropes and moves around to each individual tension traverse to complete the triangle.

Construction

A-B. The traverse rope is one continuous length of ¾-inch or 1-inch manila rope, secured to the first tree with a bowline. On each other tree the rope goes around the tree and rests on wood blocks.

---

[2] Instructions for tautening ropes and cables are given in the "General Hints" section.

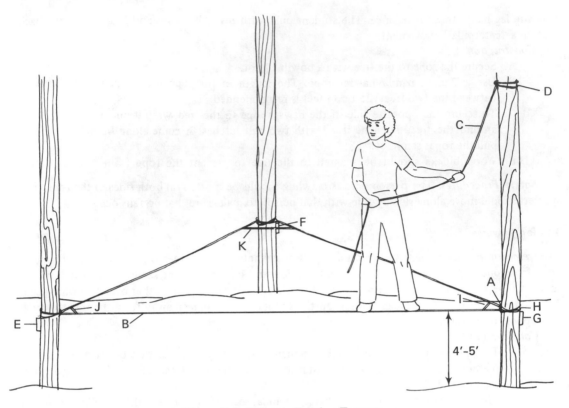

Figure 7-4. Triangle Tension Traverse

Figure 7-5. Crossing a traverse rope

C-D. The support rope is ½-inch or ¾-inch manila rope, secured to the tree with a bowline equal in length to the tension traverse. The length of the support rope is equal to the distance from the first tree to the center of the second tension traverse.

E-F-G. Secured wood blocks prevent the rope from sliding downward.

H. To secure the traverse rope above the bowline, wrap it two complete turns around the tree and tie off with two half hitches. The traverse rope should be tightened with a come-along.

I-J-K. To further tighten the traverse rope, use ¼-inch manila and tie a clove hitch to the traverse rope in front of the tree, wrap the ¼-inch rope around the opposite traverse rope, and pull tight. Tie off with two hitches. This will remove the slack in each traverse rope.

Safety Procedures. Spotters should stand on each side to help the participant regain balance as he or she moves along each tension traverse.

Kitten Crawl

Description. The participant crawls on all fours, head first, down two inclined ropes.

Construction

A. Use 1-inch manila for the crawling rope.

B-C. Secure one end of the crawling rope to the first support tree with a bowline, secure the center of the rope to the opposite support tree with a clove hitch, and return the ropes to the first support tree with an overhand knot and two half hitches.

D-E. Attach wooden blocks to each support tree to prevent slipping of the crawling rope.

Tire Swing

Description. The participant, using only the feet and hands, swings from tire to tire. No outside aids are provided to reach a tire.

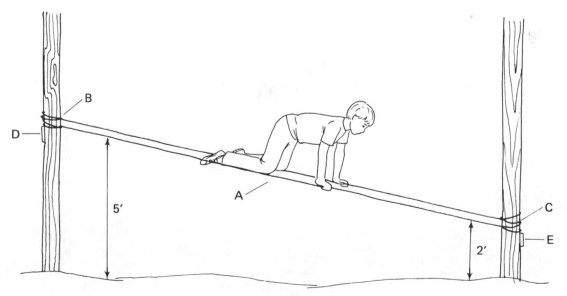

Figure 7-6. Kitten Crawl

Construction

A.   ½-inch wire cable.

B-C.   Secure wooden blocks completely around both support trees.

D-E.   To secure the cable to the first support, pass it one turn around the tree and tighten it down with two ¾-inch cable clips, from three to five feet apart and opposing each other. Tighten the cable with a come-along. Secure the cable to the second support tree in the same fashion. It should also be spiked to the wooden block with 1½-inch horseshoe spikes.

F.   1-inch manila rope, in various lengths.

G.   Secure the rope to the tires with a bowline.

H.   Place an eye splice in the 1-inch rope with rope thimble (see Figure 7-8).

Safety Procedures. The instructor should pre-check the connection between the support cable and the tire ropes for weakening.

Cargo Net Jump

Description. The participant jumps into a suspended cargo net, in a tucked position.

Construction. Use a 1-inch manila cargo net with small meshing. The center of the cargo net should be suspended about 15 or 20 feet from the ground.

A-B-C-D.   Secure a length of 1-inch manila rope to each corner of the net with a bowline.

E-F-G-H.   To secure the 1-inch manila rope to each support tree, turn it two full times around the tree and tie off with a bowline. Wooden blocks should be used to prevent slippage.

I.   Construct a jumping platform about 25 feet off the ground. The participant can climb to the platform by means of a rope ladder, which can also be used to climb out of the net.

Safety Procedures. An instructor should always be present with the students on the jumping platform. They should be instructed to jump in the tuck position and land in the center of the net. Only one student at a time should be in the net. Inspection of the securing points is mandatory before use.

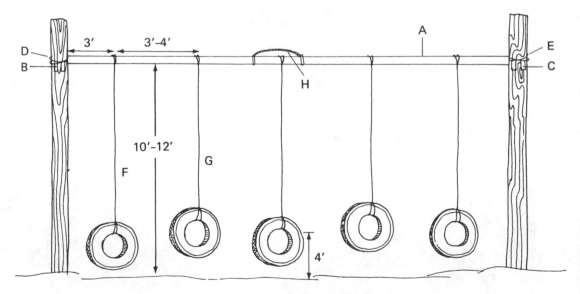

Figure 7-7. Tire Swing

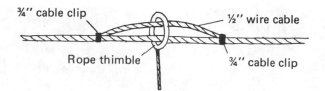

Figure 7-8. Eye Splice

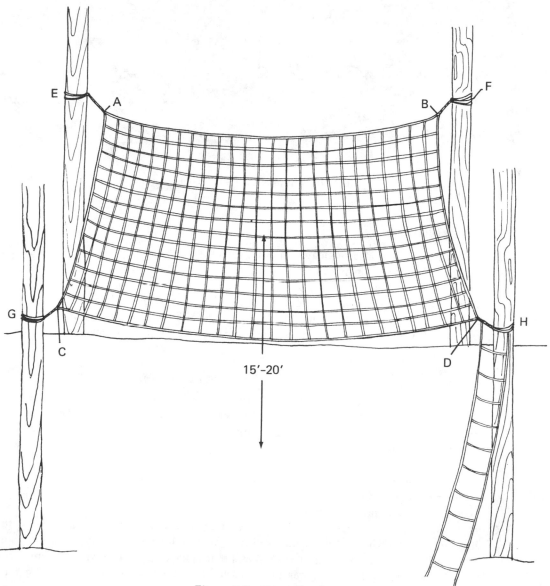

15'–20'

Figure 7-9. Cargo Net Jump

Figure 7-10. Jumping into a cargo net

Three-Rope Bridge (Burma Bridge)

Description. The Burma bridge originated in Asia, where it has been used for centuries to cross rivers, deep ravines, and mountain passes. It is a combination of three suspended ropes with side supports—one rope to walk on and two to be used for handholds. If the ropes are taut the participants can traverse the bridge with comfort and safety even with heavy loads on their backs.

The bridge can be constructed at any height, but try to place about 20 or 25 feet off the ground. If a ravine or waterfall is present on the site of your course, try to place the bridge over the natural obstacle.

Construction

    A. ½-inch wire cable.

    B-C. Fasten wooden blocks to both support trees. To secure the cable, work one end of it around a support tree and tighten it with two ¾-inch cable clips, 12 inches apart and opposing each other; pull out the slack with a come-along. Fasten in the same fashion to the opposite support tree. The cable should be spiked down to the wooden blocks with 1½-inch horseshoe spikes.

    D. Use ¾-inch manila rope for the handhold support ropes. The rope is worked two full turns around one support tree.

    E. Wooden blocks to prevent slippage.

    F-G. If possible, select a support with two limbs of equal height to use as an anchor for the handhold ropes. When limbs are not available, secure a 4 × 4 wooden post to the support tree: drill four ¾-inch holes in the 4 × 4 and then spike it to the tree with 40-penny iron spikes. Use a come-along to tighten the ropes and tie off with a clove hitch. Side supports should also be nailed to the 4 × 4 post and the support tree.

    H. $7/16$-inch nylon rope, 8½ feet long.

I-J. Clove hitches.

K. $^3/_8$-inch wire cable used for belay line.

L-M. Secure wooden blocks to the tree and fasten the cable as previously described.

Safety Procedures. A belay is mandatory. The participant is belayed by clipping a carabiner to the $^3/_8$-inch cable. Use an overhand loop to attach a piece of 1-inch nylon webbing to the carabiner. The participant should wear a swami belt (see Chapter 9). Attach the belay to the swami belt with another carabiner.

Giant's Ladder

Description. By jumping and swinging from rung to rung, the participant tries to reach the top of the ladder. The Giant's Ladder is good for developing strength, agility, and balance. The participant stands on the first rung and jumps to place his or her hands on top of the next rung, catches the rung with his or her abdomen, and allows the feet to hang free. From this position the participant pulls his or her body up to a standing position and repeats the jump to the next rung. The participant must be belayed.

Construction

A. Side support log 8 or 10 inches in diameter (hardwood).

B. Rungs 4 or 5 inches in diameter (hardwood).

C. Secure a 4 × 4 wooden post to each support; drill three $^3/_8$-inch holes into the wooden post and support and spike it with 40-penny spikes. Lash the post with ¼-inch manila rope.

D. Drill two $^3/_8$-inch holes into side of support logs for ladder, rest the ladder side support on the 4 × 4 wooden post, and again use 40-penny spikes to fasten it to the support tree. Complete by lashing the side ladder support log to the support tree with ½-inch manila rope.

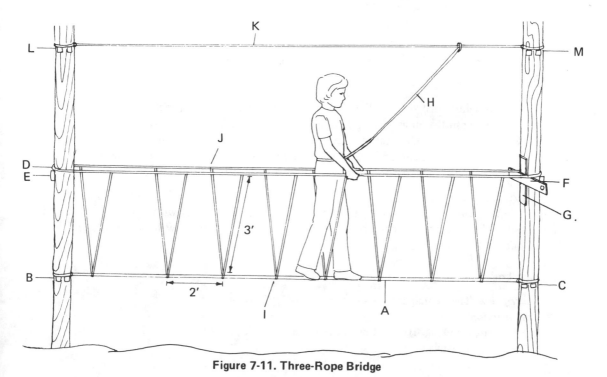

Figure 7-11. Three-Rope Bridge

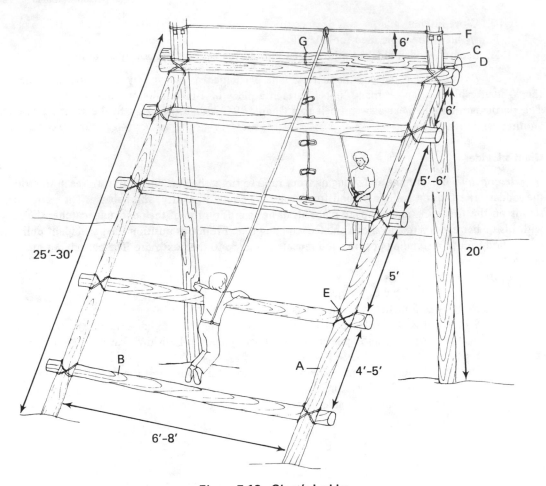

Figure 7-12. Giant's Ladder

E. To secure each rung to the side ladder support log, drill $^3/_8$-inch holes and spike on each side. Lash the rungs with ¾-inch manila rope to the ladder support logs.

F. $^3/_8$-inch wire belay cable, secured to each support tree with two ½-inch cable clips, 12 inches apart and opposing each other. Use a come-along to tighten the cable.

G. 1-inch manila rope ladder for descent after completion of the climb.

Safety Procedures. The participant is belayed from beginning to end. Attach a carabiner to the belay cable, and run a $^7/_{16}$-inch climbing rope through the carabiner down to the participant with a swami belt and carabiner. The belayer should keep a tight belay to allow for the stretch of the rope if a fall occurs.

Swinging Log

Description. The participant walks across a moving horizontal log.
Construction
    A. Hardwood log, 10 or 12 inches in diameter.
    B. 1-inch manila rope.

C. To secure the manila rope to the support tree, run it two full turns around the tree and tie off with a bowline.

D. Secure wooden blocks to support trees to prevent slippage.

E. Ring notched horizontal log and tie off manila ropes with a bowline.

F. Spike car tires to support trees to prevent damage from the swinging log.

Safety Procedures. The swinging log should never be more than 12 or 18 inches off the ground. Clear away all rocks and sharp objects from the ground six feet on either side of the swinging log.

Balance Beam

Description. The balance beam is a good obstacle to be used as a bridge from activity to activity. The participant simply walks across the beam. Many balance beams can be placed in a ropes course. If more than one beam is used, construct them at varied height levels and inclines. A beam that is six feet from the ground or lower need not be belayed, but spotting is mandatory.

Figure 7-13. A completed Giant's Ladder

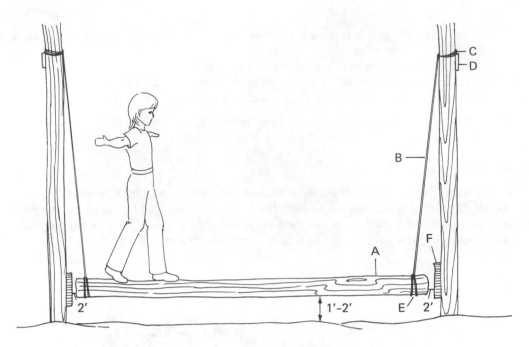

Figure 7-14. Swinging Log

Figure 7-15. Walking across a swinging log

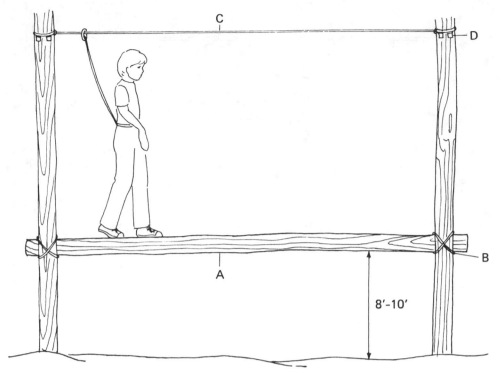

Figure 7-16. Balance Beam

Construction

    A. Straight hardwood log, 10 or 12 inches in diameter.

    B. To secure the beam to the support trees, notch the log, drill holes, and spike it with 40-penny spikes. Use ½-inch manila rope to lash down the beam.

    C. $\frac{3}{8}$-inch wire cable.

    D. Secure the cable to the support tree with two ½-inch cable clips, and use a come-along to tighten.

Safety Procedures. A beam constructed more than six feet off the ground should have a fixed belay, consisting of a carabiner attached to the cable with 1-inch tubular webbing attached to the carabiner and participant.

Inclined Log

Description. The inclined log is a balance beam constructed at an angle. The participant is instructed to walk up the log in an erect position. If the participant has difficulty after making a conscientious effort, then he or she can go on all fours or in a crawling position to complete the climb.

Construction

    A. Hardwood log, 10 or 12 inches in diameter.

    B. Notch the inclined log, drill, and spike with 40-penny spikes. The log should also be lashed with ½-inch manila rope. The opposite end of the log should be set in a small hole in the ground to prevent any backward movement.

    C. $\frac{3}{8}$-inch wire cable for belay.

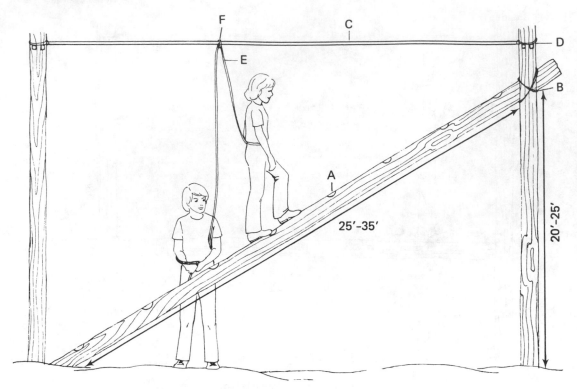

Figure 7-17. Inclined Log

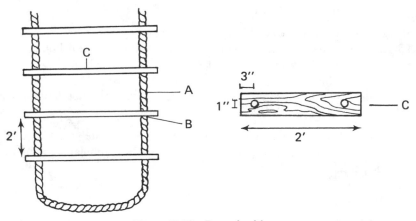

Figure 7-18. Rope Ladder

D. Secure the cable to the support tree with a wooden block and two ½-inch cable clips. Use a come-along to tighten the cable.

E. $^7/_{16}$-inch nylon goldline climbing rope for running belay.

F. Carabiner

Safety Procedures. The belay cable should be constructed slightly off center from the inclined log to prevent the participant from hitting the log if a fall occurs. As the participant moves up the log the belay person should walk alongside.

Rope Ladder

Description. A rope ladder is used to ascend or descend a station within the course.
Construction
    A. ¾-inch manila rope.
    B. Overhand knot.
    C. 2 × 4 hardwood rungs (2-foot lengths)

Determine the length of the ladder, double that length, and add six more feet for the overhand knots and tie-off. The rungs of the ladder are made of 2 × 4 wood with a hole 1-inch in diameter drilled 3 inches from each end. The first rung is placed by doubling the rope and moving up two feet from the center point; tie an overhand knot on each length and slide the 2 × 4 down to the overhand knot. Repeat the process every two feet.

Safety Procedures. Ladders that are used to ascend and descend more than 10 feet should be belayed.

Two-Rope Bridge

Description. Two parallel ropes are secured between two support trees. The participant stands sideways on the bottom rope, grabs hold of the top rope with both hands behind his or her neck, and inches the body across the rope. The two-rope bridge can be constructed at various heights. It can serve as a lead-up activity to more difficult challenges.

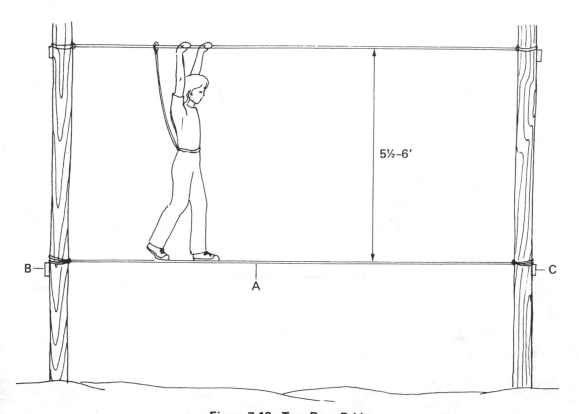

Figure 7-19. Two-Rope Bridge

Construction. Both the bottom and the top ropes are constructed in the same fashion.
  A. ½-inch manila rope.
  B. Secure to the first support with a bowline.
  C. Use a come-along to tighten the rope. Take the ropes two full turns around the tree and
     tie off with two half hitches. Use wooden blocks under each tie point to prevent slippage.

Safety Procedures. For a bridge six feet off the ground or higher, use a fixed belay or running
belay.

GENERAL HINTS

Come-alongs

A come-along is the best device for taking the slack out of a rope or cable. It is much easier to
use than a power-wrench. It is recommended that constructors use a come-along with a two-ton or
four-ton pull.

To attach a come-along to a rope, use a $\frac{7}{16}$-inch nylon prusik loop. First, pull out all the slack
you can by hand, go one turn around the tree, and attach the prusik loop about two or three feet
from the support tree. Pull the remaining slack from the rope and tie off. An important point to
remember is that the come-along should be in direct line with the ropes to be tightened. (See Figure
7-20.)

To attach a come-along to a cable, use a short length of ¼-inch or $\frac{3}{8}$-inch cable instead of a
prusik loop, and clip it to the cable that is to be tightened with two ½-inch cable clamps. Pull out the
slack with the come-along, and then remove the two clamps and the short length of cable. This
method is safer than the use of a prusik loop. (See Figure 7-21.)

Anchors

To tie off the end of a rope, wrap it one full turn around the support tree, then overlap the next
full turn over the first turn, and tie off with two hitches. (See Figure 7-22.)

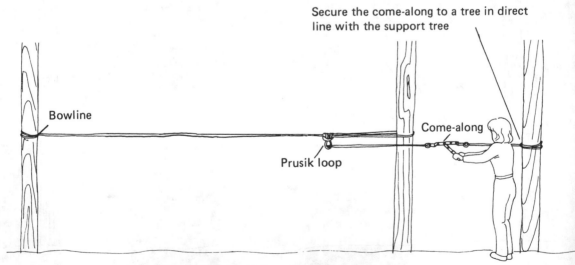

Secure the come-along to a tree in direct
line with the support tree

Bowline

Come-along

Prusik loop

Figure 7-20. Use of a come-along with a rope

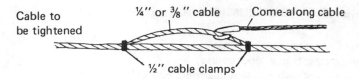

Cable to
be tightened   ¼″ or ⅜″ cable   Come-along cable

½″ cable clamps

Figure 7-21. Attachment of a come-along to a cable

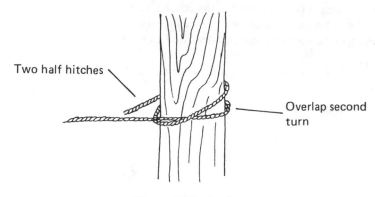

Two half hitches

Overlap second
turn

Figure 7-22. Anchor

SAFETY RULES

A ropes course, like all high-risk outdoor activities, has a definite potential for physical injury, possibly fatal, if certain safety factors are overlooked. The authors highly recommend that you seek the advice and skill of experienced ropes course builders before you construct a course. The following safety rules should be observed to minimize the risk of injuries to the students:

1. Each person should have a signed permission slip before he or she may participate in the course. The permission slip should state to the parent or guardian the exact nature of the ropes course, its benefits, and its dangers.
2. The course should be inspected before each use.
3. The ropes or cables should be replaced at the first sign of damage or dry rot.
4. Make sure that students are trained in the mechanics of proper belaying techniques.
5. Avoid using the course in wet or icy conditions.
6. Never allow students to participate in the course without proper supervision.

ROPES COURSE CONSULTANTS

Project Adventure
Physical Education Department
Hamilton-Wenham Regional High School
775 Bay Road
Hamilton, Mass. 01936

Project U.S.E. M.A.I.N.E., Ropes Course Consultants
RFD 1, Box 167
Maple Ridge Road
Harrison, Maine 04040

QUESTIONS FOR REVIEW AND DISCUSSION

1. How can a ropes course challenge students?
2. What are the basic elements in a ropes course?
3. What are the objectives of participation in a ropes course?
4. Ropes courses can be a lead-up activity for what kinds of activities?
5. What procedures should an instructor follow in introducing a ropes course?
6. How can an instructor help students to be less fearful?
7. What key factors should be considered in the construction of a ropes course?
8. What tools and equipment are necessary for construction?
9. What are some specific safety procedures that need to be followed while students participate on a ropes course?
10. What are some safety procedures for maintenance and up-keep of a ropes course?

SUGGESTED READINGS

Rohnke, Karl. *Cowstails and Cobras.* Hamilton, Mass.: Project Adventure, 1977.

eight

backpacking and camping

Backpacking is simply hiking while carrying on one's back the gear that is needed to live comfortably in the outdoors. This activity can be appreciated by families, people of all ages and of either sex, and people with differing levels of physical ability.

There are numerous reasons for the growth of backpacking: (1) It can improve mental outlook; (2) it is a good form of exercise; (3) it provides a means to explore areas of outstanding beauty; (4) it can be pursued as an inexpensive vacation and a learning experience for all members of a family; (5) it is sometimes the only mode of transportation into remote areas to pursue other outdoor activities, such as rock climbing, spelunking, fishing, and hunting; (6) it can provide relaxing escape from our complex society; (7) emotions and feelings of personal fellowship can be intensified in a natural environment; and (8) backpacking can provide a sense of accomplishment and self-worth.

EQUIPMENT

Equipment for backpacking can be divided into three basic categories. *Specific equipment* includes items that are considered to be essential, such as backpack frame, sleeping bag, sleeping pad, tent, clothes, boots, stove, and cooking equipment. *General equipment* includes items that are used for comfort but are not always essential, such as lantern, folding camp saw, axe, toilet paper, steel mirror, laundry bag, grill, binoculars, and camera. *Safety equipment* includes items needed for an emergency situation or for safety, such as waterproof matches, needle and thread, sun cream, sunglasses, maps, compass, first aid kit, and flashlight with extra bulbs and batteries.

Specific Equipment

Backpacks

The pack frame with a fitted packbag becomes a home that you carry on your back. In it, the backpacker carries all the necessary gear for a backcountry trek—food, shelter, clothing, cooking gear, safety items, and other equipment. The pack frame has evolved through many changes in design and materials. The original design was a flat board with a canvas back panel and shoulder straps. This model was developed by the army to carry large and odd-shaped loads. The modern pack frame (see Figure 8-1) is constructed of aluminum tubing, with either welded or bolted joints. Frames constructed of magnesium tubing, which is somewhat lighter than aluminum, are also available. The frame should be selected with concern for quality of workmanship and strength. Either a rigid frame or a flexible frame can be selected. The rigid frame has proven to be stronger but places a greater load on the packer when a change in direction is made. The flexible frame allows for greater comfort of

Figure 8-1. A modern pack frame
(Photo courtesy of Camp Trails
Company, Phoenix, Arizona)

movement in any directional change because the frame shifts with upper body movement. On level terrain, either the rigid frame or the flexible frame work well, but the authors have found the flexible frame to be slightly more comfortable for uphill terrain. We recommend that you try both before you buy one for a long trek.

Other components of the frame are the back panels, shoulder straps, and waist belt. The back panels are constructed of either wide canvas or nylon. Most good frames have two back panels attached to the vertical tubes of the frame, one fitting to the lower back and the other slightly below the shoulder blades. The back panel keeps the frame and pack off the back of the packer. The panel should always be drawn tight, the tighter the better. This is generally done with the turnbuckle or tie adjustment attaching each end of the back panel.

The shoulder straps are attached to the horizontal bar between the vertical bars just above the shoulders. Better frames allow the packer to adjust the placement of the shoulder straps on the horizontal bar. The straps should be close to the neck, not out on the shoulders. This placement provides the greatest comfort with a large load. Padded shoulder straps should also be used for additional comfort.

The waist belt is one of the most important features of a backpack. It can either be padded or unpadded, according to preference; however, the padded belts are more comfortable for large loads. The waist belt keeps the frame close to the body just above the pelvis, so as to take the load off the shoulders. If the waist belt is drawn tight around the waist, about 75 percent of the load should ride on the hips.

Some additional features of a good frame are rubber end plugs, which are fitted into each end of the vertical tubes in order to keep out dirt, and D rings on the vertical bars for tying on accessories.

The packbag (see Figure 8-2) is generally constructed of nylon, attached to the pack with clevis pins and split rings. More expensive bags are made of waterproof nylon duck. A bag can contain one

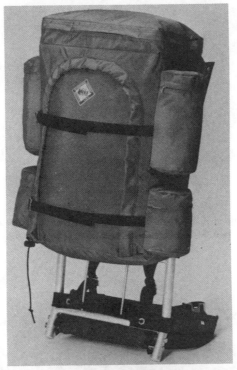

Single-compartment bag

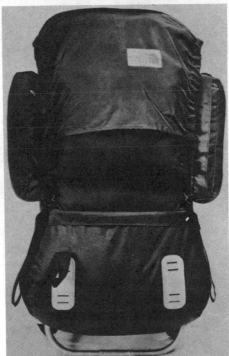

Double-compartment bag

Figure 8-2. Packbags (Top photo courtesy of Recreational Equipment Inc., Seattle, Washington; bottom photo courtesy of Roland Dare, The North Face, Berkeley, California)

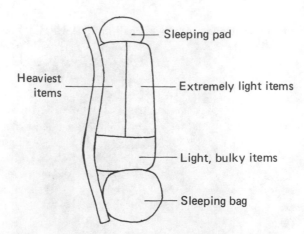

Figure 8-3. Distribution of weight in a backpack

Figure 8-4. Internal frame pack (Photo courtesy of
Camp Trails Company, Phoenix, Arizona)

large compartment or can be divided into two small ones. A good bag has four outer compartments for accessories.

Weight distribution is the important factor in packing the bag. The placement of weight can be controlled by dividing the pack into thirds. The first third is the lower part of the bag compartment and the frame; the sleeping bag (which can be the heaviest single item) should be tied to the bottom of the frame, and light, bulky materials should be stored in the lower compartment. The second third is the back half of the main compartment, where all the heavy items are placed. In the outer half of the main compartment, extremely light items are placed. (See Figure 8-3.)

A foam sleeping pad can be tied to the top of the large compartment. The outer side pockets are useful for carrying small items that must be accessible, e.g., twine, toilet paper, insect repellent, sunglasses, bottle opener, can opener, water bottles, extra matches, knife, fork, spoon, cup, needle and thread, sun cream, flashlight, maps, compass, first aid kit, and photographic equipment. In some environments, specialized items such as snowshoes, skis, crampons, and climbing rope can be tied to the D ring or leather straps on the outside of the pack.

To put the pack on your back, first adjust and tighten the waist belt, and then tighten the shoulder straps. Putting it on in the reverse order creates an uneven weight distribution with the weight resting on the shoulders, which becomes uncomfortable in a short time.

The development of the internal-frame pack (see Figure 8-4) has been a great advantage for mountain climbers and skiers as well as wilderness backpackers. This type of pack is constructed with an internal support system that suspends the weight in conjunction with the waist belt. This type of pack fits tightly to the upper body of the packer, so that it is especially helpful in climbing and skiing situations.

Sleeping Bags

Another essential piece of backpacking equipment is the sleeping bag, which should provide warmth and comfort for a good night's rest. The warmth of a bag is determined by the following factors:

1. The kind and amount of insulating material—down, polyester, or foam.
2. The structure—the shape of the bag and the manner in which the insulating material is compartmented.
3. The bag closure—zippers and drawstrings.
4. To a much lesser extent, additional covers and liners.[1]

Several kinds of insulating or filler material are used in the sleeping bags on today's market. The basic types of filler are down and polyester.

Down	*Polyester*
Goose down	Dacron Fiberfill II
Duck down	Celanese Polarguard
	Dacron "88"

Both down and polyester have advantages and disadvantages which must be considered in light of the buyer's specific requirements. The warmth of the bag is of primary importance. The price range is about the same for both down and polyester bags. Several characteristics of down and polyester fillers are compared in Table 8-1.

---

[1] Harvey Manning, *Backpacking: One Step at a Time* (New York: Vintage Books, 1973), p. 157.

Table 8-1. Comparison of Down and Polyester Fillers

DOWN	POLYESTER FILLERS
Higher in price	Lower in price
Lighter	Heavier
More compact (compressible)	Bulkier (less compressible)
Not waterproof	Virtually waterproof
Greater loft	Lesser loft
Requires more care	Easy to take care of
Warmer	Not as warm

The three basic sleeping-bag shapes are mummy, barrel, and rectangular. Mummy bags are designed to fit the contour of the body and have a single drawstring at the top that closes the bag around the head to hold in body heat. This is the most desirable type for backpacking, because it eliminates excess weight, and the contoured shape retains more warmth. Barrel-shaped bags are roomier at the midsection, for greater comfort, but they are heavier. Rectangular bags are the least desirable because they are the heaviest of the three.

The amount of dead air space between the inner liner material and the outside world is known as *loft*. This, rather than the weight of the bag, is a major factor in determining the minimum temperature in which a bag can be used. The more loft a bag has (the more dead air space), the lower the temperature rating of the bag. Down bags have more loft than polyester bags. A sleeping bag with a minimum temperature rating of –10° to –30° Fahrenheit requires a minimum of seven inches of loft.

The internal construction of a sleeping may be sewn-through, box, slant tube, overlapping tube, or laminated. (See Figure 8-6.)

Sewn-through. The sewn-through construction is the least expensive. Cold spots can occur within the bag and heat is lost through the seam. Sewn-through bags are good for use in warm weather.

Box. Most polyester and some inexpensive down bags have the box construction. The disadvantage of box construction is that the filler tends to fall away from the material walls (baffles) that trap dead air, so that cold spots occur.

Slant Tube. The major advantage of slant-tube construction is that there is very little shifting of the filler away from the baffles. High-quality bags are cut in this manner.

Overlapping Tube. Overlapping tube construction allows no shifting of the filler material, but the loft is somewhat restricted because of the cut. Overlapping-tube bags are heavier and cost more.

Laminated. Laminated construction is basically two sewn-through bags placed on top of each other. In this type of construction there are no cold spots. Laminated bags are very heavy and are the most expensive bags on the market.

Several accessory pieces of equipment can be used along with a bag for insulation and general cleanliness. A urethane foam pad or an ensolite pad is important. A large percentage of body heat is lost through conduction when one is lying on the ground. In the winter, a half-inch or three-quarter inch pad is recommended; warm weather requires a quarter-inch pad. An air mattress allows cold air to circulate beneath the body and thus increases conduction. Air mattresses are good in warm weather but poor in cold weather.

Covers and liners can be used for protection of the bag and they also add some warmth. The ground cloth is another important item when one is sleeping directly on the ground, because the bag will get dirty and wet unless it is protected in some way. A ground cloth of lightweight polyethylene or coated nylon duck is sufficient. The life span of a sleeping bag can be lengthened if the bag is

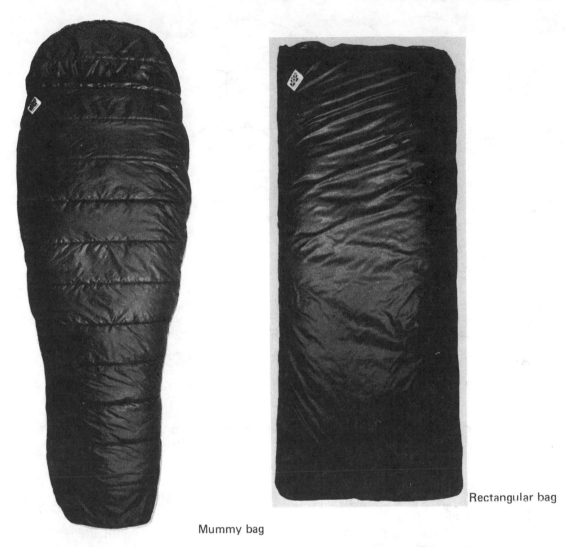

Rectangular bag

Mummy bag

Figure 8-5. Sleeping bags (Photo courtesy of Camp Trails Company, Phoenix, Arizona)

well cared for. A bag needs to be air-dried and hung up between trips. The nylon shell can be easily torn or ripped if the bag is treated carelessly. Bags should not be placed by a fire. They can be washed in warm water with a mild soap and placed in a dryer at a low cycle; consult the manufacturer's instructions for washing.

Keeping Warm at Night

The main function of a sleeping bag is to provide insulation to retain the body heat produced by the sleeper inside the bag. During sleep, the human body gains or conserves heat in three ways: (1) through the digestion of food (before getting in a bag at night, the sleeper should eat something light, because a big meal eaten just before bed causes blood to rush to the stomach and away from other body parts, so that a feeling of coldness results); (2) through external sources, such as hot drinks, sun, fire, or another body (a hot drink before bed is good, and sleeping close to another

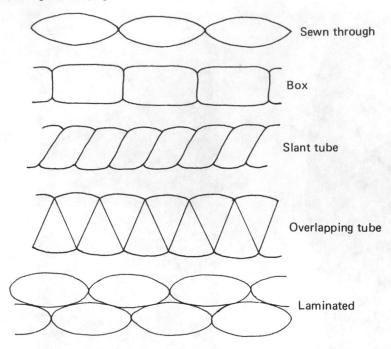

Figure 8-6. Internal construction of sleeping bags

person also helps to provide additional heat); and (3) through muscular activity, either involuntary or voluntary (if your feet are cold, move them inside the bag).

The body loses heat in five ways:

1. *Respiration.* Warm air is exhaled through breathing (this cannot be prevented unless the sleeper stops breathing); however, on very cold nights, an enclosed shelter (tent) can help to prevent the loss of warm air.
2. *Evaporation.* Perspiration from the skin that is evaporated into the air contributes greatly to a large amount of heat loss. The key is not to dress too warmly, because excess clothes cause the sleeper to perspire more. With a good sleeping bag, the sleeper should not need to wear any clothing other than what would normally be used at home.
3. *Conduction.* The body can lose heat by sitting or lying on the cold ground; a pad (ensolite or urethane) will stop conduction.
4. *Radiation.* Heat loss by radiation occurs from any uncovered body surface. Since your head contains about 40 percent of the total body heat, it is important to keep your head covered; there is an old saying that holds true—"if your feet are cold, put your hat on."
5. *Convection.* Body heat is lost as it is carried away by wind or air currents. The primary function of the filler material of the bag is to stop convection.

In short, if a backpacker follows these few simple rules, there is no need to spend a cold, sleepless night.

1. Always use a sleeping pad to stop conduction.
2. Always eat something light before going to sleep.
3. Drink a hot drink.

4. Never wear wet clothing inside a sleeping bag and do not over-dress.
5. Always keep your head covered.
6. On very cold nights, sleep inside an enclosed shelter.

Boots

Three basic types of boot are used for backpacking: trail boots, mountaineering boots, and hiking boots. (See Figure 8-7.)

The trail boot is actually not intended for backpacking. It can be used for hiking on comfortable trails and casual walking, but it is not designed for carrying heavy packs over rough terrain. A mountaineering boot is a heavily weighted boot used for rugged terrain such as ice, snow, or rock. The hiking boot is the best boot for general backpacking. The price of hiking boots ranges between $25 and $60.

One important consideration is weight. Most hiking boots weigh between three and five pounds. Each pound on your feet is equivalent (in terms of energy expenditure) to six pounds on your back.

The care and maintenance of your boots involves several different factors. Most boots are water repellent and require periodic treatment with a wax, oil, or silicone preparation in order to maintain their water repellency and to preserve the leather. After a trek, dirt should be immediately cleaned off with a stiff brush and cold water. If boots become wet, they should not be placed by a fire to dry, because this tends to dry out and ruin the leather. It is best just to let the boots dry in the open air.

The breaking in of new boots before an expedition into the wilderness is another item to consider. To start the process, wear the boots around the house for short periods of time. The next step is to take short hikes and eventually work up to hiking with a light pack.

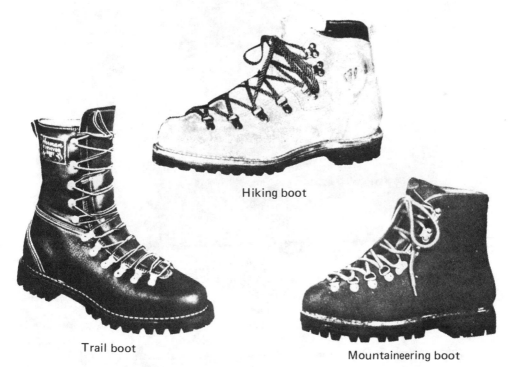

Hiking boot

Trail boot

Mountaineering boot

Figure 8-7. Types of boots (Photo courtesy of Eastern Mountain Sports, Inc., Boston, Massachusetts)

Stoves and Cooking Equipment

A small, lightweight backpack stove (see Figure 8-8) is the nucleus of the cooking gear. It is more efficient than an open fire because the temperature can be controlled. In addition, with proper use and maintenance, there is less threat of starting a forest fire and less impact on the environment with fire scars.

Before choosing a specific type of stove, you must consider what kind of fuel to use. The four basic fuels are white gas, kerosene, pressurized butane, and pressurized propane. Fuels should be considered on the basis of their availability and their cold-weather characteristics. All pressurized fuels have a very low heat output in cold weather; white gas and kerosene have a higher heat output if the stoves have pressurizing pumps. You should never buy a gasoline or kerosene stove without a safety valve. The stoves can weigh from one-fifth of a pound to as much as three and one-half pounds.

Cooking in the back country can be either a pleasant or an unpleasant experience. The principle purpose of eating is to maintain a store of body fuels. Our food keeps our bodies fueled, comfortable, and efficient. The preparation procedures, the weight, and the nutritional value of food should take precedence over its flavor.

A large variety of freeze-dried and dehydrated foods can be purchased; they are relatively expensive, but they are lightweight. Most of these foods take the form of one-pot dinners, such as pancake

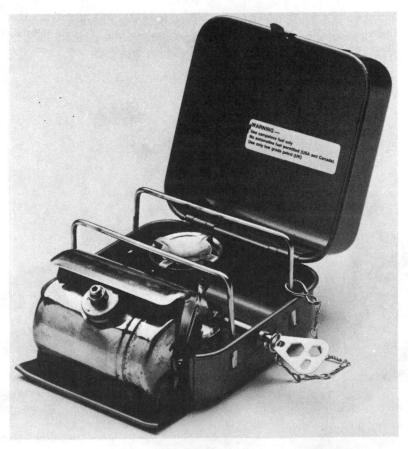

Figure 8-8. Backpack stove (Photo courtesy of Recreational Equipment, Inc., Seattle, Washington)

Figure 8-9. A-frame tent with rain fly (Photo courtesy of Trailwise Manufacturing Company, Berkeley, California)

mixes, dehydrated eggs, macaroni, spaghetti, oatmeal, and quick soups. Snacks, another important aspect of the packer menu, should consist of nuts, dried fruits, and chocolate.

It is recommended that food be packed in plastic bags to reduce weight and cut down on litter. Along with the planned menus for a trip, a small package of extra food should be assembled for emergency rations. These extra rations should be packed separately and tightly sealed for protection. Emergency rations should consist of starchy carbohydrates, fats, and proteins, in that order.

Cooking utensils should be kept few and simple. The following items are generally needed:

Two or three nesting pots with lids	Tubes or containers for margarine, pancake
Stainless steel cup	syrup, and peanut butter
Spoon and fork	Salt and pepper shakers
Sheath knife or pocketknife	Waterproof match container and book matches
	Miniature can opener

A frying pan is essential; it should be lightweight and easy to clean and should have a folding handle. A complete lightweight cook set, including pots, frying pan, cups, and plates, solves most cooking problems.

Shelter

A backpacker needs some type of protection from the elements, and some thought should be given to different kinds of shelter before one ventures into the wilderness.

A tent or an enclosed shelter adds warmth, comfort, and security to your surroundings. Several kinds of tents and tarps are available on the market. A tent should be light and compact; it should have a waterproof floor and adequate mosquito protection; and it should be constructed of a breathable fabric, preferably ripstop nylon or nylon taffeta. One style of tent that is commonly used for backpacking is an A-frame design with a rain fly. (See Figure 8-9.) This type of tent ranges from three to six pounds in weight.

A plastic tube tent (see Figure 8-10) is inexpensive and can be used in the summer, fall, and spring, but it is not recommended for cold weather or for use in snow. Polyethylene tarps (see Figure 8-11) can provide another inexpensive shelter. Tarps can be obtained in many thicknesses; the best ones are reinforced with nylon thread and grommets in each corner. Tarps can be pitched with a ridge line or in a slanted position with one end tied to a tree. Ponchos that have grommets in each corner make good emergency shelter and can be pitched in the same fashion as tarps.

Clothing

Clothing for most backpacking is not significantly different from what is worn for any other outdoor activity. The backpacker needs to be prepared for any sudden change of weather, especially in high mountain country. The most effective way to dress, and to regulate body temperature according to the weather, is to wear layers of clothing. As the body heats up or cools down, the packer can put on or take off individual garments.

One's choice of underwear depends upon the season. In warm weather a common T-shirt and ordinary underwear will be sufficient. In cold weather, thermal underwear or, preferably, fishnet underwear is a necessity. In extremely cold weather, wool underwear is best.

The pants and shirts constitute the next layer. The pants should be long, without cuffs and durable. A long-sleeve cotton shirt should be part of the outfit. In cold weather, the best clothing to have is a set of wool trousers and shirt. Wool retains warmth better than any other material when it is wet.

Next, a sweater, vest, jacket, down parka, or nylon shell jacket should be worn, according to the weather conditions. Additional outer clothing includes a brimmed hat or bandana for protection against the sun. In cold weather, a stocking cap can be worn for warmth. Mittens are preferred over gloves in extremely cold weather.

Figure 8-10. Plastic tube tent (Photo courtesy of Eastern Mountain Sports, Inc., Boston, Massachusetts)

Figure 8-11. Polyethylene tarp (Photo courtesy of Eastern Mountain Sports, Inc., Boston, Massachusetts)

Rain gear is extremely important because of the protection it provides for both backpacker and equipment. Coated nylon is lighter than rubber-coated fabric. Rain chaps can be worn to protect the legs.

General Equipment

The selection of general equipment depends on the individual preference of the backpacker. This equipment is not always essential, but it can add comfort on long treks:

Lantern	Comb
Folding camp saw	Insect repellent
Axe	Bathing suit
Toilet paper	Paper towels
Steel mirror	Detergent (biodegradable)
Laundry bag	Thermos bottle
Grill	Book
Binoculars	Paper
Camera	Pencil
Soap box and soap (biodegradable)	Razor

Safety Equipment

The following safety equipment should be carried on all backpacking trips:

Flashlight with extra bulbs and batteries	Sunglasses and sun cream—particularly in
Waterproof stick matches	deserts and in alpine and snow country
Pocketknife	Candles
Topographic maps	Change of clothes and socks
Compass	Extra food
Plastic water bottle	10 feet of rope

A good first aid kit and knowledge of first aid procedures are a must before one ventures out in the wilderness. The following items should be included in a basic first aid kit:

One dozen adhesive bandages	Razor blade
Sterile gauze pads	Moleskin
One small roll of adhesive tape	Milk of magnesia tablets
Aspirin tablets	Water purification tablets
Salt tablets	Tube of antibiotic ointment
Needles (to remove splinters)	

If one follows good safety habits, first aid should not be needed. However, if an emergency situation arises in the back country, it is important to be prepared to administer first aid. These procedures cannot be overemphasized. Statistics show that a great number of casualties have resulted from the lack of proper emergency treatment.

In closing this section on equipment, the authors would like to point out that equipment and food packaging are the most common form of litter in our nation's wilderness areas. Each and every backpacker entering the wilderness should carry a litter bag and follow this simple rule: What you carry into the woods, you always carry out, with no exceptions.

PREPARING FOR THE TREK

There are two major factors to consider before a backpacking trip: physical conditioning and the area to be covered. If a person is in reasonably good shape, he or she can just start off at a slow pace. However, if there is any doubt about one's physical condition, then arrangements should be made for a medical examination. Some pre-conditioning is advisable for all people to strengthen the feet, legs, and overall musculature. Proper conditioning can be achieved by means of jogging, cycling, or simple hiking activities. Hiking on short, easy trails is an excellent way to begin and also familiarizes you

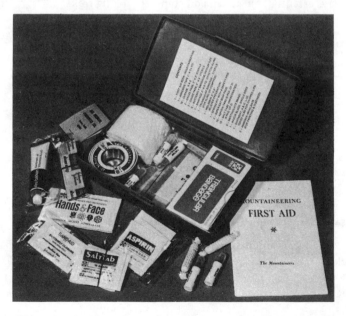

Figure 8-12. First aid kit (Photo courtesy of Recreational Equipment Inc., Seattle, Washington)

with walking in the outdoors. An excellent way to get into conditioning and to simulate the feeling of hiking up and down hills is to walk up and down stadium steps.

After a few short hikes, the next step is to acquire the feel of walking with a pack on your back. In the beginning, use a nearly empty pack load, between 15 and 30 pounds.

Trip Planning

Trip planning involves developing an outline of the expected route of travel with respect to the types of terrain, length of the trip, and tentative campsites. A copy of your itinerary should be given to a person who can notify the authorities if you have not returned by a given time. Often, registration at the trail head or park service is required and this should be checked before you start out. In developing a route, one needs the ability to read maps and use a compass. This subject is discussed in Chapter 10.

TRAIL SKILLS

A fully packed backpack for a long hike can weigh upwards of 50 to 70 pounds, which can create a problem when you try to hoist it up for placement on your back. There are a few simple techniques that can make this task a little easier. One method is to lean the pack in an upright position against a rock or tree. Then get into a sitting position on the ground with your back against the frame, slip your arms through the shoulder straps, and tighten the waist belt. Once the pack is secure on your back, go to a kneeling position and push off the ground with one leg at a time. You may need to read-just the pack once you are standing. Another method, for stronger people, is to face the frame and lift the pack to one knee while you slip one arm through the shoulder strap; then, in a single turn movement, turn and lift the pack to your back and quickly place your other arm in the shoulder strap. Then tighten the waist belt and adjust both shoulder straps. The simplest method is to ask another person to hold the pack in position while you slip into it and adjust it for proper fit. Taking the pack off your back is just the reverse of the aforementioned techniques.

Walking

Backpacking involves walking from one point to another. It is important for you to travel at a comfortable speed; do not attempt to keep up with people who are in better physical condition. It is important to conserve energy if you are going to meet the daily goal set forth in your trip itinerary. Energy can be lost by not eating the proper food, by hiking at a speed for which you are not conditioned, and by weather elements. In hot weather, you should start early in the morning, take a longer lunch break, and hike later into the evening. In cold weather, it is better to start later in the morning, take several short breaks, and stop before sunset. In both cases, it is important to drink a lot of fluids.

Walking or climbing uphill can expend a lot of energy and can completely exhaust a novice hiker if certain steps are not taken. The pace on an uphill slope should be slow and steady. It is best· not to take repeated short rest stops; push yourself and then take longer rest periods. On long, steep, uphill terrain, rest stepping—taking a short rest between steps—helps conserve energy. There are two methods of rest stepping. In the first method (see Figure 8-13), the knee of the back leg is locked with all the body weight resting on that leg, and then the front leg is brought forward, completely relaxed. After the short rest of the leg coming forward, the back leg advances and the forward leg is locked to support the body weight. This method is generally employed at high altitude with deep breathing at each momentary rest to prevent oxygen debt from occurring. The second method involves two steps followed by a brief pause and then three steps and a pause; the cycle is repeated as you climb the slope.

Figure 8-13. Rest step

Downhill travel can be equally as tiring and painful to the knees. Travel at a slow, steady pace. Tilt the upper body slightly forward and keep your center of gravity over your feet. If your upper body is tilted backward, you will lose your center of gravity and fall backwards. To help relieve the continual shock on the legs from stepping down, an extra pair of socks can be worn. In addition, it will help to consciously place the feet down with each step rather than allowing them to hit the ground hard.

CAMPING SKILLS

Campsite

The basic requirements of a wilderness campsite are a water supply, wood for a fire, and a relatively flat area for sleeping. A water supply is a prime factor for cooking and a fire safeguard. In many wilderness areas, fire permits are required before a trip starts. If fires are permitted, a supply of wood is necessary for camp selection. The area also needs to be cleaned of any small debris or sharp objects to protect your equipment.

Another consideration is the time of day to set up camp. It is important to allow enough time to set up camp and cook before you retire after a good day's hike. As a general rule, it is wise to make camp at least two hours before dark.

After a campsite has been selected, building a fire becomes one of the next steps. In a heavily traveled area, wood should be used sparingly. Use only wood that is lying on the ground. It is important that a sufficient supply be gathered before the fire is started. The simplest method of starting a fire is to arrange a small pile of dry kindling in tepee fashion and then, as the small twigs begin to burn, gradually add larger pieces of wood. It is important to position the wood in such a way that the air circulates properly, so that the fire will not be smothered by lack of oxygen. The fire should be enclosed by a formation of rocks, which hold heat and act as a safety measure. In certain circumstances, such as cases in which only wet wood is available, a fire-starter can be used to ignite the kindling. A fire-starter can be a candle, waxed cardboard, paper towels soaked in paraffin, or a small amount of stove fuel. Fires need to be thoroughly extinguished with water and dirt before you break camp.

Sanitation and Cleanliness

If our wilderness is to remain pure and beautiful, then each backpacker has the responsibility to keep this environment clean and sanitary. The selection of a latrine is a vital consideration. The following rules should always be followed in the selection of a latrine site:

1. Keep away from potential campsites and sleeping areas.
2. Keep 50 feet away from the trails.
3. Keep 100 feet away from streams, brooks, lakes or potential stream beds.

A latrine hole should be dug six or eight feet deep. A layer of dirt and rocks should be used to fill in the hole, which should be tramped down when you move away from the campsite.

Maintaining good personal hygiene to prevent illness on a trip is imperative. Bathing with soap should take place from a cooking pot and not within a stream. Cookware and eating utensils should be washed after each meal. Do not wash cookware and utensils in a stream or lake; keep at least 50 feet away. This distance is essential for environmental protection, because dirty wash water close to the bank can drain back and pollute the water source. Only biodegradable soap should be used.

SAFETY PROCEDURES

Accidents

Ignorance and panic are the two major factors involved when trouble arises with inexperienced backpackers. The greatest single step you can take to maintain health and safety is to exercise reasonable caution and common sense in everything you do. The vast majority of accidents and injuries in the outdoors are the result of carelessness.

Statistics show that more than 80 percent of all wilderness accidents are either cuts or burns; the next most common are fractures, foot infections, and eye injuries. The three main causes of death in the wilderness are heart failure from overexertion, hypothermia (exposure to cold), and drowning. Other wilderness accidents and injuries are insect and animal bites, blisters, and allergies; these can be minimized if caution is exercised.

Backpacking at High Altitudes

Acclimatization is the process by which the body becomes accustomed to hiking or climbing at high altitudes where the oxygen is limited. It is advisable to stay at one altitude for a rest period of a day or more in order to allow your body to adjust to that height. For each increase of about 2000 feet or more, the body needs additional acclimatization. The amount of rest time required to adjust at each altitude varies with the individual. "Mountain sickness" or altitude sickness occurs if the packer does not allow for the proper acclimatization period. Its symptoms are headaches, vomiting, drowsiness, chills, fatigue, and irritability. Treatment for mountain sickness is a return to a lower altitude and rest.

Fording Streams

If you ford streams or rivers, poor planning can result in injury or a very wet backpacker. Check up and down the streams for the best possible site before you cross. In some cases, rocks can be used

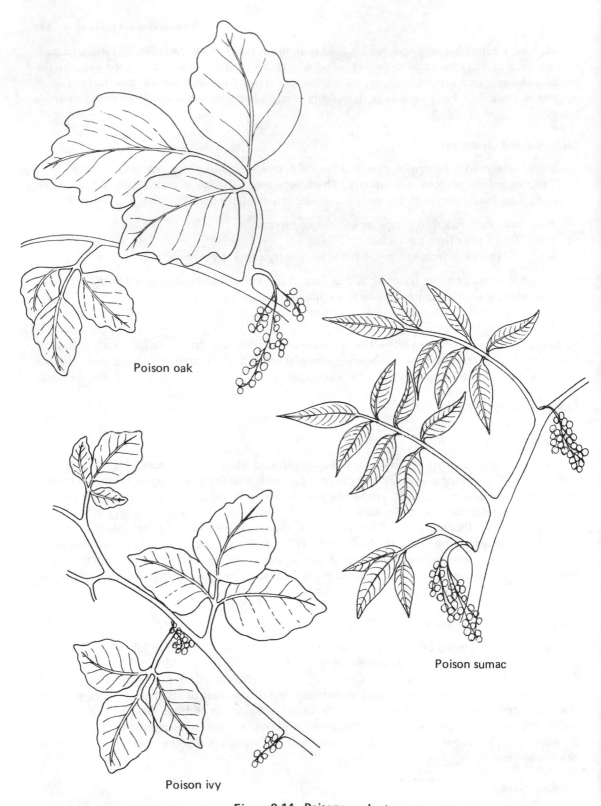

Poison oak

Poison sumac

Poison ivy

Figure 8-14. Poisonous plants

as stepping stones or a fallen log can provide passage. Before you cross, be sure to unfasten the waist belt on your backpack; if you fall, the pack can be easily removed so that it will be easier for you to stand up again. A long balancing stick or pole can be helpful. By placing the pole in the stream, facing upstream and moving sideways, one can navigate the stream with little difficulty. The current anchors the stick in the water, so that the hiker gains a sturdy base. This poling technique is useful for strong currents but is not advisable for rapids. Boots or tennis shoes should be worn to protect the feet and provide better footing.

Poisonous Plants

Severe skin irritations can be caused by three species of plants: poison ivy, poison oak, and poison sumac (see Figure 8-14). Every backpacker should learn to recognize and avoid these plants. Poison ivy, the most common poisonous plant in the United States, can grow as a vine or shrub. In the southern states and along the Pacific coast, it is more inclined to grow as a shrub than as a vine. The shrub type is more commonly known as poison oak. Both plants are recognized by beautiful, bright, compounded leaves and small, round, grayish green or white berries. Poison sumac is recognized by its bright green compounded leaves and its drooping clusters or red berries. This plant is found in swampy lowlands from New England to Minnesota and from Georgia to Texas. Symptoms of plant poisoning are itching, reddening of the skin, swelling, and sometimes blisters, which will form one or two days after contact. To treat plant poisoning, wash the area as quickly as possible with soap and water, and then apply calamine or some other suitable lotion. If you do not have calamine lotion, apply wet wood ashes to the affected area.

Animals

Animals often come into campsites looking for food. To avoid the loss of food and injury, always tie food high in a tree before you bed down for the night. The best rule for dealing with animals either large or small is to avoid them; keep a good distance away.

Safety Procedures for Special Environments

Desert Backpacking

The desert can be a beautiful but sometimes dangerous place to hike if factors such as the sun, heat, and water supply are not considered properly.

Effects of the Sun. Heat exhaustion can occur when a hiker is involved in extremely strenuous physical activity for an extended period of time. When this condition arises, the blood vessels under the skin become enlarged, so that the heat cannot escape in the form of perspiration from the skin; consequently, blood is drawn away from the brain and other internal organs, and lightheadedness or fainting occurs. Other symptoms include nausea, dizziness, headache with profuse sweating, and pale skin color. As immediate treatment for this condition, lay the victim down in a shady area and administer salt tablets and water. The victim can recover at an unusually rapid pace but should be encouraged to rest.

Heat stroke is an extremely dangerous condition and death can occur if it is not recognized and treated. In heat stroke, the cooling system of the body becomes unable to function properly and a failure of the sweating process occurs. Symptoms—confusion, lack of coordination, deliriousness, and unconsciousness—occur rapidly. During heat stroke, body temperature can soar above $105°$ Fahrenheit and the skin becomes red and hot. To treat this condition, the victim should be cooled down immediately with cold water compresses until the body temperature is lowered.

Both heat exhaustion and heat stroke can be prevented if the backpacker can avoid long periods of physical activity in extreme heat. In hot weather, the hiker should take frequent rest periods during the day in shady environments.

Sunburn can be prevented by a hat and handkerchief worn on the back of the neck. The use of a protective cream is recommended for other exposed parts of the body. Sunglasses are also helpful on bright sunny days.

Water. In the desert, the body requires seven or eight quarts of water per day to prevent dehydration. Never try to ration water in the desert. Your itinerary should include stops planned around known water sources. Do not depend on uncertain sources indicated by an outdated topography map. In emergency situations, water can be collected by the use of a desert solar still (see Figure 8-15). It should only be used in survival situations because, at best, it will produce a pint of water in about three hours. Another source of water is the barrel cactus; also, one can watch the flights of birds, particularly at sunset and dawn, because they tend to circle water holes at those times.

Cold-Weather Backpacking

Frostbite. In cold or alpine environments, frostbite and hypothermia (a lowering of internal body temperature) are two serious conditions that the backpacker or winter traveler must avoid by following several rules. Frostbite is the freezing of skin and underlying tissues. This condition is caused by a long period of exposure to freezing or sub-freezing temperatures. Other factors such as fatigue, lack of food, and dehydration can contribute to frostbite.

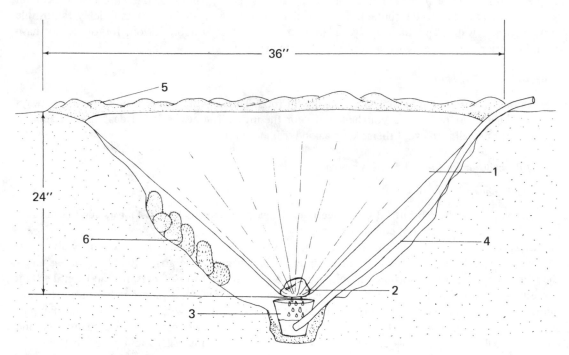

1. Plastic sheet, 6 feet in diameter.
2. Stone to form cone of plastic.
3. Jar or can to catch water.
4. ¼-inch plastic tube for drinking if available.
5. Place sand around the opening at the top
to seal the plastic. A good closure is important.
6. Line the hole with plant material; cacti are best.

Figure 8-15. Desert solar still

Frostbite is divided into two categories—superficial and deep. Superficial frostbite involves only the superficial skin and the tissues immediately beneath the skin. If superficial frostbite is not treated and cared for, it develops into deep frostbite. This condition is characterized first by a numbing of the affected area and then by a waxy skin color, which appears along with a stinging or burning sensation.

Immediate treatment for superficial frostbite is to cover the affected area with an insulating material (wool is best) and then apply firm pressure with a warm body part. For example, if the fingertips are affected, cover them with a dry wool mitten and place them in the armpit. The affected area should remain in a warm environment until it is rewarmed. Do not rub the affected area with your hands or with snow; this causes a greater risk of tissue damage and could also result in gangrene.

Deep frostbite should not be treated in the field. Attempts to thaw the affected area should be performed only by trained professionals. According to Dick Mitchell,

> Evidence indicates that a delay [in thawing] of up to 24 hours makes relatively little difference in the ultimate outcome, and might save amputation if the affected part should be refrozen before final treatment. Under no conditions should a thawed or partially thawed part be allowed to refreeze. This invariably causes far greater and more serious tissue destruction.[2]

Frostbite can be prevented by wearing proper clothing, including mittens, a hat, and wool socks. In addition, the backpacker should avoid smoking tobacco and drinking alcohol, because these substances constrict the exterior blood vessels. As the extremities become cold, the backpacker should move them around or place them next to another warm body part.

Hypothermia. Hypothermia results from continued loss of heat from the inner body. The end result of hypothermia is death by freezing. Many people have the impression that one must be exposed to long periods of subzero weather before one freezes to death. A person who is wet, however, can freeze to death at a temperature of 45° F and a wind of five miles per hour. Hypothermia is one of the leading causes of death in the wilderness. The signs, symptoms, and treatment are listed in Table 8-2. Hypothermia can be prevented if you follow these five rules:

1. Never go beyond your physical limits, and never overestimate your physical strength.
2. Always wear wool clothing and have windproof and waterproof clothing in your pack. Remember that it is best to layer your clothing.
3. Eat properly, because food is your best source of heat in cold weather.
4. Always carry an emergency shelter—tent, tube tent, or plastic tarp.
5. Stop early and set up camp in daylight hours.

TEACHING ACTIVITIES

The teaching of backpacking and camping skills can begin at the school or recreation complex. Students can be introduced to the basic equipment, skills, and safety procedures. Short trips can be taken into nearby wooded areas or campgrounds. Instructors can usually obtain permission to work on wood-cutting, fire-building, and tent-pitching skills right on the local grounds. School systems are somewhat limited by time during the school day; however, we recommend that instructors try to organize after-school programs and projects for the weekends and vacation periods. Backpacking skills are learned best on an outdoor expedition.

Students may have to provide their own equipment until a supply of equipment can be obtained from various sources. Local distributors may be able to help provide some adequate equipment at a

[2]Dick Mitchell, *Mountaineering First Aid* (Seattle: The Mountaineers, 1972), p. 54.

Table 8-2. Hypothermia—Signs, Symptoms, and First Aid

In Others	In Yourself	First Aid
Poor coordination	Intense shivering	Reduce heat loss:
Slowing of pace	Fatigue	shelter the victim from
Thickness of speech	Feeling of deep cold or	wind and weather
Amnesia	numbness	Insulate him from the ground
Irrationality, poor judgement	Poor coordination	Replace wet clothing with
Hallucinations	Thickness of speech	dry
Loss of contact with	Poor articulation	Put on windproof/waterproof
environment	Disorientation	gear
Blueness of skin	Decrease in shivering followed	Aid circulation—loosen boots,
Dilation of pupils	by stiffening of muscles	belts, constrictive clothing
Decreased heart and respira-	Blueness of skin	Add heat: put in warmed
tory rate	Slow, irregular, or weak pulse	sleeping bag; give hot
Weak or irregular pulse—	Intense thirst	drinks and food; heat from
stupor	No desire for food	canteen of water (use
		caution); huddle for body
		heat from other climbers;
		increase exercise level if
		possible under existing
		conditions.

Source: Dick Mitchell, *Mountaineering First Aid* (Seattle: The Mountaineers, 1972). p. 57. Reprinted by permission of the publisher.

reasonable price. Fund-raising ideas such as demonstration nights, car washes, and bake sales should provide your program with funding for the development of a supply of equipment.

In addition to basic backpacking skills, teachers must emphasize the importance of respecting and preserving our earth's various environments. This area of education cannot be neglected, because of the increasing number of backpackers using the outdoors. Respect for the environment can be taught by means of a series of discussions and lectures on how to use it properly. Besides regular class discussions, a variety of guest lecturers with different areas of expertise could be incorporated into the program. The following are several possibilities:

1. Red Cross personnel (first aid training).
2. Naturalists (discussions of plant and animal life in the local area).
3. Manufacturers or salespeople (discussions of new equipment).
4. Forest rangers (discussions of local forests).

Backpacking serves as a basis for many other wilderness activities, such as fishing, rock climbing, and canoeing. With the proper skills and equipment, it can be an enjoyable experience for many people. Educational and recreational programs must provide adequate services for people who want to use our environment in this manner.

QUESTIONS FOR REVIEW AND DISCUSSION

1. Why do people take up backpacking?
2. What types of pack frames are available?
3. What is the purpose of the waist belt of a pack?
4. Where should the heaviest items be packed in a backpack?

5. What procedures should be followed in adjusting a backpack to your back?
6. What factors determine the warmth of a sleeping bag?
7. Compare down filler with polyester filler for sleeping bags.
8. What is the loft of a sleeping bag?
9. Name four types of internal construction of sleeping bags.
10. Why is a ground pad important for sleeping in the outdoors?
11. What are the ways in which the body gains and loses heat?
12. What maintenance procedures should you use with a new pair of boots?
13. Why is a cooking stove recommended over an open fire?
14. What are the advantages of cooking fuels?
15. What factors should be considered in planning a trip menu?
16. What types of shelters are recommended for backpacking trips?
17. What is the advantage of wool over cotton?
18. What safety equipment is necessary for backpacking?
19. What procedures should be followed in preparation for a wilderness trip?
20. What three techniques can be used to put on a backpack?
21. What walking procedures will help conserve energy?
22. What factors are important for campsite selection?
23. What are the major causes of wilderness accidents?
24. What is mountain sickness?
25. How do you build a solar still?
26. What is the difference between frostbite and hypothermia?

REFERENCES

Manning, Harvey. *Backpacking—One Step at a Time*. New York: Vintage Books, 1973.
Mitchell, Dick. *Mountaineering First Aid*. Seattle: The Mountaineers, 1972.

SUGGESTED READINGS

Allen, Dan H. *Don't Die on the Mountain*. New Hampshire Chapter, Appalachian Mountain Club, 1972.
Cardwell, Paul, Jr. *America's Camping*. New York: Charles Scribner's Sons, 1976.
Colwell, Robert. *Introduction to Backpacking*. Harrisburg, Pa.: Stackpole Books, 1970.
Elman, Robert. *The Hiker's Bible*. Garden City, N.Y.: Doubleday and Company, 1973.
Fletcher, Colin. *The Complete Walker*. New York: Alfred A. Knopf, 1969.
Freeberg, William H., and Lore E. Taylor. *Programs in Outdoor Education*. Minneapolis: Burgess Publishing Company, 1963.
Lathrop, Theodore G., *Hypothermia, Killer of the Unprepared*. Mazamas, Oreg., 1972.
Merrill, W. K. *The Hiker's and Backpacker's Handbook*. New York: Winchester Press, 1971.
Mohney, Russ. *The Master Backpacker*. Harrisburg, Pa.: Stackpole Books, 1976.
Petzoldt, Paul. *The Wilderness Handbook*. New York: W. W. Norton and Company, 1974.
Rethmel, R. C. *Backpacking*. Minneapolis: Burgess Publishing Company, 1974.
Riviere, Bill. *Backcountry Camping*. Garden City, N.Y.: Doubleday and Company, 1972.
Van Lear, Denise, ed. *The Best about Backpacking*. San Francisco: Sierra Club Books, 1974.
Washburn, Bradford. *Frostbite—What It Is, How to Prevent It, Emergency Treatment*. Boston: The Museum of Science, 1972.
Wood, Robert. *The Best of Backpacking*. San Francisco: Sierra Club Books, 1974.

nine

rock climbing

We have all had the opportunity to observe children explore playground equipment and climb over and under various obstacles. As they climb, they experience the thrill of a new adventure, exploring a new environment and going somewhere that they have never been before. Each obstacle the child climbs is a new experience. Not only are the moves a little different, but even the angling and positioning of the body are new.

The rock climber climbs for the same reasons. No matter how many times a rock climber covers the same face, it is always a new experience.

Royal Robbins, in his book *Basic Rockcraft,* defines rock climbing in the following manner:

Historically, rock climbing is one of the components of the broad adventure sport of moun-taineering. Along with snow and ice climbing and hiking, rock climbing is one of the methods used to reach the summit of a peak. Originally this was its only justification: it was one of the roots of the tree of alpinism. Gradually, however, it has developed into a sport in its own right, and become one of the branches of the tree, with its own twigs, shoots, and branchlets running the gamut from big wall rock climbing such as is practiced in Yosemite Valley, through the various specialities of free and direct-aid climbing to bouldering, a gymnastic exercise close to the ground.[1]

The growth of rock climbing in the United States stems from the roots of general mountaineer-ing. In the latter part of the 1800s, mountaineering clubs were formed primarily by scientists wishing to study mountain phenomena. Men and women were admitted on equal terms, in contrast with European clubs, which were exclusively dominated by men. Organized mountaineering clubs within the United States were the Appalachian Mountain Club, with its headquarters in Boston; the Sierras, in California; the Mazamas, in Oregon; and the Mountaineers' Local, in Seattle. Members were mostly middle-class people from sedentary occupations. A club would organize trips into various mountain environments during holidays.

Founded in 1902, the American Alpine Club today is the leading club in America which fosters the growth of mountaineering. Its endeavors include publishing the *American Alpine Journal, Accidents in North America Mountaineering,* and several regional guide books. The club also helps by supporting expeditions to various parts of the world and is actively involved in conserving and pre-serving mountain environments.

---

[1] Royal Robbins, *Basic Rockcraft* (Glendale, Calif.: La Siesta Press, 1971), p. 7.

TYPES OF ROCK CLIMBING

Bouldering

Bouldering, or boulder gymnastics, is a climbing sport, especially popular in the West, in which the climber has the thrill of climbing a high wall but is relatively close to the ground. The intensity of the climb comes from various gymnastic moves performed on the boulder.

Technical Climbing

Technical climbing involves the use of special equipment, ropes, and a variety of protection devices. Technical climbing can be divided into two areas: (1) *technical free,* in which the climber is belayed but only natural handholds and footholds are used to gain a higher position on the rock; and (2) *aid climbing,* in which artificial climbing aids are used to gain a higher position. Such aids are stands or a piton, pulling on a runner, etriers, and mechanical ascenders.

Solo

Many climbers refer to solo climbing as the ultimate experience, but it can also become the ultimate tragedy. There are two types of solo climbing: (1) solo with equipment and self-belays; and (2) solo free, without ropes and equipment.

Clean Climbing

With the increasing popularity of rock climbing, many areas are starting to show the effects of overuse and misuse of pitons and climbing bolts. Popular routes are becoming polished and reveal many piton scars. Clean climbing does not use the piton or hammer. Climbers protect themselves with nuts and runners. Clean climbing leaves no scars and keeps the rock in its natural form.

Doug Robinson describes clean climbing in the following manner:

> There is a word for it, and the word is clean. Climbing with only nuts and runners for protection is clean climbing. Clean because the rock is left unaltered by the passing climber. Clean because nothing is hammered into the rock and then hammered back out, leaving the rock scarred and the next climber's experience less natural. Clean because the climber's protection leaves little trace of his ascension. Clean is climbing the rock without changing it; a step closer to organic climbing for the natural man.[2]

Each rock climber should take responsibility for preserving an environment that provides so much pleasure. The development and practice of clean techniques will be better insurance for the environment.

CLASSIFICATION OF CLIMBS

In describing a climbing route, climbers have found it desirable to grade each route on the basis of its difficulty. A standard grading system enables the climber to know the skill level required and the difficulties presented by a particular route. At the present time most rock climbing routes in the United States are graded by the Sierra Club system or a modification of it. The Sierra Club system distinguishes five classes, with a sixth class (the *A* class) representing technical aid:

---

[2] Doug Robinson, "The Whole Natural Art of Protection," in *Clean Climbing* (Tillson, N.Y.: The Eastern Trade, 1974), p. 2.

Class 1   —Hiking, on even or uneven surface, no special equipment needed, hands are also not needed.

Class 2   —Scrambling, hands and special equipment helpful but not always needed, should be carried for safety.

Class 3   —Climbing, knowledge of elementary climbing techniques is needed. Climbing equipment is carried for safety and to assist inexperienced climbers.

Class 4   —Roped climbing with belaying. General class 4 climbs are roped climbs, with belay person anchored and with low degrees of exposure.

Class 5   —Roped climbing, requiring special climbing equipment, runners, nut chocks and pitons for protection. Belay person is always anchored. Class 5 climbs have a high degree of exposure.

Class 6 or A—Roped climbing with an aritificial assist, such as pulling up on runners and the use of etriers (pre-tied stirrups).[3]

In class 5 routes, the degree of difficulty and exposure varies from pitch to pitch. Therefore, a decimal system has been added to further clarify the difficulty of each route. The decimal system starts with .0 and continues through .10. For example, a route might be classed as a 5.0, a 5.4, or a 5.10. A 5.10 climb has the greatest amount of exposure and requires the highest skill and knowledge level. A class 5 route is graded by its most difficult pitch. If a route has five pitches, each pitch may have a different grade (for example, first pitch 5.5, second pitch 5.6, third pitch 5.4, fourth pitch 5.7, and fifth pitch 5.3; the complete route would be graded 5.7).

A rock climber should be aware that the grading or climbing routes vary from area to area. A 5.7 climb in Yosemite might be only a 5.5 route in another area. In addition, one climber might grade a climb 5.5 on the basis of his or her skill level, whereas another might consider the same route 5.6 or 5.7. Weather conditions affect the grading of routes: a climb is graded 5.7 dry but 5.9 wet. A climber's performance also varies from day to day. One day a climber might have little difficulty with a 5.5 climb, but the next day the same climb might prove to be a 5.8 on the basis of the climber's performance.

At best, grades of climbing routes do not always indicate the true level of difficulty for that climb. Every climber should always be aware of this grading factor and be careful to select climbs on the basis of his or her current ability level.

EQUIPMENT

In the early stages of growth in rock climbing, the climbers' equipment consisted of a sturdy pair of hunting boots, a durable pair of trousers, and a large-diameter rope made of natural fibers. The equipment was limited, and the general rule was that the lead climber was not to fall.

A beginner needs very little equipment. As the skill level increases, the need for equipment also increases. Equipment can be divided into two categories—personal and technical. Unlike snow or ice climbing, personal equipment in rock climbing is kept to a minimum, consisting of boots, clothes, helmet, and miscellaneous items (e.g., first aid kit, knife).

Footwear

A beginning rock climber needs no more than a good pair of tennis shoes. As one advances in skill, shoes can become more specialized to meet the demands of the climb.

---

[3]Climbing Committee of the Mountaineers, *Mountaineering: The Freedom of the Hills.* (Seattle: The Mountaineers, 1974), p. 109.

Three types of rock climbing boots are available. The *kletterschuhe* (German) is a good all-around technical boot; the uppers are constructed of leather with rubber sides on the toe and heel caps to facilitate jamming into cracks. The soles are fairly stiff lug type. The kletterschuhe is a good boot for outcrop climbing, but at times is poor for long friction climbs.

The best boots for friction climbing have smooth rubber soles. This type was originally designed by Pierre Allain of France under the name of PAs, which are made of canvas and are extremely lightweight. Many manufacturers have taken Allain's idea and have developed different models. These boots should fit very tight and should be worn with thin socks or without socks. Climbers have found that pulling a sock over this type of boot can help to provide a securer base on wet rocks.

For the beginning climber a lightweight mountaineering boot is generally recommended.

Clothing

A loose-fitting pair of pants should be worn. Any type of tight-fitting clothes will restrict movements. Shorts, knickers, or lederhosen are also recommended. Long-sleeved shirts are better than short-sleeved shirts to protect against abrasions.

Helmets

Protective headgear should always be worn by a climber, and any participant in the climbing area should wear a helmet for protection from falling rocks or debris. In 1975 four climbers were killed as a result of not wearing a helmet.[4] The only helmets that should be worn are those designed specifically for rock climbing or mountaineering. The outer shell of the helmet should be constructed of plastic and fiberglass with a crush liner for an inner shell. The inner shell should also consist of a suspension system so that the climber's head does not touch the outer shell. This provides for better shock absorption. The chin strap should be secured to the helmet at four points, which provides a better transfer of impact. A climbing helmet should be selected on the basis of the following criteria:

1. Impact strength.
2. Ability to absorb shock from top and side positions.
3. Ability to stay on the head during a fall and at impact.

Technical Equipment

The development and use of technical equipment for rock climbing has doubled in the last decade. Many climbers now find that advances in equipment have eliminated many of the challenges of climbing. But improved equipment has meant greater security and has allowed climbers to cover routes once considered unclimbable. A complete book can be written on technical equipment and the application of such devices because there are so many on the market. Only the basic technical equipment for rock climbing is described here.

Rope

The climbing rope is the climber's lifeline. It is the umbilical cord between the climber and the belay person. A climber should know the essential qualities and the proper use and care of rope. A climbing rope should be made of nylon. Natural-fiber ropes should never be used for rock climbing, because they do not have the strength or shock-absorbency of nylon. Kernmantel is the most popular type of climbing rope because of its handling qualities. The rope is of core-and-sheath construction.

---

[4] American Alpine Club, *Accidents in North American Mountaineering* (New York: American Alpine Club, 1976), p. 21.

Figure 9-1. Hawser-laid rope (goldline)

The core (kern) consists of parallel strands of nylon surrounded by a tightly braided nylon outer sheath (mantel). This type of construction is less prone to kinking. The average test strength of kern-mantel is about 500 pounds. The UIAA (*Union Internationale des Associations d'Alpinism*) gives its seal of approval to a rope having an impact force value of 2,650 pounds, which will sustain most lead climb falls.[5] A standard climbing rope is 11 mm in diameter and 150 feet in length, but many climbers prefer a length of 165 feet. In Europe a double rope (two 9-mm ropes) is preferred over a single 11-mm rope.

Another type of climbing rope is a hawser-laid rope, which is also known as a goldline. A hawser-laid rope is made of three groups of nylon filaments plaited together. (See Figure 9-1.) The main advantage of this type is that the construction increases the elasticity up to 30 percent of its length, but hawser-laid ropes tend to kink badly. A standard hawser-laid rope for climbing is $7/16$ inch in diameter and 150 feet long.

The life of a climbing rope depends on the frequency of use, care, and the kind of rock on which it is used. With average use, a rope can be used for about two years. If a rope receives any extreme stress it should be retired immediately, for example, a long lead climber fall, damage from falling rocks, or improper care.

All climbing ropes should be stored in a dry place away from sunlight and should never be stepped on.

Sling

Also known as webbing or tape, the sling is constructed of nylon, either tubular or flat, and is used for rappelling seats, swami belts, and runners. Nylon tubular or flat slings should only be tied with a water or fisherman's knot. One-inch tubular or flat slings should always be used in relationship to any body ties or runners.

Carabiners

The carabiner (see Figure 9-2) is the most useful item of mountaineering equipment. Climbing carabiners are oval or *D*-shaped devices constructed of aluminum alloys for lightweight properties and strength. They are either locking (screw-gate) or nonlocking (with no gate). Locking carabiners offer greater security. With the gate screwed down there is little chance that the carabiner might open. When nonlocking carabiners are used for attachment to the body sling, two should be used with the gates in opposite directions. Carabiners have the following uses:

1. To join a climber to a climbing rope or rappel.
2. To join a belay rope to a climber.
3. To join the climbing rope to a protection point.
4. To ensure smooth running of the climbing aid equipment to a protection point.

Only carabiners that have been tested for more than 3,500 pounds should be used for climbing.

---

[5] Climbing Committee of Mountaineers, p. 114.

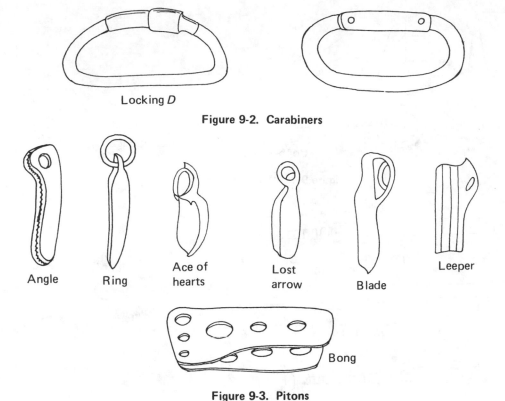

Locking *D*

Figure 9-2. Carabiners

Angle   Ring   Ace of hearts   Lost arrow   Blade   Leeper

Bong

Figure 9-3. Pitons

Climbing Hardware

Generally, climbing hardware consists of pitons, nuts, and bolts. Climbing hardware is used mainly for protection points. At the present time, climbing nuts are becoming more popular. With the growth of clean climbing, which eliminates the use of a hammer and drill, pitons and bolts are becoming less popular because of the scars and damage they cause to the climbing route.

Pitons. A piton is a nail-like device with a fixed eye or ring, which is hammered into a crack for a protection point. They are made from steel, nickel alloy, or chrome-moly steel and come in a variety of sizes and shapes. (See Figure 9-3.)

Nuts. British climbers are credited with the development of nuts, also referred to as *chocks*. The climber should pick out various sizes and shapes. On their hike to climbing areas they would place a chock into a crack and attach a runner in much the same way a climber would hammer in a piton. Modern technology has long replaced the skillful art of searching for chockstone. Nuts come either wired or with perlon-tied loops. (See Figure 9-4.)

Bolts. When no cracks are available for inserting a nut or piton, a bolt is used to provide protection to the leader. Bolts require drilling a hole into the rock. There are three types of bolts: (1) expansion, (2) nail drive, and (3) rawl drive. A hanger must accompany the bolts on which to attach the carabiners. (See Figure 9-5.)

A climber should take exteme care in placing a bolt. Royal Robbins describes the use of bolts in the following passage:

> They make possible some of the finest rock climbs on earth by opening up stretches of blank and otherwise unclimbable rock. But they also diminish the value in climbing by making it

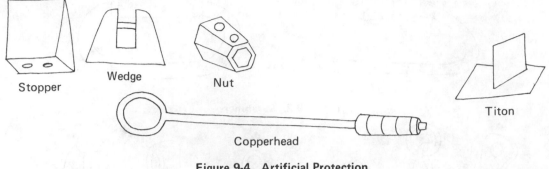

Figure 9-4. Artificial Protection

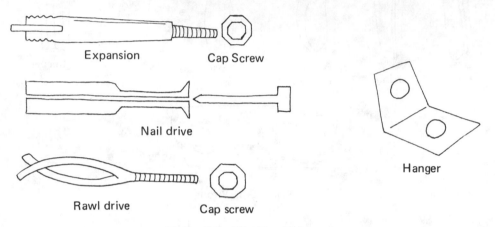

Figure 9-5. Climbing Bolts

possible for anyone to go anywhere if they were willing to drill. Bolts should never be placed on established routes unless the route has since been changed so it is impossible without them.[6]

KNOTS

There are almost an unlimited number of methods for tying knots: joining ends of ropes together, securing an object, lashing, etc. Of all the numerous knots available only a few are chosen for rock climbing. A rock climbing knot is selected on the basis of the following criteria: (1) strength, (2) easiness to tie and untie, (3) ability to stay tied, and (4) efficiency. In selecting a knot, efficiency is a prime consideration. (See Table 9-1.) A knot tied in a rope can cause a considerable loss of strength because of the uniform stress it places on the individual rope fibers; for example, if a knot is 70 percent efficient, the strength of the rope is reduced to 50 percent.

The knots that are generally used in rock climbing and mountaineering are described below. It is recommended that each of these be backed up with an overhand knot or half hitch to prevent slippage. The use of such a back-up system is called *boomproofing*.

Bowline. This strong knot is used for anchoring a rope to a fixed object, tying loops, or securing an end person.

[6] Robbins, p. 18.

Bowline on a Bight. This is used for tying in the middle person. (*Caution:* An error in tying this knot will cause a slip knot.)

Bowline on a Coil. This provides more protection to the climber's midsection and will better equalize the tensions on the climber.

Figure Eight. This knot is used for tying a loop and is also suitable for joining two rope ends together.

Secure with an overhand
knot for safety
(boomproofing)

Figure 9-6. Bowline

  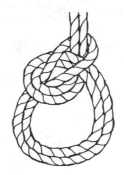

Figure 9-7. Bowline on a bight

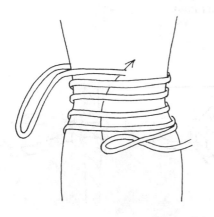 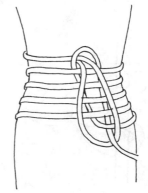

Figure 9-8. Bowline on a coil

Figure 9-9. Figure eight

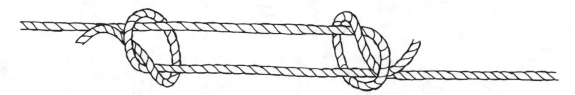

Figure 9-10. Fisherman's knot

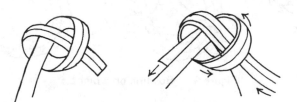

Figure 9-11. Water knot

Figure 9-12. Prusik

Table 9-1. Knot Efficiency

KNOT	EFFICIENCY
Bowline	70–75%
Figure eight	75–80%
Fisherman's (single)	60–65%
Fisherman's (double)	65–70%
Water knot (ring bend)	60–70%

Fisherman's Knot. This is the most effective knot for tying two ropes together or for making runners. A double fisherman's is the most secure for joining perlon ropes to tubular webbing since it has a lesser tendency to slip. It is also one of the few knots that does not need to be boomproofed.

Water Knot. This knot is also known as a *ring bend.* It is useful when joining two ends of flat or tubular webbing.

Prusik. This is a special knot used by climbers, in much the same way that mechanical ascenders are used. When the knot is tied around another rope, it will slip away from the direction of pull. Climbers use prusik loops to ascend a fixed rope.

BASIC SKILLS

Belaying

Belay is a universal term used to describe the safety system for protecting the climber in case of a fall. There are two types of belays, dynamic and static. Dynamic belays bring the falling climber to a gradual halt. In a static belay system the climber is brought to a halt as quickly as possible. In rock climbing, static belays are generally preferred over dynamic belays.

Anchors

The belay person should always be anchored down to prevent him or her from being pulled off the belay position during the fall. An anchor is secured by attaching the belay person to a fixed object. An anchoring point could be a fairly large diameter tree, pitons, or nuts. In climbing, hardware is used for anchoring points. The belay person should be anchored at two points, preferably three points, independent of each other. These points should be placed on the same line as the climb, or directly behind the belay person to prevent the belayer from being pulled off balance during the fall.

Hip Belay

The hip belay is a standard method, and beginners should master it. In this system the belayer can either stand or sit, although sitting in a braced position provides a stronger base during a fall. These steps are followed in the execution of a hip belay:

1. Anchor down the belay person.
2. The climbing rope goes around the back of the belayer, above the anchoring ties of the player.
3. The end of the climbing rope that is attached to the climber is handled with the right hand, pulling hard. The left hand (braking hand) holds the other end of the rope next to the climber's left hip. If the belayer is left-handed, the left hand is the pulling hand and the right hand is the braking hand.

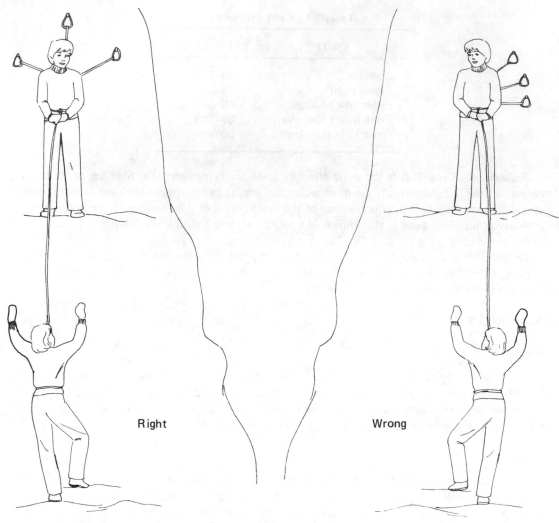

Figure 9-13. Belay anchors

4. As the climber moves up, the slack is taken out of the rope with the pulling hand, pulling back towards the body, while the braking hand pushes the rope away from the body.
5. When the hands are parallel to each other, the pulling hand holds both ropes momentarily and the breaking hand slides back to the belayer's hip. The pulling hand then pulls up more rope.
6. The holding and pushing process continues until the climb is completed.
7. Braking. In the event of a fall the braking hand is brought across the body, undercutting the pulling hand, and both hands hold tight.

In this system the pulling hand and braking hand should never leave the ropes. Avoid any practice of having a large amount of slack in the climbing ropes, but not to the point where the belayer is pulling the climber up the face.

In belaying a lead climber, the process is the same, but the belayer is feeding the rope out. (See Figure 9-14.)

Communications

A communications system between climber and belayer is essential for safety. No climber should start the climb unless the belayer tells the climber that everything is okay. (See Table 9-2.)

CLIMBING TECHNIQUES

As in any sport, rock climbing is one that the participant masters only after long hard hours of practice. The climber can read materials and be instructed in the equipment, knots and various techniques, but once the climber is on the rock, it's up to the climber.

Figure 9-14. Lead belay

Table 9-2. Climbing Signals

BELAYER	CLIMBER
On belay—everything is set, you can now start to climb	*Up-rope*—pull up the slack
	That's-me—the slack is out of the rope
Climbing away—start to come up.	*Climbing*—the climber is climbing
	Slack—the rope is too tight
	Up-rope—the rope is too loose
	Tension—use only when more security is needed
	Falling—I'm falling, hold tight
Off-belay—the belayer is no longer belaying the climber	*Off-climb*—the climber is in a secure position, or has completed the climb*

*The climber should always shake the belayer's hand, just to say thank-you for a good belay.

Figure 9-15. Body position

Figure 9-16. Edging

In mastering the skill, boulders are one of the best places to start. Bouldering allows the climber to develop the balance and feel for the rock, without the great fear of going very high off the ground.

Body Position

One of the biggest mistakes a beginner climber makes is hugging the rock. A climber should always try to stand up as straight as possible as this will keep the body off the rock, giving the climber a better center of gravity. The body weight should always be placed directly over the feet. (See Figure 9-15.)

Three Points of Contact

As the climber moves up the rock, the first holds he or she should look for are footholds followed by handholds. You can push up with your leg much easier than you can pull with your arms. The climber should always have three points of contact on the rock, that is, two footholds and one handhold, or two handholds and one foothold. Avoid crossing your feet and never try to move both feet at the same time. Rock climbing is a slow concentrated series of movement, each one thought out in advance. A good rock climber moves with grace and ease, with little wasted motion—planning, moving and planning again, avoiding holds that will cause fatigue.

Climbing Holds

A climber makes contact with the rock through a series of holds, either hand or foot. Footholds can be classed as friction holds, edging, or jams. In friction holds, the climber places the greatest amount of boot surface on the rock in order to gain acohesion to the face and provide a nonslip hold. The center of gravity must be directly over the feet. Edging is placing the side of the foot on any convex surface of the rock (see Figure 9-16). Jams involve placing a portion of the whole boot, leg, or knee into a crack to provide a wedge for pushing off from the face (see Figure 9-17).

Handholds use the same principles as footholds (see Figure 9-18).

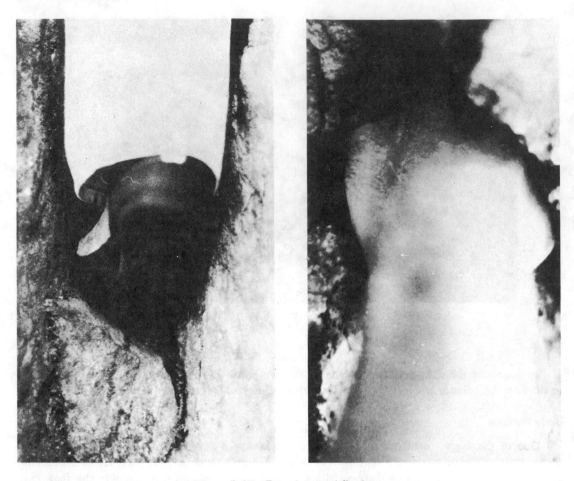

Figure 9-17. Foot jam and fist jam

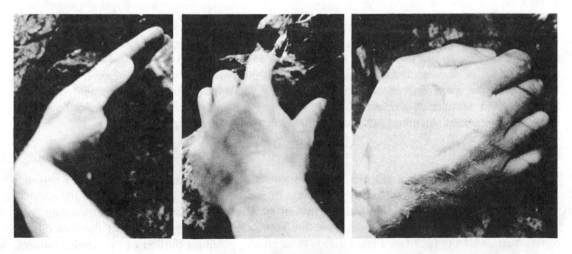

Figure 9-18. Handholds

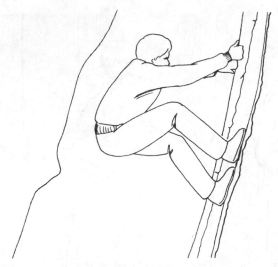

Figure 9-19. Lay back technique

Special Holds

By putting together a series of holds a climber establishes a move. A move could be just a hand-hold, a foothold, or a combination to gain height, a lay back, a chimney, an undercling, or a jam series.

Lay Back. This technique is used on vertical cracks. Cracks in corners are especially conducive to lay back techniques. The climber assumes position with both feet on the wall and both hands in the crack. The arms should be locked to place body weight on the bones of the arms rather than the muscle. The hips are held tight to the wall. (See Figure 9-19.)

Chimney. When a vertical crack is big enough so that the climber can have his or her whole body inside, a chimney technique is used. (See Figure 9-20 and Figure 9-21.)

Undercling. This is used for traversing a slightly tilted large crack. Hands are placed as flat as possible on the under wall, and the climber then inches along, keeping equal pressure on the hands and feet. (See Figure 9-22.)

Jam Series. When a vertical crack is not big enough for full body placement, a series of foot jams should be used.

RAPPELLING

A method of descending over a rock face, or for retreating when unforeseen difficulties or emergencies arise is known as rapelling, or *abseil* (German). The principle of the rappel is to slide down a fixed rope, either with a body wrap or by a mechanical device to create friction on the rope to control the rate of descent.

Preparation for Rappelling

Rappelling Seats

Rappelling seats are generally tied with one-inch tubular nylon webbing, and are selected for safety and comfort.

Diaper Sling. The most popular seat is the diaper sling. (See Figure 9-23.) It is constructed with about 10 feet of webbing. The ends of the sling are tied with a ring bend or fisherman knot (see the

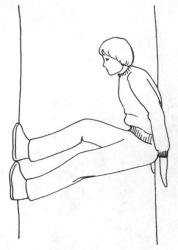

Both feet are placed flat against the wall front. The back is flat against the back wall.

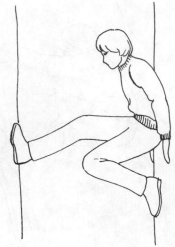

One foot is placed on the back wall and the climber pushes up, raising the hands and back to the highest position.

Alternate foot is placed back and the body is raised again.

Back is pressed against the back wall and the knees lock in a resting position.

Figure 9-20. Execution of chimney technique

section on knots). Once the loop is created by tying both ends of the sling, the seat is ready to be attached to the body. Place the center of the sling around the small of the rappeller's back. Reach through the rappeller's crotch and pull the sling back through to the stomach. The end result is three loops. Connect the loop with a carabiner. A swami belt should also be worn with the diaper sling.

Double Loop Seat. Another seat that can be used for rappelling or climbing is the double loop seat. (See Figure 9-24.) This seat has several advantages over the diaper seat and swami belt because it can be tied early in the morning and then worn all day through climbing and rappelling activities. It also provides greater security and comfort for the person. This seat can be tied with at least 16 feet

Figure 9-21. Chimney technique

Figure 9-22. Undercling technique

Front   Back

Figure 9-23. Diaper seat

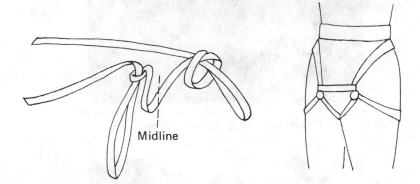

Midline

Figure 9-24. Double loop seat

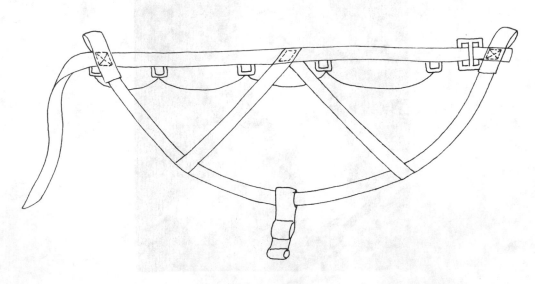

Figure 9-25. Whillans seat

of sling by first finding the middle of the sling and then tying two overhand knots to create two loops that will fit around the top of the thighs. These loops should be about three inches on either side of the middle of the sling. After you put the loops on your legs, bring the sling around the outside of your hips and then crisscross the remaining sling around your waist. Finish by tying a water knot on your hip.

Whillans Seat. The authors have found that the most effective and comfortable seat is a commercially manufactured seat designed by Don Whillans. (See Figure 9-25.) This seat is the strongest and most versatile seat on the market today. It can be used for all types of climbing, belaying, rappelling, and caving. The Whillans seat has been effective in handling forces greater than 5000 pounds. The weakest point of the seat is in the buckle. As a consequence, the waist strap must be brought back through the buckle and a piece of flat rope tied through the three loops with a water knot. (See Figure 9-26.)

Swami Belt

Also known as a waist loop, the swami belt has replaced the bowline on a coil for attaching the climbing rope or belay rope to the climber. (See Figure 9-27.) A swami belt is tied with about 15 feet of one-inch tubular nylon webbing. Start with the center of the 15 feet of webbing in the center of the back just below the rib cage, and wrap five or six times around the waist. The ends should be tied with a water knot and two half hitches.

The big advantage of the swami belt is that it provides a wider surface area over the body rather than a rope tie-in. It also is more comfortable if a fall should occur.

Rappel Anchors

The rappelling rope can be anchored to a large tree or an outcropping of rock. If natural anchors are not available, pitons, nuts, or climbing bolts can be used. With artificial anchors, the rappelling ropes should be anchored at two points, and preferably three. The rope can be doubled for rappels

Figure 9-26. Whillans seat with tied waist strap

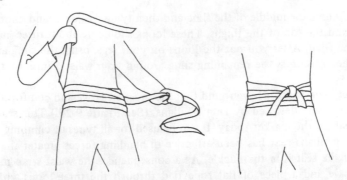

Figure 9-27. Swami belt

Figure 9-28. Braking system

shorter than 75 feet. If the rappel is longer than 75 feet, two climbing ropes tied together with a double fisherman's knot should be used. In both cases, a figure eight knot should be tied at the free ends of the climbing rope to prevent rappelling off the rope.

Braking System

The function of the braking is to create friction on the ropes to control the speed of the descent. (See Figure 9-28.)

Rappel Techniques

After the anchors have been selected and tied into, and the rappelling seat has been attached to the rappeller, the rappeller is ready to begin. The rappeller stands with feet shoulder-width apart looking back toward the anchors. The left hand holds the ropes about six inches above the braking system (this hand is only a guide hand). The right hand holds the rope just behind the right hip (this hand is the rappeller's brake hand). The rappeller then leans back and walks backwards, moving the brake hand away from the hip. To stop, the rappeller simply pulls the right hand back to his or her hip. As the rappeller moves to the edge of the rappel, gravity will begin to act upon the body. The rappeller should stay perpendicular to the incline of the rappel, with both feet touching the face of the rock. As the rappeller continues down, he or she should start gaining a sitting position, again with both feet touching the face of the rock. On an overhang, the rappeller should remain in the sitting body position.

The rappeller should avoid any jumping or jerking movements as this will place unnecessary strain on the rope. Upon completion of the rappel, the rappeller calls back to the belay person with "Off rappel!" Only one person can rappel on a rope at a time.

Belaying

In belaying a rappel, the belay person is anchored down in the same manner as if the belay person were belaying a climber. The belay person holds the belay rope in each hand, allowing the ropes to slide easily through, as the rappeller moves down the rappel. If the rappeller loses contact or must stop, the belay person tightens his or her grip on the rope and crosses his or her arms across the body.

Body Rappels

Arm rappelling can be used on low-angle slopes. The rappeller faces down the slope with ropes wrapped around each arm and behind the back. The rate of descent is controlled by the rappeller's grip on the ropes. (See Figure 9-29.)

Dulfersitz. The ropes pass through the crotch up across the chest and over the shoulder. The dulfersitz can be used on higher angled faces. (See Figure 9-30.)

Figure 9-29. Arm rappelling

Figure 9-30. Dulfersitz

Placement of Hardware

The lead climber is primarily concerned with the placement of hardware (protection points). Lead climbing should not be attempted by a beginner until he or she has experienced many climbs as a second person. Therefore, the authors recommend many top-roped climbs before one tries lead climbing. Protection placement and lead climbing can be practiced on a large boulder before vertical faces are attempted. A discussion of the techniques of protection placement does not fall within the scope of this chapter, which is intended for beginning climbers.

ARTIFICIAL CLIMBING AREAS

Artificial climbing areas or simulation of climbing skills can be constructed on school or recreation facilities. Examples of such areas can be tops of buildings for rappels, stone walls for climbing, stone chimneys, stairwells and narrow halls for chimney teaching, bleachers in a gymnasium, and so forth.

Artificial Climbing Walls

The simplest of all practice climbing walls can be constructed out of a solid brick wall and hardwood blocks cut at various angles and bolted to the wall. (See Figure 9-32.) Construction of the wall is done in the following manner.

1. Select a brick or flat stone interior or exterior wall about 20 or 25 feet high. Avoid cinder block walls, which are hollow and will not hold the bolts.
2. Use a hardwood block (oak is preferred) for the handholds and footholds. The block should be cut and placed at different angles and sizes. Each block should also have two $5/16$-inch holes drilled and countersunk for the starter block and three holes for longer blocks.

Figure 9-31. Artificial climbing wall (Photo courtesy of Paul Ross, International Mountain Equipment, North Conway, New Hampshire)

³/₈-inch climber bolt

Figure 9-32. Construction of artificial climbing wall

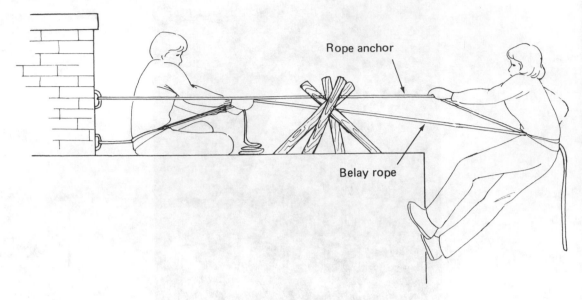

Figure 9-33. Building rappel

3. The design of the climb is up to the builder; many routes and variations of routes can be placed on one wall. Each block is attached to the wall with $5/16$-inch lag screws with sheaths. The builder will need a heavy-duty electrical drill with masonary drill bits.

4. A $3/8$-inch climber bolt should be placed at the top of each route for the belay point. The climber is belayed from the bottom of the wall.

Building Rappels

The sides of most buildings can provide good practice rappelling areas. Avoid anchoring the rappelling rope to aluminum air ducts or pipe vents. The best anchors are brick chimneys or small block houses found on building tops. (See Figure 9-33.) Also, a tripod should be constructed on top of the building to keep the rappelling rope above the rappeller's shoulders; this allows for greater balance as the rappeller steps over the edge of the building. The tripod should also be anchored down. Avoid areas in which windows would interfere with the rappeller's route of descent. Doorways and walkways should also be avoided.

QUESTIONS FOR REVIEW AND DISCUSSION

1. What are the four basic types of rock climbing?
2. What is aid climbing?
3. Why is clean climbing so important today?
4. How can a climber help to preserve rock faces?
5. Explain the Sierra system for classification of climbing routes.
6. Which climbing classification includes routes that require the use of artificial aides such as etriers?
7. What type of boots are best for friction climbs?
8. What criteria should be used in the selection of a climbing helmet?
9. What are the characteristics of a kernmantel climbing rope?

10. What factors determine the life of a climbing rope?
11. What types of knots should be used with tubular or flat rope?
12. Explain three specific uses for a carabiner.
13. What is the difference between nuts, bolts, and pitons?
14. Which knot should be used for anchoring a rope to another object?
15. What is a figure eight knot used for?
16. What knots are used for joining two ropes?
17. Explain two different types of belays.
18. What communications are important between a climber and a belayer?
19. What are some examples of special climbing holds?
20. What is a rappelling seat?
21. Explain proper rappelling techniques.
22. What safety procedures should be followed in building an artificial climbing wall?

REFERENCES

American Alpine Club. *Accidents in North American Mountaineering.* New York: American Alpine Club, 1976.

Climbing Committee of the Mountaineers. *Mountaineering: The Freedom of the Hills.* Seattle: The Mountaineers, 1974.

Robbins, Royal. *Basic Rockcraft.* Glendale, Calif.: La Siesta Press, 1971.

Robinson, Doug. "The Whole Natural Art of Protection," in *Clean Climbing.* Tillson, N.Y.: The Eastern Trade, 1974.

SUGGESTED READINGS

Aleith, R. C. *Bergsteigen Basic Rock Climbing.* Scottsdale, Ariz.: Bergsteigen, 1971.

Crew, Peter. *Encylopaedic Dictionary of Mountaineering.* London: C. Tinling & Company, 1968.

MacInnes, Hamish. *International Mountain Rescue Handbook.* New York: Charles Scribner's Sons, 1972.

May, W. G. *Mountain Search and Rescue Techniques.* Boulder, Colo.: Rocky Mountain Rescue Group Inc., 1973.

Meldrum, Kim, and Brian Royle. *Artificial Climbing Walls.* London: Pelham Books, 1970.

ten

map and compass reading

An exciting, adventurous way of exploring the great outdoors is through the use of a map and compass. This method of exploring and navigating the land is now commonly known as orienteering.[1] A wide variety of orienteering games and activities are becoming popular, for example, cross-country, point-to-point, score, route, line, window, and memory orienteering. All of these require skill in the use of map and compass, rapid decision making, and running endurance. These activities can take place during either the day or the night. They can provide an enormous amount of fun and adventure.

Maps and compasses have been in use for many years (Marco Polo may have had knowledge of the compass in 1250), but their use for orienteering activities began in Sweden in 1917. Orienteering gained popularity there and in other parts of Europe, especially in Norway, Denmark, Finland, and Switzerland. This popularity has slowly drifted to the United States and Canada, primarily through the scouting movement. Many schools (such as Ohio State University, East Stroudsburg State College, and Brigham Young University) and community recreational programs now offer orienteering activities.

Orienteering can be adapted so that almost anyone can participate. It can be organized in the form of group- or family-centered activities, and it requires a minimal financial outlay. A blend of physical and mental skills is required of participants. Organization time is minimal for the participant. Another advantage is that these types of activities can be used in conjunction with a variety of other outdoor activities, such as camping, hiking, hunting, fishing, geography studies, bicycling, and running. Many people also promote orienteering because it helps to develop self-reliance and the ability to make decisions.

TYPES OF ORIENTEERING ACTIVITIES

Cross-Country or Point-to-Point Orienteering

Cross-country, or point-to-point, orienteering is probably the most popular orienteering activity. A series of markers or control points is set up to form a course over an area of varied terrain that covers from three to nine miles, according to the skills of participants. The control points are usually marked with red and white nylon bags, or sometimes a plastic bottle is used. The markers should be placed in an area where they are visible and accessible from the ground. Participants are each given a map on which the control points are circled and numbered in a specific order. They must then decide

---

[1] *Orienteering* is the trademark and service mark of SILVA Division of Johnson Diversified, Inc.

which route will provide the quickest access to each control point. For example, courses are laid out so that participants must decide whether to go around or over a hill. Each control point should have a coded punch or some type of identification card to provide evidence that a participant has actually visited there; the punched cards are turned over to the course officials at the end of the race. Participants are timed with a stopwatch, and their decisions about which routes to take are evaluated on the basis of how long they take to complete the course.

Table 10-1 is an example of a point-to-point orienteering meet card. A topographic map marked with a point-to-point orienteering course is shown in Figure 10-6.

Score Orienteering

The object of score orienteering is to accumulate points in a given time period. Each control point is assigned a point value on the basis of the distance and the type of terrain to be traveled by the participant. There is no sequence to be followed; the participant tries to visit as many control points as possible within the time limits. The time period can vary according to the particular circumstances. Points can be deducted if a person returns to the starting point after the allotted time period has elapsed; usually, one point is deducted for each minute beyond the limit.

Table 10-1. Point-to-Point Orienteering Meet Card

CONTROL NUMBER	GRID REFERENCE	DESCRIPTION OF CONTROL
Start	038 845	
1	038 868	Lone tree
2	045 853	Gate at track junction
3	045 860	Green patch in wood (path)
4	056 865	Gate against bank
5	049 880	Concrete post
6	033 874	Fallen trees
7	039 858	Green trees near mud patch
8	033 852	Tree with fractured trunk
Finish	037 844	Clearing

Magnetic Variation—8 degrees
Scale of map—1:25,000
Maximum time allowed—120 minutes

Observe the rules of the countryside

Cross roads directly

No smoking or fires please

All competitors must report to the finish on completion of
   the event
Course setters
   C. Walker
   A. Ross

Source: W. P. Adams, "Geography and Orienteering," *The Journal of Geography* 71 (November 1972):475. Reprinted by permission of the publisher.

Figure 10-1. Point-to-point orienteering

John Disley points out some advantages of score orienteering activities:

1. They can be held in reasonably open country, for as the linking together of controls is a matter of personal preference there is not likely to be a procession formed as when the orienteers all move in the same pattern of progress. This means that fairly open park land can be used without good visibility detracting from the enjoyment of the event.
2. Competitors of all standards can compete together in the same event. The strong performers can cover six to eight miles in 90 minutes, while the novices, women and juniors can complete the event to their own standards, probably covering three to four miles in the time allowed.
3. The event can be confined to a comparatively short period of time. A flock of competitors can be sent off at the same time so that the whole entry can be started within half an hour. With a time limit set for the return, most of the competitors will be within a two hour period. This means that fairly large meetings can be held in the summer evenings and even night events can be over in winter by nine o'clock.[2]

Route or Line Orienteering

Route orienteering involves following an irregular line marked on each participant's map. Control points are not marked on the map but are found along the route. The participants mark on the map exactly where they find each control point. Participants must stay exactly on course or they miss the

---

[2] John Disley, *Orienteering* (Harrisburg, Pa.: Stackpole Books, 1973), p. 79.

control markers. Scores are determined by the number of control points found and the accuracy of plotting their positions on the map.

Since the competitors follow essentially the same course, it is necessary to allow a short interval between their starting times. If a competitor finds out that he or she has missed a control, he or she must decide whether to backtrack and look for it or whether to continue to the finish and avoid further delay. A time penalty is usually assessed for missed controls.

Window Orienteering and Memory Orienteering

Window orienteering is usually used as a practice drill for the other types. Participants are given a map that has been blacked out except for the area around each control point. They must then follow a compass azimuth between control points. They must remain on that bearing regardless of the terrain it crosses.

Memory orienteering is another excellent training method. The participants must memorize a portion of the map between two points, for example, from the starting point to the first control or from the first control to the second control. Participants race from point to point in this manner, and scoring is determined by the time taken to complete the course.

Night Orienteering

Night orienteering can be a very exciting and adventurous activity. The abilities to find directions and to judge distances are of prime importance. Only experienced orienteers will be successful at night orienteering; beginners should not engage in it.

Night orienteering can take advantage of terrain that is not suitable for daytime orienteering, such as parks that are either too open or too crowded for use during the day. Safety and lighting equipment are important considerations for night orienteering.

Relay Orienteering

A variety of relays can be set up to utilize various forms of orienteering. Relays emphasize competition and teamwork in an orienteering program. Every member of the team can make a contribution to the overall success of the maneuver. A good example of such activities is the cloverleaf relay (see Figure 10-2).

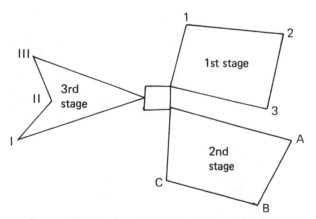

Figure 10-2. A cloverleaf relay (From John Disley, *Orienteering.* © 1973. Reprinted by permission of Stackpole Books, Harrisburg, Pennsylvania, and Faber and Faber, London.)

BASIC SKILLS FOR ORIENTEERING

Setting Up a Course

The most important aspect of successful orienteering is a well-organized and well-planned course. The level of difficulty must be determined, so that the course can provide the participants with a sufficient challenge but not be too difficult for them to experience some measure of success. Some factors to be taken into account by a course-setter are the following:

1. All orienteering skills should be utilized—map reading, compass reading, concentration, choice of routes, running, distance judgment, and decision making. The course should require participants to use a combination of all these skills, not just one or two of them.
2. Landowners should be contacted and permission should be obtained before construction of the course is started. Many landowners are willing if they are asked properly.
3. Maps must be obtained. These are available through various agencies, to be discussed later in this chapter. The organizers should check the accuracy of the maps.
4. The course-setter should pick out aspects of the terrain that will provide problems for the participants, for example, hills, lakes, rock faces, and thickly wooded areas.
5. The course-setter should avoid setting up a course with dogleg angles at the control points, because these would causes participants who are leaving a control to use the same path that is used to enter the area. In that case, one could find a control point simply by observing the path of an exiting participant.
6. Control points should be set so that their position is deceptive without careful map analysis. Straight routes should be much more difficult than zigzag routes. Alternative routes should be available. Railroads, paths, and power lines should be used to tempt participants into longer but safer routes that may or may not be faster.
7. Control points should not be located near an open area, such as a field or lake, because they would be too easily sighted. The markers should be placed in a spot that corresponds to a landmark on the map, such as a large tree, a boulder, a hilltop, or a building.

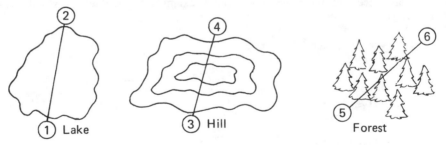

Figure 10-3. Terrain problems

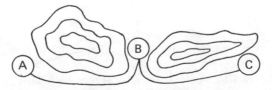

Figure 10-4. Dogleg angle

Map Reading

Orienteering activities can be limited by the type of maps that are available. The best ones for most activities are topographic maps prepared by the United States Geological Survey. Most of the United States has been mapped at the scale of 1:24,000, which means that for every 1 unit on the map there are 24,000 units on the ground. This scale is usually the most satisfactory for orienteering activities; however, a scale of 1:62,500 is also satisfactory. Map information in your state can be obtained by writing to:

Map Information Office
U.S. Geological Survey
Washington, D.C. 20242

The maps usually cost 75 cents for a quadrangle. Maps of areas east of the Mississippi can be obtained from:

Distribution Center
Geological Survey
Washington, D.C. 20242

Maps of areas west of the Mississippi can be obtained from:

Distribution Section
Geological Survey
Denver Federal Center
Denver, Colorado 80225

Each map has a name and a number, which you will have to obtain before you can order. It may be necessary to order two or three maps in order to show enough terrain.

Once you obtain a map of your particular area, you should start by just walking the terrain with your map. Try to pick out available routes and familiar markings, such as buildings, roads, hilltops, power lines, and lakes.

Orienteers must become familiar with all aspects of a map, including these basic parts:

1. *Map scale.* The scale expresses the relationship between the map and the earth's surface. The most common scales are 1:24,000 and 1:62,500; every unit on such maps represents either 24,000 or 62,500 units on the earth's surface. The smaller the second number of the ratio, the more detail the map shows.
2. *Contour lines.* Points of equal elevation are connected by contour lines on a topographic map. These lines reflect the shape of the land; between two adjacent lines is a 10-foot decrease in elevation.
3. *Grid lines.* Grid lines are solid block lines, parallel to the borders of the map; the distance between them represents one kilometer. The grid enables orienteerers to pinpoint spots on the map.
4. *Map symbols.* Symbols commonly used on topographic maps are shown in Figure 10-5.

Figure 10-6 is a topographic map that is marked with a point-to-point orienteering course. Note how the location of the control points requires participants to make decisions about their route.

Figure 10-7 is a topographic map that is marked for a score orienteering event. The point values vary according to the difficulty of the terrain and the distance of the control point from the starting point.

TOPOGRAPHIC MAP SYMBOLS

VARIATIONS WILL BE FOUND ON OLDER MAPS

Hard surface, heavy duty road, four or more lanes ......

Hard surface, heavy duty road, two or three lanes ......

Hard surface, medium duty road, four or more lanes ....

Hard surface, medium duty road, two or three lanes .....

Improved light duty road............

Unimproved dirt road and trail.............

Dual highway, dividing strip 25 feet or less.............

Dual highway, dividing strip exceeding 25 feet.........

Road under construction.........................

Railroad, single track and multiple track ....

Railroads in juxtaposition.........................

Narrow gage, single track and multiple track.........

Railroad in street and carline......................

Bridge, road and railroad ....

Drawbridge, road and railroad ....

Footbridge...................................

Tunnel, road and railroad ....

Overpass and underpass ....

Important small masonry or earth dam ....

Dam with lock...............................

Dam with road...............................

Canal with lock...............................

Buildings (dwelling, place of employment, etc.)........

School, church, and cemetery.....................

Buildings (barn, warehouse, etc.)..................

Power transmission line...........................

Telephone line, pipeline, etc. (labeled as to type).......

Wells other than water (labeled as to type)............ oOil.....oGas

Tanks; oil, water, etc. (labeled as to type)............. ● ● ● ⊘Water

Located or landmark object; windmill.............. o.........

Open pit, mine, or quarry; prospect.................. ✕......... x

Shaft and tunnel entrance..........................■.........⅄

Horizontal and vertical control station:

    Tablet, spirit level elevation...................... BM △ 5653

    Other recoverable mark, spirit level elevation .... △ 5455

Horizontal control station: tablet, vertical angle elevation VABM △ 9519

    Any recoverable mark, vertical angle or checked elevation △3775

Vertical control station: tablet, spirit level elevation..... BM ✕ 957

    Other recoverable mark, spirit level elevation .... ✕ 954

Checked spot elevation .... x 4675

Unchecked spot elevation and water elevation .... ✕ 5657.... 870

Boundary, national.......................

    State...........................

    County, parish, municipio.....................

    Civil township, precinct, town, barrio...............

    Incorporated city, village, town, hamlet............

    Reservation, national or state...................

    Small park, cemetery, airport, etc.............

    Land grant.........................

Township or range line, United States land survey .....

Township or range line, approximate location ....

Section line, United States land survey ....

Section line, approximate location.................

Township line, not United States land survey ....

Section line, not United States land survey ....

Section corner, found and indicated .... +.........+

Boundary monument: land grant and other............ ▫.........▫

United States mineral or location monument........... ▲

Index contour		Intermediate contour..	
Supplementary contour........		Depression contours ..	
Fill............		Cut............	
Levee........		Levee with road....	
Mine dump........		Wash............	
Tailings............		Tailings pond........	
Strip mine........		Distorted surface.....	
Sand area............		Gravel beach........	

Perennial streams		Intermittent streams..	
Elevated aqueduct........		Aqueduct tunnel......	
Water well and spring. o........		Disappearing stream..	
Small rapids........		Small falls........	
Large rapids........		Large falls........	
Intermittent lake.....		Dry lake............	
Foreshore flat.......		Rock or coral reef....	
Sounding, depth curve.	10	Piling or dolphin.....	
Exposed wreck......		Sunken wreck......	

Rock, bare or awash; dangerous to navigation ....

Marsh (swamp)........		Submerged marsh	
Wooded marsh.......		Mangrove	
Woods or brushwood ..		Orchard............	
Vineyard............		Scrub............	
Inundation area......		Urban area	

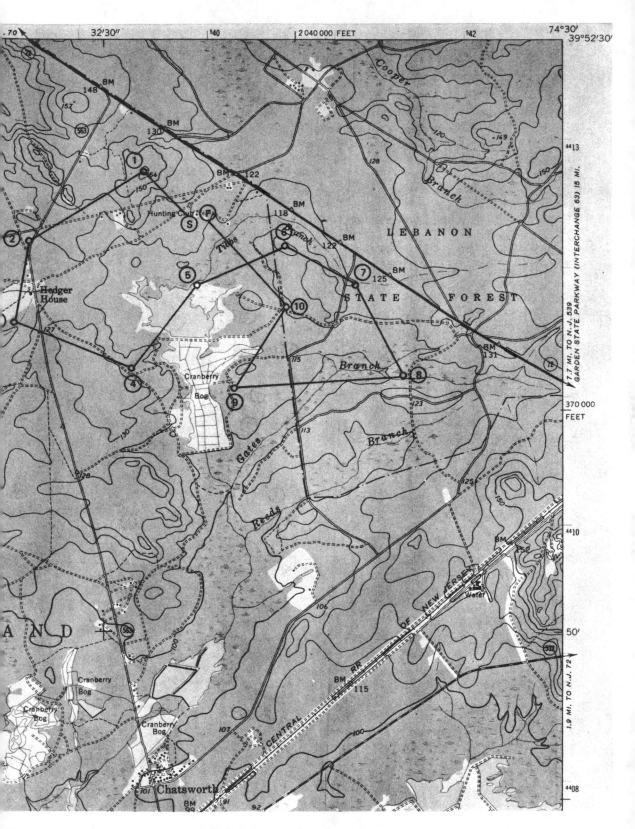

Figure 10-6. Point-to-point orienteering course

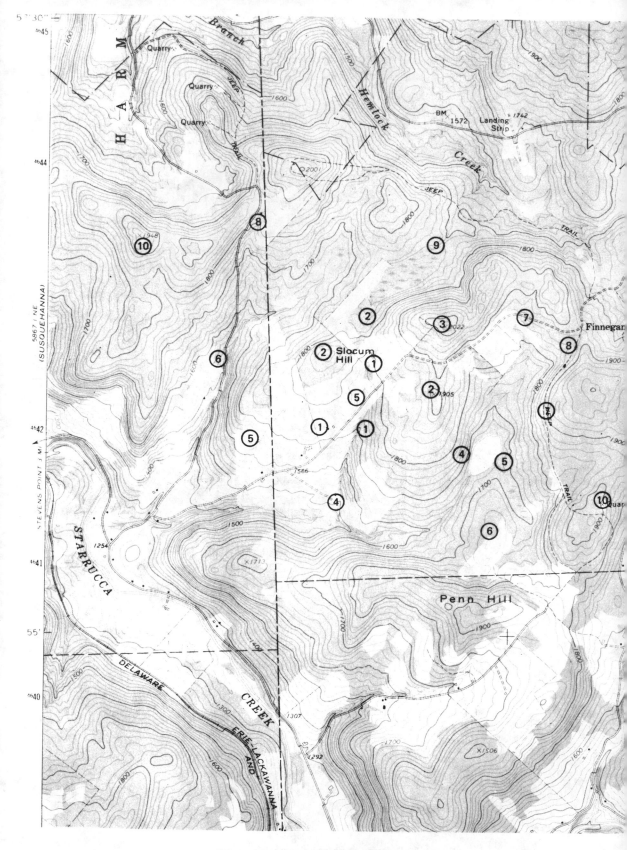

Figure 10-7. Score orienteering event

Compass Reading

Many styles of orienteering compasses and accessories are available. The Silva Company, a Swedish firm directed by the Kjellstrom brothers, is a major supplier. Compasses and accessories range widely in price. We suggest that you take a look at what is available at your local sporting goods store and ask for a trial with a low-priced compass. After you gain some experience, you should be able to make better decisions about the styles and prices that are right for you.

Orienteerers must become familiar with their compasses in order to succeed at these types of activities. (See Figure 10-8.)

The *housing* is a movable circular metal or plastic portion of the compass, which indicates directions (*N, S, E,* and *W*) and contains degree markings and orienting lines. The *magnetic needle,* suspended in the housing, always swings to the north. *Orienting lines* are marked on the housing to orient maps and to determine bearings. The *direction-of-travel arrow* helps line up bearings to find the proper direction in which to travel. In addition to knowing the parts of the compass, orienteerers should become familiar with the following terms:

Bearing—the direction of a given point from an observer; it is given by the horizontal angle between that point and north (the angle is measured in degrees in a clockwise direction from the north).

Quadrant—one of four 90° segments of the compass, namely, northeast (0°-90°), southeast (91°-180°), southwest (181°-270°), and northwest (271°-360°).

Azimuth—the direction of a celestial body (such as the moon, the sun, or a star) from an observer; it is given by the horizontal angle between north and a point on the horizon that represents the position of the celestial body (the angle is measured in degrees in a clockwise direction from the north).

Magnetic north—the direction in which a magnetic needle points.

True north—the direction of the North Pole.

Declination—the horizontal angle between true north and magnetic north.

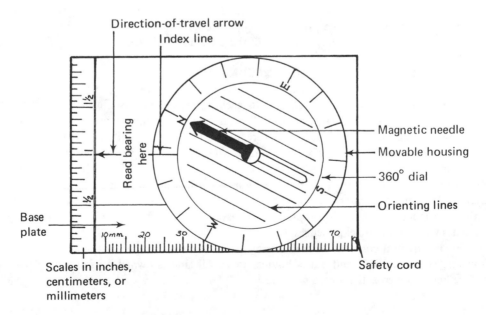

Figure 10-8. Parts of a compass

Besides a magnetic needle, an orienteering compass is equipped with a protractor, which not only enables a person to locate a correct direction from the map, but also allows one to point out the correct direction on the ground. There are essentially three steps in taking a bearing from a map, according to Disley:

1. Place the long edge of the compass along the desired line of travel, i.e., join up where you are to where you wish to reach. Check that the Direction of Travel arrow points towards your destination.
2. Turn the compass housing until the orienting lines and arrow are parallel to the grid lines.
3. Read off the number of degrees at the index pointer. This is the Grid Bearing.[3]

This bearing may have to be converted to a magnetic bearing, because the difference between true north and magnetic north is usually too great to ignore.

Skill in reading and using a map and compass requires a good deal of time and effort. These skills cannot be acquired just through reading this chapter or another book about orienteering. Try to obtain a compass and a topographic map for your area, and then walk the area to become familiar with the respective map symbols. Use the compass to help orient the map, and take bearings of particular points of interest. You should gradually gain confidence with your map and compass.

LEARNING ACTIVITIES WITH MAP AND COMPASS

A little creativity and ingenuity can go a long way in the development of learning activities. The Minnesota Department of Natural Resources (Bureau of Information and Education) has developed an excellent orienteering program for secondary schools in that state. The program, which includes beginning, intermediate, and advanced activities, could be adapted to suit different schools and recreational agencies. Several of the activities geared for beginners are presented in Appendix D. A pamphlet of beginning orienteering activities has been put together by John W. Horstman, of Meadow Lake School of Robbinsdale (Minnesota) Area Schools. Any school could adapt his ideas for use in its own program. Mr. Horstman has also developed and used a variety of map and compass activities, which were presented at the National Conference of Outdoor Education held in March 1976 at Duluth and Isabella, Minnesota, and some of these are also included in Appendix D.

SAFETY AND ENVIRONMENTAL CONCERNS

The safety factors that are relevant to each age group vary somewhat according to students' needs and interests. The best rule to follow is to use common sense in the woods. Instructors, directors, or teachers should become aware of the hazards that might exist in a certain area. They need to inform and remind children of various safety problems. Procedures should be established for emergencies and unplanned problems that might arise, for example, one should know the location of the nearest telephone, doctor, or hospital. Various woods and wilderness areas have inherent dangers that students must learn about, such as dangerous animals, treacherous terrain, or problems of orientation. Teachers must use appropriate progressions and teaching techniques in order to provide students with successful experiences.

Environmental concerns in orienteering include showing respect for fences, trees, crops, animals, housing, streams, lakes, and out-of-bounds areas. All land is owned by someone. Secure permission before beginning an activity on a new site.

---

[3]*Ibid.*, p. 54.

An additional safety precaution is to make sure that all students return to a specific place. This helps ensure that all students are safe, and can eliminate an unnecessary search.

QUESTIONS FOR REVIEW AND DISCUSSION

1. What is involved in the sport of orienteering?
2. What is point-to-point orienteering?
3. What are the advantages of score orienteering over point-to-point orienteering?
4. What is a cloverleaf relay?
5. How can an orienteering course be set up that incorporates all available terrain?
6. What is a map scale?
7. How is a topographic map different from a road map?
8. What are contour lines?
9. What are map symbols for roads, schools, rivers, lakes, and swamp areas?
10. What are the major parts of a compass?
11. Why are bearings and quadrants important to an orienteerer?
12. What steps should be followed to take a bearing from a map?
13. How is the direction-of-travel arrow used in orienteering?
14. Which learning activities would be good for a beginning orienteerer?

REFERENCES

Disley, John. *Orienteering.* Harrisburg, Pa.: Stackpole Books, 1973.

SUGGESTED READINGS

Carlson, L., J. Lee, A. S. Peepre, and Mall Peepre. *Introduction to Orienteering.* Canadian Orienteering Service, 446 McNicoll Ave., Willowdale, Ont., 1971.
Disley, John. *Your Way with Map and Compass.* Silva Ltd., 446 McNicoll Ave., Willowdale, Ont., 1971.
Devine, Barry. "Run for Your Life." *JOHPER* 43 (November-December 1972):44-46.
Kjellstrom, Bjorn. *Be Expert with Map and Compass.* Harrisburg, Pa.: Stackpole Books, 1967.
Pirie, D. A. G. *The Challenge of Orienteering.* London: Pelham Books, 1968.

eleven

cycling

Cycling, or bicycling, has become a popular outdoor activity. The continual rise in the cost of oil, gasoline, automobiles, and automobile repairs and the national concern for health and physical fitness have caused people of all ages to take up cycling as a serious activity. Bicycles are used for a variety of purposes: (1) for transportation to and from work, school, or shopping, (2) for physical conditioning, (3) for fun, (4) for touring, traveling, or sightseeing across the country, and (5) for highly competitive racing. Cycling means many different things to many different people, from the pure enjoyment of riding for several short hours in the outdoors to the intensive competition of racing in the Olympic games.

In a number of towns, cities, and states across the United States, community efforts are being made to encourage cycling to and from work and school. Bike paths are becoming a common sight as the promotion of cycling and cycling safety increases. In 1971, the Oregon state legislature passed a law requiring the state highway department to spend a minimum of 1 percent of all gasoline taxes to build bicycle and pedestrian paths.[1] Similar legislative action has been introduced in 30 other states. The city of Davis, California, has an extensive system of bicycle paths. Most large universities have an organized network of bike paths across their campuses.

In addition, large industrial companies throughout the United States are encouraging their employees to cycle to work. Bicycle racks and shower facilities are provided by some companies, such as Goodyear Tire and Rubber Company in Akron, Ohio. Companies are also promoting cycling clubs for recreation.

Many colleges and universities (for example, Ohio State University, the University of Utah, East Stroudsburg State College, and the University of Maine at Portland-Gorham) offer courses in cycling, often with interdisciplinary approaches that include weekend or vacation trips. Catonsville Community College, in Baltimore, Maryland, offers a two-week bicycle tour that combines instruction in cycling with ecology and personal and community health.[2] Students can earn as many as six credits for this course. They cover more than 350 miles on bikes and additional distance by van, canoe, and ferry. Learning packets are distributed 30 days before the trip.

Cycling instruction and trips have also become more popular at the high school, junior high school, and elementary school levels. Kittitiny Regional High School and West Morris Mendam High

Special thanks to Dr. Lee N. Burkett, of Arizona State University, for writing the first draft of this chapter.

[1] Robert Cantwell, "Where All Roads Lead to Roam," *Sports Illustrated* 42, no. 21 (26 May 1975):37-44.
[2] "Fresh Ideas for College Physical Education—Interdisciplinary Bike Tour," *JOPER* 46 (February 1975): 40-41.

School in New Jersey offer cycling as an elective. Chandler Junior High School, in Chandler, Arizona, offers a bicycle safety course, which uses an obstacle course and a nearby racetrack to develop cycling skills. Jefferson Elementary School, in Gahanna, Ohio, also uses an obstacle course in its bicycling safety program.

In Missouri, a pilot program on bicycle safety was conducted with fourth- and fifth-graders.[3] This program used a packet of instructional materials developed by the Missouri Department of Elementary and Secondary Education under the direction of Dr. Robert M. Taylor, the director of health, physical education and safety for the state. The packet includes motivational and problem-solving teaching strategies along with pre-tests and post-tests and information on bicycle safety, first aid, history, rules, maintenance, games, and purchasing procedures. The results of the program were encouraging, because the children showed large gains in their knowledge of bicycles.

Cycling is an excellent form of physical exercise; it can serve as a complete physical conditioning program or as a part of one. The bicycle ergometer, which is a stationary bicycle, has been used in cardiac stress testing. Cooper rates bicycling as an excellent activity. In his book, *Aerobics,* he explains a rating system based on points accumulated over a week; for example, cycling three miles in 11 minutes and 30 seconds, twice a day and five days a week, is a sufficient weekly routine to maintain an excellent level of fitness.[4]

If you embark on a regular cycling program, you should receive the following benefits:

1. Weight control (mild cycling burns 5 calories per minute, or 300 calories per hour).
2. Improved cardiovascular conditioning.
3. Improved muscular endurance.
4. Better muscle tone.
5. Enjoyment of the outdoors.
6. A cleaner environment.
7. Save money on gas, oil, and automotive repairs.
8. Help reduce dependence on foreign energy sources.

EQUIPMENT AND CLOTHING

Bicycles are made in various sizes and have many different speed ranges. You can buy 1-speed, 3-speed, 5-speed, 10-speed, or 15-speed bicycles. *Speed* refers to the number of gears. Just as a car has several gears, from low to high, so do many bicycles.

The price of bicycles ranges from $50 to more than $1,500, depending upon the quality and type of components such as exotic frame materials like graphite and titanium. A one-speed bicycle with a coaster brake and balloon tires is the least expensive.

Most people today buy the 10-speed bicycle. The price of a 10-speed depends on the quality of the frame, wheels, gears, and gear changers, the type of materials, and craftsmanship. We recommend a price range from $125 to $250 for a new bike. Good used models can often be purchased at auctions or through newspaper ads. Bicycles sold at police auctions usually are in bad shape or have been stripped of their parts, but we have found that they can be repaired with a little skill and a few parts. Take along a friend who knows bicycles, and keep in mind that it is better to get a high-quality bicycle (Raleigh, Schwinn, Centurion) than a low-quality bicycle that runs well. Good bicycles sometimes have been painted over and look rather cheap. The quickest way to check quality is to examine the frame, brakes, and derailleur.

---

[3] Irwin W. Davenport, "Missouri Bicycle Safety Program," *School and Community* 62, no. 8 (April 1976): 36-37.
[4] Ken Cooper, *Aerobics* (New York: Bantam Books, 1968).

The major parts of a 10-speed bicycle are shown in Figure 11-1. The frame is shown in more detail in Figure 11-2.

Most good-quality frames are brazed into lugs at their joints. A frame construction in which the tubes are inserted into each other and welded is usually not as strong. (See Figure 11-3.) However, there are some good frames that are not lugged (Viscount, Schwinn) and are just as strong.

Bicycle brakes also reflect quality in a bike. Inexpensive one-speed bikes usually have a coaster brake, which works by back-pedaling. More expensive bicycles have front and rear caliper brakes, which are operated by levers on the handlebars. For the beginner, we recommend a center-pull brake rather than a side-pull brake, because it provides an even, smooth, powerful pull, and is usually more reliable, and requires less maintenance. There are also several effective side-pull models (Shimano, Campagnolo) that can be used with tubular tire rims. (See Figure 11-4.)

Besides the essential parts listed above, you may want to acquire other pieces of equipment:

1. Lights (See "Safety," below)
2. Water bottle

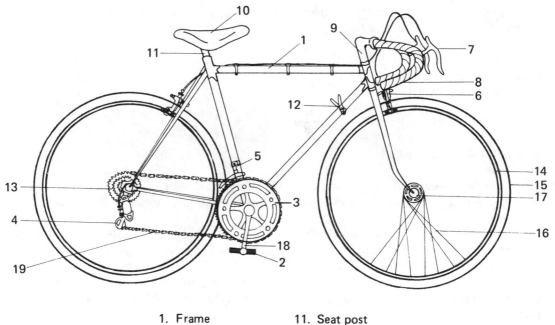

1. Frame	11. Seat post
2. Pedal	12. Gearshift
3. Chain wheel	13. Freewheel gear
4. Rear derailleur	14. Rim
5. Front derailleur	15. Tire
6. Caliper brake	16. Spokes
7. Brake levers	17. Hub
8. Handlebars	18. Crank
9. Handlebar stem	19. Chain
10. Saddle	

Figure 11-1. Major parts of a 10-speed bicycle

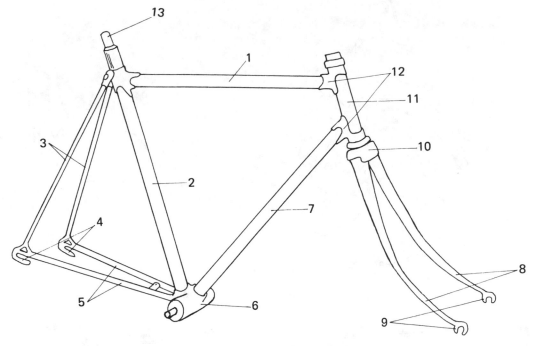

1. Top tube
2. Seat tube
3. Seat stay
4. Fork end (rear)
5. Chain stay
6. Bottom bracket (hangar)
7. Down tube
8. Fork blade
9. Fork end (front)
10. Fork crown
11. Head tube
12. Lugs
13. Seat post

Figure 11-2. Parts of a frame

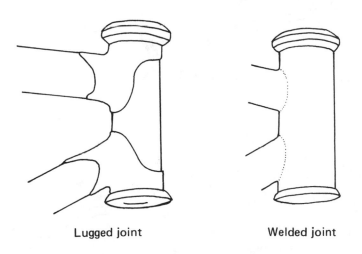

Lugged joint   Welded joint

Figure 11-3. Frame construction

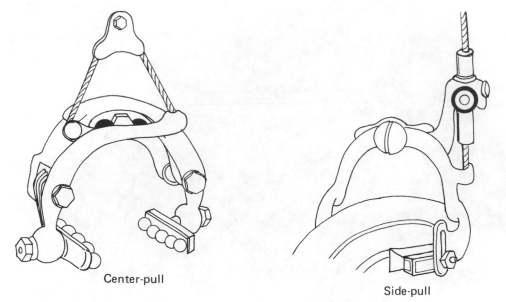

Center-pull   Side-pull

Figure 11-4. Caliper brakes

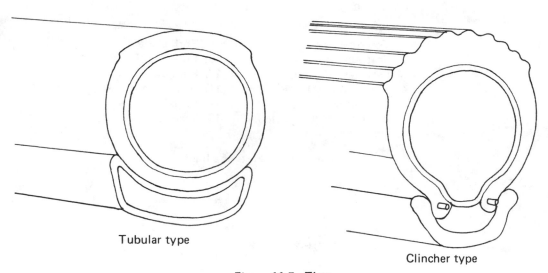

Tubular type   Clincher type

Figure 11-5. Tires

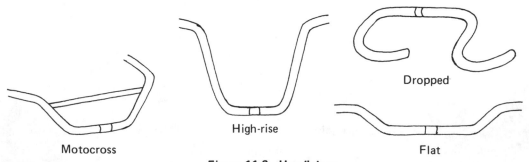

Dropped

Motocross   High-rise   Flat

Figure 11-6. Handlebars

3. Camping equipment
4. Tandems
5. Baskets
6. Body seat
7. Locks (Buy one that takes at least five seconds to break, has no lock cable, and is stealproof. This way you increase the length of time it takes to steal the bicycle.)
8. Kickstand
9. Odometer and speedometer
10. Tire pump
11. Horn
12. Radio (We do not recommend radios for safety reasons; you should be able to hear the traffic.)

The two basic types of tires are the tubular and the wired-on, clincher model (see Figure 11-5). Tubular tires are sewn all the way around the tire, so that the tube and the tire form one complete unit. They are light, flexible, compact, and offer a minimum of rolling resistance. They must be cemented to the rim and thus are impractical to repair on the road. An entire spare tire must be carried at all times. Consequently, we recommend the use of the wired-on or clincher-type tire because it is more durable, heavier, and easier to repair. Clincher tires are also easy to obtain at most bicycle shops.

Fitting a bicycle to you is extremely important. Fitting your bicycle starts with the proper frame size. A rule of thumb is to select a frame that allows you to straddle the top bar with comfort. Another rule of thumb is to select a frame that is about 10 inches shorter than your leg. If you buy a frame that is either too large or too small, proper saddle and handlebar adjustments will be impossible or very difficult.

There are four basic types of handlebars that are available: (1) flat, (2) dropped, (3) high-rise, and (4) motocross (see Figure 11-6). The flat handlebar is found on the conventional 3-speed bicycle. The dropped handlebar is found on the 10- or 15-speed bicycle. The high-rise handlebar is found on the Sting Ray bicycle. Motocross handlebars are found on motocross bikes (see "Bicycle Motocross," below).

Fitting the handlebars to you will make a great difference in cycling comfort. Three adjustments can be made on handlebars: (1) stem height, (2) tilt of the handlebars, and (3) the horizontal distance from the saddle. The last of these can be altered only with an adjustable stem, which is rather difficult to find.

To get an approximate height adjustment for the handlebars, make them level with the nose of the saddle. The horizontal distance from the saddle can be changed a little by moving the saddle forward or backward; however, its position should not be changed radically (saddle position is discussed in the following paragraphs). A good way to find the correct horizontal distance is to measure your hand-to-forearm length; this length should approximate the horizontal distance from the rear edge of the handlebar to the nose of the saddle. If you follow the two rules of thumb for selecting a frame, you can get the proper stem for height and horizontal length. The typical tilt of the handlebar is a 10-degree downward tilt of the lower handle. All of these adjustments should be made and changed only after you have put at least 100 miles on your bicycle. If you wish to make adjustments after that, comfort is the criterion.

There are many types of saddles. The most comfortable are the leather models and the new ensolite-padded models with a plastic body. The steel-bodied saddles are the least comfortable.

Saddle adjustment is probably the most important adjustment in fitting a bicycle, since it determines the efficiency of the cyclist's leg muscles. Three saddle adjustments can be made: (1) saddle height, (2) distance of saddle nose from crank, and (3) saddle tilt.

Saddle height is extremely important for efficient cycling. Scientific studies have been conducted in order to determine the most efficient saddle height. One such study was completed by Thomas

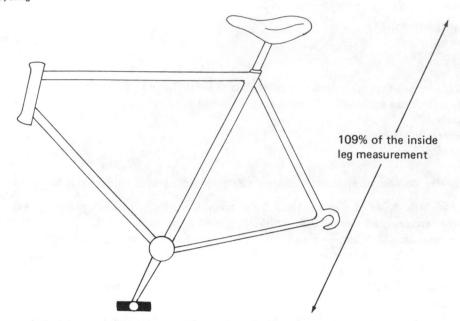

Figure 11-7. Measuring for saddle height

Vaughn and appeared in *American Cycling*.[5] He showed that adjustment of saddle height by 4 percent of the inside leg measurement affects power output by approximately 5 percent. Vaughn's final recommendation was that saddle height should be 109 percent of the inside leg measurement. This adjustment can be made as follows:

1. Measure the length of your leg on the inside, from the floor to the crotch.
2. Multiply this length by 1.09.
3. Turn the crank until it is parallel to the seat tube (see Figure 11-7).
4. Measure the distance from the pedal to the top of the saddle and adjust it to the calculated height.

Although this adjustment might not feel comfortable at first, saddle height is something one can become accustomed to in time. If you follow the saddle adjustment formula, you will be a more efficient cyclist.

The saddle nose should be adjusted so that it is between one and one-half and two and one-half inches behind the crank hanger. The tilt of the saddle is important only for your comfort. Many bicyclists feel that the saddle should have its nose slightly higher than its rear for best distribution of weight.

Another adjustment that should be made on your bicycle is the position of the brake levers. Position the levers where they are easiest for you to reach. We also recommend that you use a clip-on rearview mirror for cycling in city traffic. The mirror should be adjusted so that you can see behind you without moving your head.

Adjusting toe clips is rather easy. Just remember to keep them loose if you use them in traffic. It is important to get the correct size—small, medium, or large. If your shoes are (men's) size 8 or smaller, get a small toe clip; if your shoes are between size 8½ and size 10, use a medium clip; if your shoes are bigger than size 10, use a large toe clip.

[5] Thomas Vaughn, "Scientific Setting of Saddle Positions," *American Cycling*, June 1967, p. 12.

The details of upkeep and maintenance are beyond the scope of this book. We suggest that you refer to *The Complete Book of Bicycling,* by Eugene Sloane. For basic maintenance, however, we recommend the following lubrication schedule:

Chain. Use LPS #3 or Drislide every 30 days. If you ride on a dusty road, lubricate more often. Remove the chain, clean it, oil it, and remove the excess oil.

Front wheel hub. Every six months. Remove and regrease the bearings.

Fork bearing. Every six months. Remove and regrease.

Bottom bracket. Once a year. Remove crank and grease bearings.

Pedal. If you have the type that cannot be dismantled, place several drops of LPS #1 at both ends of the pedal every 30 days. If you have the type that can be dismantled, remove and regrease every 30 days.

Cables. Once a month. Spray with a silicon lubricant or use light oil.

Caliper brake. Every 30 days. Spray silicon lubricant on pivot.

Derailleur. Every 30 days. Apply light oil or silicon spray on moving parts. (Every six months, remove and regrease idler wheel.)

Freewheel. Every 30 days. Lube with light oil. (Remove every six months, clean and oil.)

We suggest that you buy the following tools to work on your bicycle:

1. Chain rivet remover (about $2).
2. Mafac ultralight tool kit (about $4).
3. Freewheel remover (about $4). Make sure that you purchase the proper freewheel type.

Clothing is a matter of personal taste in cycling. However, there are several rules that you should consider with respect to the type of cycling in which you will be involved. The weather is always going to be a factor, especially if you will be traveling any distance. Cycling will always create a wind-chill factor; you must consider the temperature along with the windchill factor in order to determine the type and amount of clothes to be worn. Most cyclists use some type of windbreaker, cycling jersey, poncho, or rain slicker to protect them from the elements. It is also important to remember that loose-fitting, baggy pants can get caught in the chain and cause an unforseen fall.

In addition to the warmth and rainproofing of cycler's clothing, their colors should also be considered. Bright, highly visible colors, such as red or orange, should be used. Many stores sell the light-reflective or phosphorescent colors that you see on road workers. Clothing that is highly visible is essential, especially in poor weather conditions.

Gloves, special shoes, and helmets should also be considered depending upon your tastes and the type of cycling in which you are involved. Summer and winter gloves are available and can be useful to brush debris from your tires and also as protection during a fall. Special cycling shoes with a steel shank for even foot pressure increase your efficiency for racing and long-distance touring. Special shoe cleats can also be used to pull pedals up and push them down without letting your feet slip off the pedals. These cleats should not be used if you have to do a lot of starting and stopping. Helmets are another important piece of clothing that should be considered, especially in heavy city traffic or in racing. Features of helmets to be considered are color, ventilation, durability, strength, and comfort. Many shapes and models are available for different weather conditions. It is important to remember that most of your body, except the head, can repair itself. Common sense is the rule to follow in the selection of clothing for your type of cycling.

SAFETY

The most important aspect of cycling is safety. One very real fact concerning accidents involving bicycles and cars is that, no matter who is right, the bicycle rider gets the worst of the accident. If you are lucky, an accident will result in just a few broken parts of your bicycle; if not, a few broken parts of you.

The first step is to obtain a quality bike with quality parts in order to ensure proper functioning. In addition, it is important to adjust the bike properly and keep up a regular maintenance schedule. If you are not sure about any cycling aspect, be sure to seek the advice of an expert.

Donald J. Pruden points out that over 1,000 bicycle fatalities occurred in 1973.[6] Of accidents involving children 14 years or younger, virtually all were the fault of the children. He suggests consistency of behavior in order to reduce cycling accidents.

We recommend the following rules to enable you to enjoy cycling and yet maintain safety.

1. Remember, *YOU* are subject to all traffic regulations.
2. Always wear clothing that can be easily seen by cars.
3. Always ride *with* traffic as close to the right side of the highway as possible or on a bike path.
4. Stay off city streets, if possible, where curb parking is allowed.
5. In traffic, always ride with your hands on or next to the brake levers.
6. Use streets that have bicycle paths or that are parallel to the main street.
7. Avoid riding during busy traffic hours.
8. Watch very closely for cars that might turn right at intersections.
9. When in doubt, give anything or anyone the right of way.
10. Watch for people opening car doors, and look through the rear windows of parked cars for people inside.
11. Do not weave from side to side.
12. Watch for other cyclists. Be ready to take evasive action. Other cyclists can be your worst enemy.
13. Be very careful when you approach driveways.
14. Be very careful when you change road surfaces, especially from paved to dirt.
15. When mornings are cold, watch carefully for spots of ice in shaded areas.
16. Watch for grated storm sewers. You can be seriously hurt if your front wheel drops into the grating.
17. Remember when you approach an overpass that on cold days it will have frost on it if it is protected with an overhang.
18. Do not brake with the front brakes first. Start with the back brakes, then apply the front.
19. Do not apply the front brakes hard or you will cartwheel.
20. Always expect drivers *not* to see you: *ride defensively*.
21. Approach intersections with caution.
22. Stay in control and *watch your speed*.
23. Always ride on your provided seat; do not try to be a clown or stunt driver.
24. Do not give passengers a ride on the handlebars, crossbar, seat, or rear fender.
25. Do not pull passengers on skateboards, bicycles, or roller skates, and never hitch a ride on cars.
26. Avoid riding more than two abreast, to prevent the backup of traffic.
27. Avoid carrying packages in your arms; you need both hands for an emergency. If you must carry packages, use a backpack or a proper rack or carrier.
28. Never ride on freeways.
29. You may want to walk your bike across busy streets at an intersection.
30. Get off the road if you must make repairs.

---

[6]Donald J. Pruden, "Collision Probability and Bicycle Safety," *The Science Teacher* 43, no. 1 (January 1976): 40-41.

If you find that you are going to be hit by a car from the side, try to get your legs up to protect them. If you fall from a bicycle, try to absorb as much of the blow with the arm, but don't keep it stiff.

Safety for riding at night is extremely important. A good front light that can be seen 500 feet ahead and a good red light in the back are necessities. Bicycles are very hard to see in the daytime and almost impossible to see at night. A must for safe night riding is a device consisting of a red rear light and a white front light, which can be strapped to the left leg (see Figure 11-8). Such lights can be purchased at almost any store that carries bicycle parts. When one is riding, the light makes a circular motion and can easily be seen by people in passing cars.

A few words should be said about clothing and cycling safety. We have already pointed out that clothes should be highly visible and that pants legs can get caught in the chain. It is easy to clip pants back with a rubber band or a ready-made clip (see Figure 11-9). Such clips can be bought at any bicycle shop. It is very important to keep clothing away from the chain, because a caught pants leg could lead to serious injury.

Reflectors are also advisable. Buy reflector strip tape and put it anywhere it will hold (heels, saddle, helmet, pedals, carriers, and so forth).

When you are cycling in very heavy traffic and wish to make a left turn, it is best to go straight through the intersection on the right-hand side and walk your bicycle across the street. This takes more time, of course, but it will also increase your chances of being around to enjoy future times.

Some cyclists say that it can be fun to ride in the rain; however, it is also very dangerous. Your visibility is cut down, and so is the visibility of the people driving cars. Wet pavement makes it very

White light ————   ———— Red light

Figure 11-8. Bicycle night light

Figure 11-9. Pants clip

tricky to control your bicycle when you are cornering. It should also be noted that caliper brakes are almost useless if the rims get wet.

TIPS ON RIDING A BICYCLE

Proper cycling technique is very important for efficient cycling. A very important aspect of proper riding is that the bicycle should be fitted to the person. However, there are several other important aspects to proper cycling technique.

One such technique is the ankling method. You should never cycle with the arch or heel on the pedal. The ball of the foot should be placed on the pedal. With the foot placed this way, you should push on the pedals so that the foot rotates downward. This technique allows the muscles of the lower leg to be used to aid your cycling. The more muscles you can use, the easier it is to cycle. Toe clips assist the ankling technique. Some people feel that toe clips can double pedaling efficiency because they can be used to pull up on the pedal as well as to push it down. Toe clips also keep the foot in proper pedaling position. Beginning cyclists should not use toe clips in heavy city traffic until they become familiar with how they function. All cyclists should keep the straps fairly loose in city cycling to facilitate emergency stopping.

Proper pedaling cadence is another important technique in cycling. Different people have different natural cadences. For most people, from 60 to 80 strokes per minutes feels natural. To find your natural cadence, ride for a distance in the lower gears and then shift up until you are comfortable. On distance rides, find your natural cadence and shift gears only to maintain the cadence. Of course, wind velocity and hills can cause you to change gears.

Changing gears on a 10-speed bicycle takes very little practice, but a few words of caution are needed:

1. *Never* shift derailleur gears unless you are pedaling.
2. Do not jump through all the gears at one time.

The reason for these simple rules is that they prevent damage to the derailleur. If you park your bicycle in a public place, always check the gears when you come back; someone could have moved the gearshift so that you might damage the gears or derailleur. Therefore, check the gears and start slowly to be sure the derailleur is properly adjusted. Note that there are no slots on the gearshift to tell you what gear you are using. You will have to get used to your particular shift. If a grating or grinding noise is produced when you shift, then the gearshift lever is not in the correct position; readjust it until the noise disappears.

With three-speed bicycles, the gears will not change until you stop pedaling.

If you wish to cycle long distances, you should engage in a physical conditioning program. We suggest the following noncycling exercises:

1. *Jogging.* The final objective is to reach a heart rate of 130 or more beats per minute and to maintain that rate for 20 minutes or longer.
2. *Step running.* The final objective is to run approximately seven stadium flights up and down, depending on the height of the flights.

Remember, start any conditioning program *slowly*. You can also use your bicycle to develop and maintain conditioning. It is a good idea to break in your body and your bicycle slowly. Breaking in the saddle is important to prevent soreness on long trips.

TEACHING CYCLING IN A SCHOOL OR RECREATION PROGRAM

Many possibilities are open to teaching cycling in a school or recreational program:

1. Present instructions on equipment, getting parts, maintenance, and safety.
2. Set up an obstacle course.
3. Organize a weekend trip or overnight trip.
4. Combine cycling with orienteering.
5. Organize a bicycle club.
6. Set up a bicycle co-op for repairs and parts.
7. Offer a safety program for the school and the community.
8. Set up races.
9. Use a marathon race for money-raising activities.

If you plan overnight or orienteering activities with your class or group, refer to the chapters on back-packing and orienteering for suggestions about equipment and ideas.

Bicycle clubs can be a real adventure. Usually members of a club have sufficient knowledge among themselves to make any repairs and to operate a co-op for repairs and parts. Clubs can also hold marathon races to raise money to fund their own activities or to donate to charity. Most marathons are long-distance races with no individual winner; rather, all participants who finish the course are winners. Members can persuade individuals and businesses to donate money for each mile they complete. For example, if Suzy had a pledge of 10 cents a mile from each of four people and the course was 20 miles long, she would earn eight dollars for the club or for charity. The more sponsors a cyclist can get, the more money he or she can raise. Marathon races in support of a common cause are an excellent means to promote bicycle safety and to stimulate community involvement.

Obstacle courses are also fun. They should include sharp turns, stops, low-speed and high-speed cycling, precision cycling, hills, and downgrades (see Figure 11-10). Time trials could be set up so that students can test their skills under pressure. Several schools have used nearby minicar racetracks to run time trials on bikes. The students seem to enjoy it and the business gets a little free publicity. In setting up an obstacle course, you might try using small blocks of wood to outline the course; these provide precise feedback if students stray from the course guidelines. An outline could be painted on the parking lot, and then the blocks of wood could be placed on the painted lines.

Cycling in a school or recreation center is limited only by the ingenuity and creativity of those offering the program. Depending upon their ages, participants are usually able to obtain bicycles for themselves. You may be able to work out an arrangement with a local cycle shop for buying or renting secondhand bicycles. It may also be possible to purchase bicycles from a local police auction and repair them with your classes, giving groups of students a specific project to work on for the unit.

Many local police departments and traffic control departments have people in charge of bicycle safety who speak to classes or groups. A variety of movies, films, pamphlets, and literature focus on bicycle safety and maintenance and other relevant topics. In addition, local merchants are usually glad to make presentations on the various bicycles that they sell and may also be willing to discuss topics such as maintenance, repair, accidents, and safety. Literature and materials are also available from several large companies and state departments of education (for example, the Goodyear Tire and Rubber Company and the states of Missouri and Pennsylvania).

It is important to teach safety skills in a controlled environment, preferably on the school grounds or recreational complex, before you organize trips through the city. Lectures and visual instructional devices that involve students in problem-solving situations facilitate this type of learning. Obstacle courses on the school grounds or in nearby areas should provide an opportunity for students to practice these skills. After they have developed a minimal level of competence (ability to control the bike and safety procedures), you may want to organize several short trips through the city, so that students can practice turning, stopping, starting, signaling, and other skills. It is a good idea to contact local police for suggested routes and local rules or regulations. It would be wise to start on isolated or untraveled roads and then slowly progress to busier streets. A large class with a wide range of abilities can create supervision problems for cycling trips because of the distance between those in

Stop line (stopping)

Straight line (precision)

Circle (precision)

Figure 8 (precision)

Varying speeds (control)

Rectangle (cornering)

Intersection (use of signals, stopping and starting)

Figure 11-10. Tracks for an obstacle course

the front and those at the end of the group. The class should proceed in single file to eliminate traffic backup; student leaders could be used at various points in the line; they should be given directions on what to do in specific situations.

If there is a wide range of abilities among students in your class, you may want to group them by ability level so that they can experience some measure of success. The learning environment can be arranged so that these different groups can work on different activities at different times. Instructors may also want to consider individual learning contracts to provide students with a specific incentive.

Bicycle races on a track or through the city can be fun, but they can also be dangerous if proper safety procedures are not followed. If you hold races on a circular track, be aware that accidents usually occur on the first turn. One way to avoid this problem is to use a staggered start with lanes and require contestants to stay in their lanes until they are past the curve. They should not be allowed to cut inside unless they have a lead of one cycle length. Races through the city should receive permission from local authorities and should avoid any dangerous streets or intersections. These races could be run in heats, with times used as the qualifying or ranking factor, so that cyclists are not racing in large groups.

Teachers should be aware of the wide range of cycling abilities among students in their classes. It is important for students to leave the bicycling unit with a positive attitude and a desire to take up more cycling activities. Teachers should arrange environments so that all ability levels can have some type of success and develop this positive attitude.

BICYCLE MOTOCROSS

Bicycle motocross is a form of racing, which is gaining tremendous popularity across the United States, especially in California, Arizona, Colorado, and Florida. A variation of motorcycle motocross or dirt bike racing, this activity involves a great deal of controlled risk, adventure, and competition. The race takes place on obstacle courses that utilize sharp turns, jumps, hills, bumps, and mud. Obstacles vary from course to course, depending upon the terrain available and ingenuity of the developers. Bicycle motocross has become quite popular with students, primarily in the age range from 8 to 16 years. Many parents have become actively involved in supporting this activity for their

Figure 11-11. Motocross racing (Photo courtesy of
B.M.X. Products, Inc., Chatsworth, California)

MAG® SCRAMBLER®

Figure 11-12. Motocross bicycle (Photo courtesy of
Schwinn Bicycle Company, Chicago)

children because of various reasons, for example, physical fitness, safety concerns, and competition. It is likely that many children and parents will be seeking proper instruction for bicycle motocross activities.

Motocross bicycles are quite different from traditional bicycles (see Figure 11-12). They come equipped with a variety of special parts and accessories:

1. Special diamond-shaped, heavy-duty frame with a raised crank hangar for extra ground clearance and suitable for the use of an extra long crank.
2. Heavy-duty rims, hubs, spokes, and fork.
3. 20-inch tires with knobby grip tread.
4. Single speed with a coaster brake.
5. Padding on the frame and crossbar to protect the rider.

Motocross bicycles also can be equipped with fenders, imitation gas tanks, banana style saddles, dual or mono shock absorbers, numerous styles of frames, and other accessories. Most of these parts are not necessary for successful motocross racing. They are a matter of personal preference and provide you with a chance to "do your own thing." The price of these bicycles ranges from $90 to $200.

Motocross racers also have their own special dress code, which includes helmet, goggles, face mask, gloves, jackets, and pads for the knees and elbows. It appears that this cycling activity will continue to grow rapidly and could become an exciting addition to school and recreation programs.

CYCLING ORGANIZATIONS

Amateur Bicycle League of America
4233 205th Street
Bayside, Long Island, New York

American Youth Hostels, Inc.
20 West 17th Street
New York, New York 10011

Bicycle Institute of America
122 East 42nd Street
New York, New York 10017

British Cycling Federation
26 Park Crescent
London W1, England

Canadian Youth Hostels Association
268 First Avenue
Ottawa, Ontario, Canada

Cyclists' Touring Club
Cotterell House
69 Meadrow
Godalming, Surrey, England

League of American Wheelmen, Inc.
5118 Foster Avenue
Chicago, Illinois 60630

International Bicycle Touring Society
846 Prospect Street
La Jolla, California 92037

National Bicycle Dealers Association
29025 Euclid Avenue
Wickliffe, Ohio 44092

Scottish Youth Hostels Association
7 Bruntsfield Crescent
Edinburgh 10, Scotland

QUESTIONS FOR REVIEW AND DISCUSSION

1. List four reasons for the increasing popularity of cycling.
2. What physiological benefits occur from a controlled cycling program?
3. What does it mean to say that a bicycle has 10 speeds?
4. What are the most important parts of a quality 10-speed bicycle?
5. What is the difference between a lugged joint and a welded joint?
6. What are the two types of caliper brakes?
7. What are the advantages and disadvantages of tubular tires and clincher tires?
8. What parts of a bicycle require proper fitting?
9. What maintenance and upkeep is necessary on a 10-speed bike?
10. What guidelines should a person follow for proper cycling clothes?
11. What are some specific safety rules that a cyclist should follow?
12. What are ankling and pedaling cadence?
13. What types of conditioning activities could be used for cycling?
14. How would you set up a bicycle obstacle course?
15. What is bicycle motocross and what are the characteristics of a motocross bicycle?

REFERENCES

Book

Cooper, Ken. *Aerobics*. New York: Bantam Books, 1968.

Articles

Cantwell, Robert. "Where All Roads Lead to Roam." *Sports Illustrated* 42, no. 21 (26 May 1975): 37-44.
Davenport, Irwin W. "Missouri Bicycle Safety Program." *School and Community* 62, no. 8 (April 1976):36-37.
"Fresh Ideas for College Physical Education—Interdisciplinary Bike Tour." *JOPER* 46 (February 1975):40-41.
Pruden, Donald J. "Collision Probability and Bicycle Safety." *The Science Teacher* 43, no. 1 (January 1976):40-41.
Vaughn, Thomas. "Scientific Setting of Saddle Positions." *American Cycling*, June 1967, p. 12.

SUGGESTED READINGS

Ballantine, Richard. *Richard's Bicycle Book*. New York: Ballantine Books, 1974.

Baranet, Nancy Neiman. *The Turned Down Bar*. Philadelphia: Dorrance and Company, 1964.

Bowden, Den, and John Matthews. *Cycle Racing*. London: Temple Press Books, 1965.

Cuthbertson, Tom. *Bike Tripping*. Berkeley, Calif.: Ten Speed Press, 1972.

English, Ronald. *Cycling for You*. London: Clutterworth Press, 1964.

Green, George. *Story of the Cyclists' Touring Club*. London: Cyclists' Touring Club, 1953.

Kraynick, Steve. *Bicycle Owner's Complete Handbook*. Los Angeles: Floyd Clymer Publications, 1960.

Moore, Harold. *The Complete Cyclist*. London: Isaac Pitman and Sons, 1960.

Murphy, Dervia. *Full Tilt: Ireland to India on a Bicycle*. New York: E. P. Dutton and Company, 1965.

Pullen, A. L. *Cycling Handbook*. London: Isaac Pitman and Sons, 1960.

Sloane, Eugene. *The Complete Book of Bicycling*. New York: Trident Press, 1970.

twelve

skin diving, tubing, and rafting

The great variety of water environments, including streams, rivers, ponds, lakes, and oceans, have attracted millions of people for many years. Trends indicate that more people than ever are making use of our earth's waterways for fun and recreation. These environments provide an opportunity to explore an unknown and uncrowded natural setting that is free from roads, buildings, cars and planes. People have experimented with a wide range of methods and devices for traveling on top of bodies of water and for exploring beneath the surface.

Bodies of water can provide much fun and adventure if people adhere to the proper safety techniques and procedures. Water safety varies according to the specific activity that is involved; however, it is important for every person who engages in any type of water activity to be able to swim adequately. It is a sad fact that drowning statistics indicate that many people have overestimated their swimming ability, have not been able to recognize hazardous conditions, or have not followed proper safety procedures. People must become skilled in all aspects of water safety before they take part in outdoor water activities that have inherent dangers or risks.

This chapter focuses on six topics related to outdoor water activities. As an introduction, the first three sections deal with drownproofing and survival floating; currents, undertows, and weeds; and elementary forms of rescue. This general introduction leads into discussions of three outdoor water activities in particular: skin diving, tubing, and rafting. Anyone who attempts to participate in these activities should already have mastered basic swimming techniques.

Skin diving, tubing, and rafting are very popular today. Scuba diving, which is closely related to skin diving, has also enjoyed much popularity recently, but it is not discussed here because of the intensive training and program required. We feel that it is too dangerous to attempt to condense all the necessary information on scuba diving into one chapter. Therefore, we suggest that people who are interested in scuba diving should sign up for a course with a local YMCA or some other reputable instruction program, such as the Professional Association of Diving Instructors (PADI) or the National Association of Underwater Instructors (NAUI). Also, many college programs offer an instructional course for both skin diving and scuba diving. These programs can provide the proper equipment and instruction for these activities.

DROWNPROOFING AND SURVIVAL FLOATING

Drownproofing, or survival floating, as defined by the American Red Cross, is a method of remaining afloat in water for long periods of time with minimal expenditures of energy.[1] It was

---

[1] American National Red Cross, *Lifesaving—Rescue and Water Safety* (Garden City, N.J.: Doubleday and Company, 1974), pp. 165-166.

developed by the late Fred R. Lanoue, former professor of physical education and head swimming coach at the Georgia Institute of Technology. This technique takes advantage of the fact that nearly everyone can be taught to float. From a face-down position in the water, the body usually assumes a semivertical position. If one holds one's breath and relaxes, the face and head will rest just below the surface, and the upper portion of the back will rise above the surface of the water. Thus, little movement, and therefore little energy, is required to bring the face and head to the surface of the water so that one can breathe. The important point to remember is relaxation: it assures an advantageous position in the water and affords better breath control.

Survival floating includes five phases.

1. *Resting position.* Take a breath and hold it. Relax the arms and legs, and allow the face to rest in the water. The body will naturally assume a relaxed floating position. The authors have found through teaching experience that, due to differences in body builds, the body will not always assume a semi-vertical floating position. Remember that relaxation is the most important principle behind drownproofing; don't fight your body's natural floating position.
2. *Preparation to exhale.* Slowly lift the arms to shoulder height and separate the legs into a modified scissors kick.
3. *Exhalation.* Gently pull the arms down toward the hips and push the legs together. At the beginning of this movement, gradually exhale through the nose or the mouth (or through both). The eyes should be open to help judge the position of the mouth and nose in the water.
4. *Inhalation.* As the mouth clears the surface, take a breath.

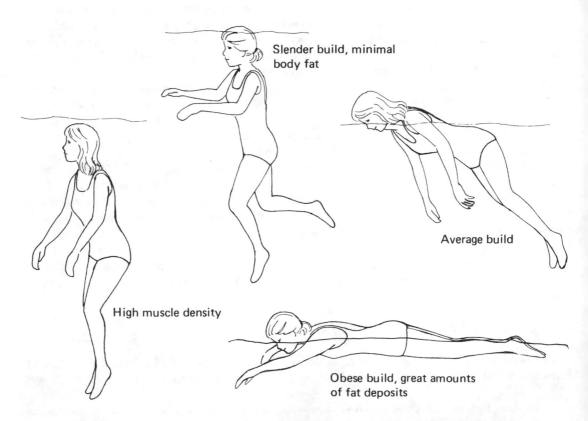

Slender build, minimal body fat

Average build

High muscle density

Obese build, great amounts of fat deposits

Figure 12-1. Drownproofing resting positions in relation to body build

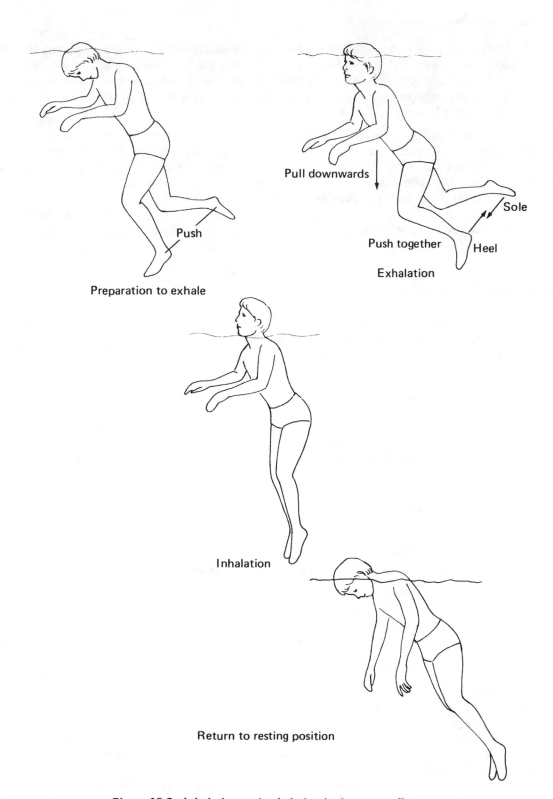

Figure 12-2. Inhalation and exhalation in drownproofing

5. *Return to resting position.* Allow the body to assume its natural floating position, with the face resting just under the surface. At this point, the body will sink below the surface, but due to the air in the lungs the upper back will float back up. Remain submerged only until you desire a breath, *not* until you need one. After this exercise has been performed for an hour, the average rest is about 10 seconds.

The basic technique of survival floating can easily be modified into a travel stroke or to help a poor floater remain afloat. To achieve a forward traveling movement, increase the width and vigor of the scissors kick and, with the raising of the back leg, follow the kick with a straight-arm pull down towards the thigh. After inhalation, the body should assume a more vertical position so as to be able to glide toward the surface at an angle and thereby achieve forward movement.

A person with a lot of muscle mass often has difficulty remaining afloat near the surface. To correct this problem, a wider scissors kick and a more powerful arm movement are needed. All these movements must be performed slowly and in a relaxed manner to prevent pushing the body further downward.

PERSONAL FLOTATION DEVICES

The American Red Cross provides instruction at the swimmer's and advanced swimmer's levels of ability in the use of clothing for flotation devices. Such devices work on the principle that trapped air bubbles can aid the swimmer in staying afloat. Shirt flotation is used with survival floating, and pants flotation is used with a back float.

Shirt Flotation

If the shirt has buttons, they must first be buttoned. A shirt with tails should be secured with the two tails tied together. A pullover shirt must also be tied so that the trapped air cannot escape. Make sure that the shirt is made tight at the neck. The swimmer might find it necessary to grasp the neck of the shirt firmly to help trap the air.

The swimmer now takes a deep breath, assumes a survival floating position, and with the head submerged exhales between the second and third buttons of the shirt. An air bubble should form at the upper back portion of the shirt. A pullover shirt is exhaled into at the neck and then held secure to hold the trapped air.

The swimmer continues the cycle of survival floating until the air bubble begins to diminish. The procedure is repeated to form a new air bubble as often as necessary.

Slacks Flotation

Slacks flotation differs from shirt flotation in that the slacks must first be removed. The swimmer assumes a jellyfish float, takes a deep breath, unsnaps the pants and unzips the zipper, and begins lowering the pants. One leg should be removed at a time, and a breath should be taken as often as necessary. It is especially important to remember that there is no need to hurry. Attempting to hurry only exhausts the swimmer and creates a panic situation.

Once the pants are removed, the swimmer begins treading water and inflates the pants. They must be zipped up and snapped at the waist. A knot must then be tied at the end of each leg, or both legs can be tied together. If the legs are tied separately, the resulting flotation device resembles water wings. If both legs are tied together, the swimmer slips the head into the opening between the legs and uses it like a Mae West (inflatable life jacket).

After the knots are tied and the zipper is closed, the swimmer can follow one of two procedures. Gather the waistband together as if in preparation to blow up a paper sack. Assume a jellyfish float, take a good breath, submerge the head, and exhale into the pants. After each breath, be sure to grasp the opening tightly, so that the air does not escape. The pants should begin to fill with air and float towards the surface. Once this occurs, the swimmer is ready to assume a back-floating position. While floating, the swimmer must hold the waistband closed, so that the air bubble does not escape.

The second procedure for inflating the pants calls for the swimmer to grasp the back of the waistband and hold the pants with one hand at the surface of the water. The free hand then splashes the air into the open waist by striking downwards toward the waist. As the pants fill with air, they rise to the surface.

CURRENTS, UNDERTOWS, AND WEEDS

Since many of the water activities discussed in this chapter take place in moving water, such as rivers, streams, or oceans, it is important to discuss several hazards that participants might encounter.

Currents are horizontal movements of water, which can carry objects or swimmers from one place to another. They can be a nuisance or a great help, depending upon how a person makes use of them. Currents have a tendency to carry swimmers away from shore, and this can occur even before the swimmer is aware of what is happening. According to the American Red Cross, the rule of thumb is: *If you are caught in a current, never fight it.* The swimmer should move diagonally across the current and with the flow and, once freed from the current, can then turn and head for shore. Keep in mind that a long walk is much safer than trying to fight a current and exhausting yourself in the water.

Since currents vary significantly from place to place, divers and river runners should make the water's flow an important part of their knowledge. Surface currents can be studied by observation of floating objects. Subsurface movement is hard to determine, due to the contours of the bottom surface of the body of water. Information on subsurface movement should be obtained from people who are familiar with the area.

A current that is commonly found along ocean beaches is called an undertow, backflow, or backwash. It is caused by the fast return of water along the bottom of a shore after the waves have brought it into the shore. (See Figure 12-3.) The backflow lasts only a short time and then usually dissipates at the line of breaking waves. The water is usually only about waist deep where the undertow ends. These currents are most dangerous to young children, who are not adequate swimmers and are surprised by the strength of the undertow. Divers and swimmers can take advantage of these currents for an easy beach entry or a fun ride.

Another current that causes more trouble and accidents for swimmers is called a rip current. It is caused by water moving fast through a gap or opening in a bar or a reef due to a buildup of water

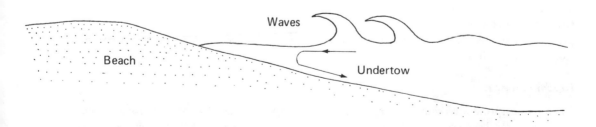

Figure 12-3. Undertow current

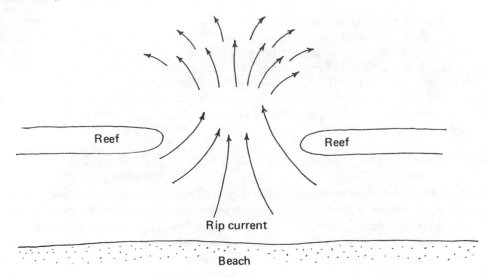

Figure 12-4. Rip current

caused by wave action. (See Figure 12-4.) These currents are usually much stronger and faster than an undertow and can quickly carry an unsuspecting person out to sea. If you get caught in a rip current, simply ride out with the current and then swim off to the left or right as the current begins to dissipate.

Water weeds are another hazard for an unexperienced swimmer. If caught in weeds, do not panic, because hurried, thrashing movements only tend to wrap the weeds more securely around the limbs. Gentle, slow, shaking movements and moving with the current will release the weeds. When surfacing where weeds on the surface of the water may be present, surface with the hands over the head so that they can help to part the weeds. It may be necessary to surface for a breath, and then submerge again and swim underneath the weeds to clear yourself from this hazard.

ELEMENTARY FORMS OF RESCUE

The safety procedures previously described are intended for self-survival. However, water safety rules stress that no water activities should ever be undertaken alone. When participating in water activities, you should always have a partner, or buddy. The rescues discussed here are methods by which you can help your buddy if he or she is in distress. It is best to remember to reach, throw, row, then go. Even a certified lifeguard would go into the water and make contact with a distressed swimmer only if all other forms of rescue were not effective. A person who is in a potential drowning situation is panicky, and his or her main concern is to stay above the water to breathe. An untrained person can get too close to the victim and find himself or herself being used as a stepladder, a situation in which a double drowning becomes a very real possibility.

Reaching Rescue

In attempting a reaching rescue, the rescuer must make sure that he or she has a secure base of support. A reaching rescue can consist of an arm reach or extending the body towards the victim. The rescuer should have a firm hold on a canoe, branch, or some other solid object. Be sure to keep your eyes on the victim at all times and provide constant reassurance and encouragement to remain calm.

Extension Rescue

An extension rescue consists merely of extending your reach. The principles of the reaching rescue apply here. Objects that can be used to extend a reach include an oar, a paddle, a towel, articles of clothing, a pole, a tree branch, and even a snorkel. Keep in mind that the purpose of the rescue is to avoid contact with the victim. Once the victim has a secure hold on the extension, he or she can then slowly be pulled to safety.

Free-Floating Support

If the victim is too far away to be saved by a reaching or extension rescue, the rescuer might find it necessary to wade or swim with a floating object to the victim. Objects such as a floating cushion, a life jacket, an oar, a styrofoam cooler, or a branch can be used. If the rescuer is a strong swimmer, the victim can be towed to shore. Keep the towing arm extended, and keep your eyes on the victim at all times. A panicking victim might attempt to climb on the object and grasp your arm. If the rescuer is not a strong swimmer, direct the victim to hold on to the object and begin to kick towards shore.

It is strongly recommended that methods of self-survival and elementary rescues be practiced in a pool and mastered before participation in any activities on open water. If you have doubts about your swimming capabilities, a life jacket carrying the United States Coast Guard seal of approval should be worn at all times.

All participants in water activities should be skilled in performing mouth-to-mouth resuscitation. It is highly recommended that a course be taken in cardio-pulmonary resuscitation (CPR). Check with your local heart association to find out about course offerings.

SKIN DIVING

Three-quarters of the surface of the earth is covered with water. It is only natural that since the beginning of human existence there has been an insatiable interest in the seas, lakes, rivers, and streams for both commercial and recreational use.

Skin diving, also known as breath-hold diving, is an ancient skill, carried on today much as it has been for centuries. For generation after generation the commercial ama divers of Japan have harvested abalone and pearl oysters on a lungful of air, and food-seeking Polynesians have made long, breath-holding dives to spear fish for food. As a sport, however, skin diving is only about twenty years old, having started—as have so many underwater developments—on the French Riviera, as a competitive spear fishing game.[2]

The sport of skin diving is for the purist—it requires very little equipment—a mask, a snorkel, and fins. Skin diving has no effect on the environment if divers restrict themselves to observation of nature. It is a sport of total freedom, and the only limit is the length of time that divers can hold their breath.

A diver should be physically fit and have good swimming ability. When a person enters a water environment, there is always some degree of danger. Pre-training is essential to overcome the physical and psychological difficulties of swimming above and below the surface. The Council for National Cooperation in Aquatics recommended the following requirements in swimming ability before a person starts a training program in underwater activities:

[2] Henry Ketels and Jack McDowell, *Safe Skin and Scuba Diving* (Boston: Education Associates—Little, Brown and Company, 1975), p. 91.

1. Tread water, feet only, 3 minutes.
2. Swim 300 yards without fins.
3. Tow an inert swimmer 40 yards without fins.
4. Stay afloat 15 minutes without accessories.
5. Swim under water 15 yards without fins—without a pushoff.[3]

A diver should also be able to demonstrate the proper technique of survival swimming and drownproofing. Jogging and swimming laps in a pool are good exercises for developing good overall physical fitness for skin diving. Jogging is an excellent activity for the development of cardiovascular fitness, and swimming is good for the development of body strength, because of the resistance of water against the body. A diver should practice all diving techniques in a pool or in shallow water before venturing out into the open water. Practice in a controlled area enables the diver to become accustomed to the underwater environment, and thus helps him or her circumvent many of the physical and psychological risks that are encountered in the sport.

Equipment

Because it does not require a large capital outlay, skin diving is a sport that can be enjoyed by people of all different economic levels. The essential equipment for skin diving includes mask, fins, snorkel, and knife.

Mask

The mask is the most important piece of equipment in skin diving. It creates a pocket of air between the eyes and the water; without this air space, vision underwater is distorted and foggy. The mask is worn over the eyes and nose. Masks come in a wide variety of shapes and sizes, consisting of circular, rectangular, and oval designs. The choice of design is a personal preference. A good diving mask should be constructed of a pliable rubber skirt with a shatterproof clear glass (not plastic). The glass face plate should be held in place with a noncorrosive frame. Some masks also feature exhaust valves for purging water and nose-pinching devices for equalizing air pressure.

Proper fit can be determined by holding the mask to the face; the diver should breathe in through the nose to cause suction and the mask should remain in place without the diver handling it. If suction cannot be created, then the mask fits improperly, and a different shape should be tried.

Swimming goggles should never be worn in place of a mask in skin diving. Since the pressure of goggles cannot be equalized, a diver can easily rupture the blood vessels in the eye.

Fins

Swim fins are used by the diver to swim more efficiently. They have either open or closed heels. Closed-heeled fins provide greater protection to the soles of a diver's feet; however, they have a tendency to come off in the open surf. Closed-heeled fins come in shoe sizes; open-heeled fins come in small, medium, large, and extra-large sizes. The selection of open- or closed-heeled fins is a matter of personal preference.

The muscle tone of the diver's legs and overall leg strength are important considerations in the selection of fins. Stiff fin blades provide greater power but also fatigue the legs much faster, whereas more flexible blades provide less power but do not require as great an energy expenditure.

---

[3]Council for National Cooperation in Aquatics, *The New Science of Skin and Scuba Diving* (New York: Association Press, 1970), p. 19.

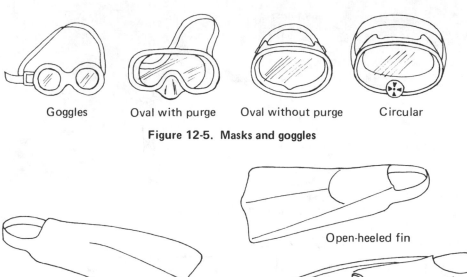

Goggles   Oval with purge   Oval without purge   Circular

Figure 12-5. Masks and goggles

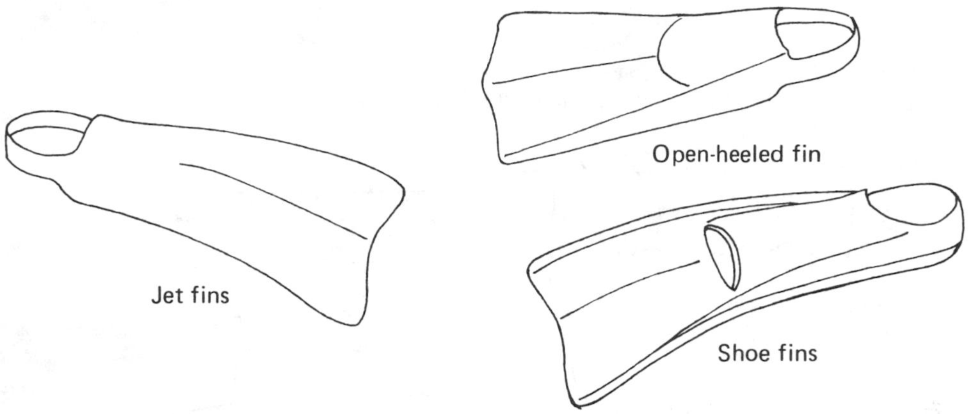

Open-heeled fin

Jet fins

Shoe fins

Figure 12-6. Fins

Since fins are made for swimming and not for walking, a diver should not walk with fins on the feet. If certain circumstances require walking with fins on, the diver should walk backwards. If fins are fitted too tight, they can cause cramps in the foot, and if they are too stiff for the diver, they can cause cramps in the lower leg muscles.

Snorkel

A snorkel is a *J*-shaped tube constructed of plastic or rubber, which enables the diver to breathe while swimming face down in the water. A snorkel should have a flexible mouthpiece and should be from 12 inches to 14 inches long, with a large enough barrel to minimize inhalation resistance. Any attachments for keeping water out of the barrel should be avoided. Such attachments tend to restrict inhalation and can be dangerous if they become stuck.

Knife

A diver's knife is not intended to be a weapon for warding off demons of the deep; rather, it is an all-purpose tool. It is used for freeing the diver from entanglements underwater (marine life, monofilament fishing line) and for digging, prying, and chipping. A diver's knife should be made of stainless steel.

Physiology of Skin Diving

Atmospheric pressure at sea level is 14.7 pounds per square inch (psi); for every foot below the surface, the pressure increases 0.445 psi. If a diver was to dive to a depth of 10 feet, the surrounding pressure would be 20.15 psi. This increase in surrounding pressure—ambient pressure (the pressure of the water together with the pressure of the air above it)—causes various physiological effects to occur.

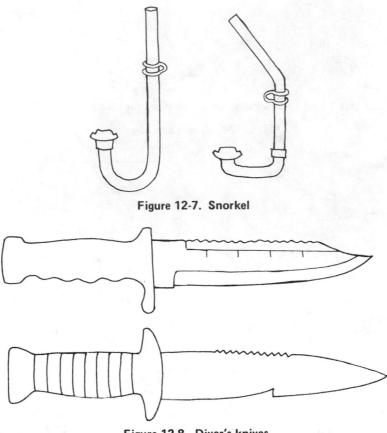

Figure 12-7. Snorkel

Figure 12-8. Diver's knives

The effect of a pressure differential between two structures is called *squeeze*. In skin diving, the diver is faced with the problems of middle ear squeeze, sinus squeeze, thoracic lung squeeze, and mask squeeze. All these are first recognized by pain in the area where the ambient pressure is not equalized with the pressure of air trapped in the mask or within the body.

Middle Ear Squeeze

When a diver is at the surface, the air in the middle ear is at surface pressure. As he or she descends, the ambient pressure increases, but the pressure of the air in the middle ear does not and thus a pressure differential is created. This occurs at depths of five feet or more. If the pressures are not equalized, the eardrum eventually ruptures. Symptoms are extreme pain and blood oozing from the outer ear. Dizziness and disorientation occur as cold water enters the middle ear. This condition persists until the water warms up in the middle ear.

Middle ear rupture can be prevented by equalization of the pressure, either by means of swallowing, yawning, or using nose pinchers in the mask. Ear plugs should never be worn by a diver.

Sinus Squeeze

The skull contains five air-filled cavities, known as the sinuses, which are connected by hollow passages to the nasal cavity. If the mucus membrane lining the nasal cavity becomes swollen due to a cold or some obstruction, air will not pass freely through the sinus cavities, and squeeze will occur.

Symptoms of sinus squeeze are pain above the eyes or in the cheeks and sometimes a reddish mucus draining from the nose. To prevent sinus squeeze, never dive while you have a bad cold. Nose drops that contain an antihistamine preparation sometimes help, but beware of side effects.

Thoracic Lung Squeeze

The lungs of an average person at the surface hold about 10 pints of air. As the diver descends, the pressure increases and the volume of the lungs decreases according to Boyle's law: *At a constant temperature, the volume of a given quantity of any gas varies inversely as the pressure to which the gas is subjected.* The deeper a diver descends, the smaller the lung and thorax become. Squeeze occurs if the diver goes deep enough to compress the lungs totally into their minimum volume; its results are bleeding in the thoracic cavity and damage to the lungs. This condition rarely occurs if the skin diver avoids trying to set diving records and leaves this activity to trained individuals with unusual lung capacities.

Mask Squeeze

In descent, a pressure differential occurs in the air space between the face and the outer face plate of the mask. Ruptured blood vessels around the eyes and cheekbones can result. Mask squeeze can be prevented by always wearing a mask with a flexible rubber skirt and blowing air from the nose into the mask on descent.

Shallow-Water Blackout

If a diver tries to extend his or her breath-holding capacity, carbon dioxide intoxication can occur; this is also known as shallow-water blackout. This mishap is the second most frequent type of accident in skin diving, with drowning being the first. Shallow-water blackout can also occur if one uses a snorkel that is more than 14 inches long. To prevent shallow-water blackout, always stay within your breath-holding limits.

Hyperventilation

Hyperventilation is taking large deep breaths with concentration on exhaling. Many people think that, if they purge the respiratory system of carbon dioxide, the system can hold more oxygen. Actually, the respiratory system only uses about 25 percent of total oxygen intake; the remaining 75 percent is exhaled. Hyperventilation should not be practiced. Breath-holding powers can be expanded by repeated practice of swimming underwater for increasing lengths over a period of time.

Medical hazards of skin diving are summarized in Table 12-1.

Basic Skills of Skin Diving

Skin diving, as a water activity, requires swimming skill. It requires good kicking strokes, because in skin diving the arms are rarely used. The kick most often used is the face-down flutter with two variations: (1) face-up flutter and (2) on-the-side flutter.

Types of Kicks

Face-Down Flutter. The body should form a normal prone position with the hips below the waterline. The arms should be in front of the body with a slight flexion of the elbow and with the back of the hand breaking the surface. This position will streamline the body causing less resistance in the water creating a greater propulsion from the kick. The leg should be straight with toes pointed back. The kick is an alternating sweeping motion of about 18 to 24 inches. The feet should not be lifted above the surface of the water.

The flutter kick can be easily practiced by holding on to the side of a pool in the correct body position and kicking at various frequencies and lengths of sweeps. Emphasis should be placed on the efficiency of the kick, not on the speed.

Table 12-1. Medical Diving Hazards

HAZARD	SYMPTOMS	PREVENTION	FIRST AID
Middle ear squeeze	Sharp pain, bleeding from ear canal, dizziness	Equalize ear by swallowing or yawning, or use mask nose pinchers	Stop diving, see doctor
Sinus squeeze	Pain above the eyes or at both sides of the nose; blood and mucus come from the nose	Never dive with a head cold	Relieved by ascending; use nose drops (antihistamine)
Thoracic lung squeeze	Pain in chest; difficulty in breathing on surfacing; bloody, frothy sputum comes from mouth	Avoid deep descents while skin diving	Maintain an open airway, treat for shock, see doctor
Shallow-water blackout	Numbness of fingertips; confusion, cyanosis, unconsciousness	Always breathe normally (do not hyperventilate); no deep breath-holding dives	Treat for shock
Mask squeeze	Pain and swelling around face, bruises above eye or on cheekbones	Equalize mask; avoid rapid descents	Cold compact for swollen and bruised areas

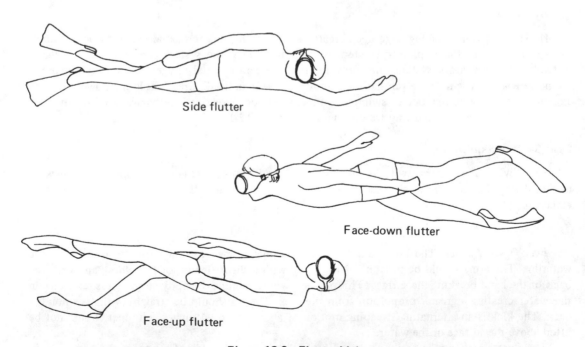

Side flutter

Face-down flutter

Face-up flutter

Figure 12-9. Flutter kick

Face-Up Flutter. The body is positioned on its back, with the palms facing down. The hip should be slightly bent, but not in a sitting position. The kick is the same as the face-down flutter kick. Generally, the error in technique is that the swimmer tends to assume a sitting position, which causes greater resistance in the water and thus a loss of propulsion. The face-up flutter is good for towing something in the water.

Side Flutter. The swimmer is positioned nearly in a straight line on his or her right or left side, with the arms at the sides. The head should be just resting on the surface of the water with the ear in the water. The kicking action is a scissor motion.

Another variation of the flutter kick is used for treading water (holding position). The body is in a vertical position, and the kicking action is the same as that for the face-down flutter. The arms should be slightly out to the side with the hands moving counterclockwise. The kick and hand action should just be fast enough to keep the head above the surface.

Mask Skills

The mask is a window, which provides a clear field of vision while a diver is under the water's surface. This window requires some care and practice in its use, as it can sometimes become fogged or flooded.

The face plate on a mask initially fogs upon being placed in water because of the difference between air temperature and water temperature. To prevent the fogging, an antifogging preparation can be purchased at most diving stores. Saliva, which is cheaper and at times much more effective, can also be used. Both antifogging preparation and saliva are used before the diver enters the water. If the mask becomes fogged under the surface, the diver can vent it with a small amount of water. Venting is accomplished by pulling the mask away from the nose slightly and then holding the face down and moving it both clockwise and counterclockwise.

Another problem the diver must contend with is clearing a flooded mask under water. This skill should be practiced over and over until one can just react to the situation without thinking. Several methods are used to clear a flooded mask.

1. If the mask has a purge valve, it is easily cleared if a slight pressure is applied on top of the face plate and the diver exhales through the nose. The speed and efficiency of clearing a mask by this method depends on the size and placement of the purge valve.
2. If the mask is not equipped with a purge valve, the diver first places pressure on top of the face plate and then pushes the bottom of the face plate away from the face. Once an opening has been created between the bottom of the face plate and the face, the diver exhales through the nose. The air rushes to the top of the mask, where it pushes the water out the bottom. The important thing to remember is that there must be a tight seal between the top of the face plate and the forehead to clear the water efficiently.
3. The mask can also be cleared from the horizontal body position. The diver turns on his or her side while swimming under water using a side flutter kick. The top arm places pressure on the side of the face plate so that the bottom side is pushed away from the face, and the diver exhales through the nose. This is the best method for clearing a flooded mask while one is swimming horizontally under water.

Snorkel

The snorkel is an extension of the airway from the body to the outside environment. A snorkel enables the diver to swim in a horizontal, face-down position while continuing to breathe. The diver should practice breathing with a snorkel at a normal rate, without a deep rhythm of inhalations and exhalations.

The snorkel is cleared by exhaling deeply into the mouthpiece, to force the water out of the open end of the barrel. An additional aid for clearing the snorkel once the diver has broken the surface is to tilt the head backward slightly and exhale. Upon clearing the snorkel, the diver should

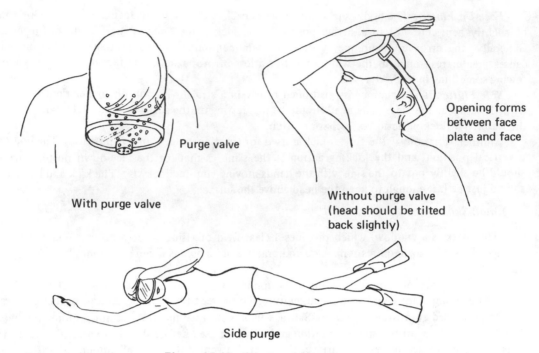

With purge valve

Purge valve

Opening forms
between face
plate and face

Without purge valve
(head should be tilted
back slightly)

Side purge

Figure 12-10. Clearing the mask

not take a deep breath, since a small amount of water can be left in the barrel, and it can cause choking if it is inhaled. It is better to take small breaths right after the snorkel is cleared and then to work slowly into a normal breathing rhythm.

Water Entries

Entries into the water should be made from a maximum height of six feet. Entries from a deck or rock platform more than six feet above the water can be dangerous because of the impact force of hitting the water. If a fixed object (deck or platform) is used, the front jump entry is recommended. The diver should hold the mask tightly to his or her face and jump with the body in a straight verticle plane. The heels of the fins should hit first. A step entry is performed by holding the mask, taking a long step, and pushing off with the back foot. Once the body is completely in the water, bring both feet back together in a scissor motion, which creates an upward propulsion that returns the head and shoulders to the surface.

A forward roll entry can be used from a boat: simply tuck the head and roll into the water, to land on the back of the neck and shoulders. The forward roll entry should be made from a very low height, no higher than the sides of a small boat.

Surface Dives

The surface dive is an effective way to submerge under water with small energy expenditures. There are two basic methods: (1) the head-first pike position and (2) the feet-first position.

Head-first Pike Position. When the diver reaches the point where he or she will make the dive, the legs are pulled up into a tuck position; the upper torso dips below the surface while the legs are straightened out in a pike position. Upon completing the pike, the diver tucks the legs at the knees

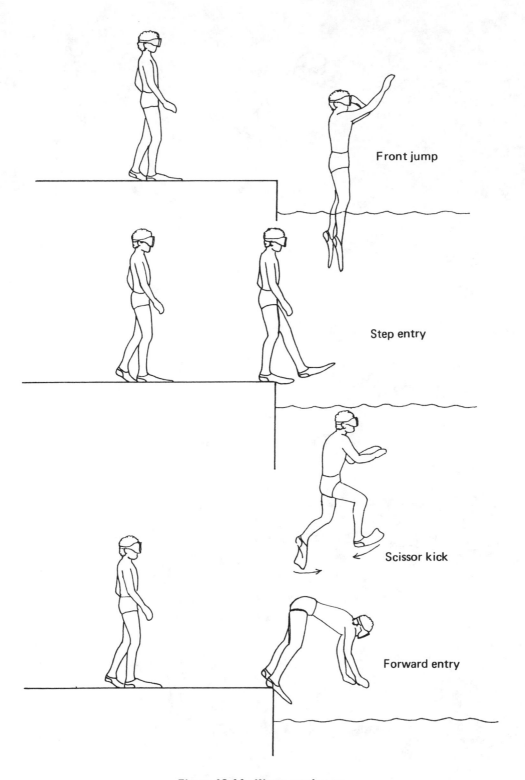

Figure 12-11. Water entries

Figure 12-12. Head-first surface dive

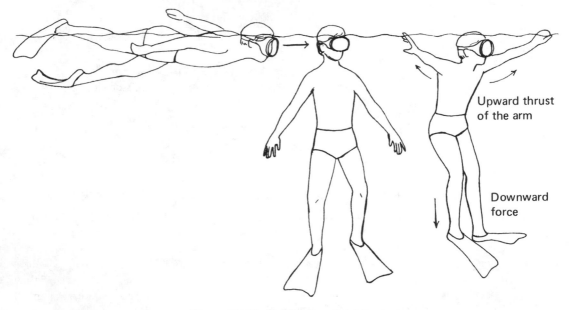

Figure 12-13. Feet-first surface dive

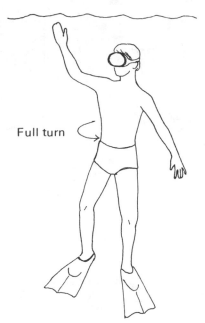

Full turn

Figure 12-14. Surfacing

and kicks up. If the dive is performed correctly, the body will assume a straight, vertical plane position. This position should be held until the diver loses momentum; then the diver starts to flutter kick and continues to go deeper or levels off.

Feet-first Position. At the point of the dive, the diver changes from a horizontal to a vertical body position. Once in the vertical position, the arms are thrust away from the side of the body to an overhead position. This action creates an opposite reaction, which pushes the body downward. Once momentum slows, the diver levels off to a horizontal position.

Surfacing

Upon returning to the surface, the diver should be looking up with one hand overhead and, just before breaking the surface, should continue to look up and turn a full 360°.

All divers should mark their location with a "diver down" flag (see Figure 12-15). Boat operators should not approach any closer than 100 feet of the flag. It is recommended that the diver surface as close as possible to his or her flag to avoid being hit by an oncoming boat. A diving flag can be easily displayed by attaching it to an inflated inner tube on a shaft that is not less than three feet long.

Water Temperature

Variations in air and water temperature are of great importance to the diver. Water temperature in fresh-water bodies (lakes, rivers, streams, and quarries) varies greatly, depending upon seasonal changes, whereas seawater will only vary 9° on an average from season to season.

Swimming in cold water (below 65°) can cause a rapid reduction in body heat, which results in fatigue and muscle cramps. Heat reduction from the body takes place 240 times faster in water than on land. However, swimming in warm water (73° or warmer) can cause heatstroke. The most comfortable water temperature for an unprotected skin diver ranges between 68° and 71°.

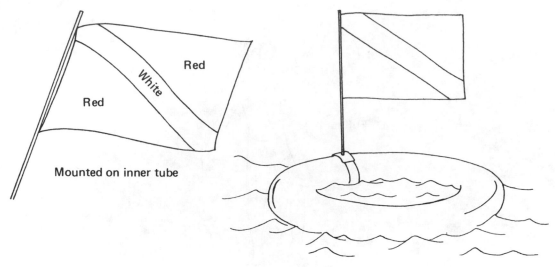

Red

White

Red

Mounted on inner tube

Figure 12-15. Diving flag

Marine Life

A complete discussion of all the various forms of marine life that a diver might encounter is beyond the scope of this chapter. The authors recommend the references listed at the end of this chapter.

The species that seem to cause the greatest concern among divers are sharks. Perry W. Gilbert makes the following points:

> Probably only a few species have made unprovoked attacks on humans in clear water that does not contain blood or refuse. But in turbulent or murky water, or under conditions in which a man is bleeding or is transporting a wounded fish or is attempting to net, spear, or otherwise capture a shark while in the water, many species are capable of inflicting injury to humans. Even the common nurse shark (*Ginglymostoma cirratum*), which many consider completely harmless, will occasionally bite man.[4]

To avoid any injuries or run-ins with sharks, remember these few simple rules:

1. Never transport a wounded or bleeding fish.
2. Avoid any undue thrashing or jerky movements in the water.
3. Avoid wearing or towing any bright, shiny object in the water.
4. Never dive where sharks have been recently sighted.

A diver should always keep in mind that observing marine life is much safer than disturbing or tampering with it. If a diver follows these simple rules, he or she can enjoy many long hours of spellbinding beauty with no fear of harm from marine animals.

Teaching Activities

Kick Relays. Divide the class into an equal number of teams. Each team divides equally, with half at one end of the pool and half at the other end. With fins only, each member must flutter kick to the opposite end. Start with the face-up kick, then switch to the face-down and side kicks.

---

[4]Perry W. Gilbert, ed., *Shark and Survival* (Lexington, Mass.: D. C. Heath Company, 1963).

Table 12-2. Marine Life Hazards

HAZARD	SYMPTOMS	PREVENTION	FIRST AID
Sharks Barracuda Moray eel	Torn flesh, bleeding, pain	Avoid transporting wounded or bleeding fish Keep hands out of holes No shiny objects Don't swim in area of of sighting	Stop bleeding (compress points) Treat for shock Loss of limbs Tourniquet
Portuguese man-o-war Jellyfish Fire coral Sea wasp Sea anemone Sea worms	Swelling Burning Severe pain Paralysis Respiratory arrest Unconsciousness Shock	Don't swim in area of sighting Observe, don't disturb Don't touch if you do not know the species	Neutralize with ammonia, white vinegar (heat to 105°), baking soda and water, alcohol Antihistamines Mouth-to-mouth resuscitation for respiratory arrest Treat for shock Remove bristles with adhesive tape

Equipment Recovery. The instructor throws mask, snorkel, and fins into the pool. The student surface dives, recovers all equipment, and puts it on before returning to the surface. It is recommended to break this activity into three progressions: (1) recover mask, (2) recover mask and snorkel, and (3) recover mask, snorkel, and fins.

Golf Ball Addition. Use a marker to number two sets of 10 golf balls from 1 to 10. Then, drop the balls into the deep end of the pool. The instructor calls out a number—such as 12 or 17—and a diver wearing mask, snorkel, and fins descends to recover, in one dive, balls adding up to the total number given.[5]

Follow the Leader. Anchor 8 or 10 three-foot plastic rings on the bottom of the pool in any arrangement (hula-hoops work well). One student is appointed leader, and the rest, wearing mask, snorkel, and fins, follow the leader through each ring.

Contracts

Student contracts are an effective method of teaching diving skills. Four skin diving contracts designed for junior high school students are shown in Tables 12-3 through 12-6.

TUBING

Tubing, which has rapidly become popular in the past few years, involves the use of an inner tube from a tire for navigation on a stream or river. Tubes can range in size, shape, and age as long as they hold air and can support the weight of the navigator. People have used tubes to cover all sections of various waterways, including rapids, white water, rocky sections, and areas with overhanging brush.

[5] Ketels and McDowell, p. 113.

Table 12-3. Skin Diving Contract: Face Mask

Write the date when each performance objective is met.

_____ 1. Adjust the face mask strap to your head size.

_____ 2. *Fog preventative.* Apply saliva to the face mask—rub all around the face plate, *do not rinse.*

_____ 3. *Vertical tilt.* Fill the mask with water and hold it to the face without the strap. In chest-deep water, go under in a vertical position and, by tilting the head backwards from the chest, push against the upper edge of the mask and exhale gently. Completely clear the mask in three out of five attempts.

_____ 4. *Horizontal Roll.* Fill the mask with water and hold it to the face without the strap. While in a horizontal position, roll on the left shoulder, push gently with the right hand against the side of the mask, and exhale gently. Completely clear the mask in three out of five attempts.

_____ 5. Repeat objective 3 with the strap attached to the back of the head.

_____ 6. Repeat objective 4 with the strap attached to the back of the head.

_____ 7. In six feet of water, submerge to the bottom of the pool; by pinching the nostrils, gently exhale into the mask until you feel the pressure equalize in your ears. Successfully equalize the pressure in four out of five attempts.

_____ 8. Repeat objective 7 in nine feet of water.

_____ 9. Repeat objective 3 in deep water.

_____ 10. Repeat objective 4 in deep water.

_____ 11. Throw the mask into shallow water, submerge, and put the mask on. Complete a vertical tilt and clear the mask in one breath in four out of five attempts.

_____ 12. Throw the mask into shallow water, submerge, and put the mask on. Complete a horizontal roll and clear the mask in one breath in four out of five attempts.

_____ 13. Repeat objective 11 in six feet of water.

_____ 14. Repeat objective 11 in nine feet of water.

_____ 15. Repeat objective 12 in six feet of water.

_____ 16. Repeat objective 12 in nine feet of water.

Table 12-4. Skin Diving Contract: Fins

Write the date when each performance objective is met.

_____ 1. Wet feet and fins. Put on fins by pushing the toes to the front of the fin and then slipping the backs on.

_____ 2. At the shallow end of the pool, hold on to the side with the face down and practice a slow, fairly wide flutter kick.

_____ 3. Swim two lengths of your modified flutter kick without arms (one length with arms at the side, one length with arms extended forward).

_____ 4. Swim two lengths of your modified flutter kick with a wide breast stroke movement of the arms.

_____ 5. Begin as in objective 2, but with a regular scissors kick.

_____ 6. Begin as in objective 2, but with an inverted scissors kick.

_____ 7. Repeat objective 3, but with a regular scissors kick.

_____ 8. Repeat objective 4, but with a regular scissors kick.

_____ 9. Repeat objective 3, but with an inverted scissors kick.

_____ 10. Repeat objective 4, but with an inverted scissors kick.

_____ 11. Throw the fins into shallow water, submerge, and don the fins in one breath in four out of five attempts.

_____ 12. Throw the fins into deep water. Submerge and don the fins in one breath in four out of five attempts.

The activity can provide a great deal of risk, adventure, and challenge, depending on the nature of the river. It can become a dangerous, however, if certain safety precautions are not followed by all participants.

Equipment

Inner tubes can be obtained or purchased from various sources, including gas stations, automotive junkyards, automotive parts stores, tire stores, some recreational departments, and some campgrounds located on a prime tubing source. There are no exact specifications or requirements for a satisfactory inner tube, but it must not have any leaks and it must be able to hold the weight of the user. Tubes are inexpensive, costing from one to five dollars. Older, used tubes can sometimes be obtained for free. A thrifty tuber should look for tubes long before he or she gets within close proximity of a possible tubing site because of the obvious increase in the price range.

Possible tubing sites in your immediate vicinity should be checked out thoroughly prior to a tubing excursion. This information is available from a local parks and recreation department, nearby community members, or people with previous experience on the river. It is important to find out as much as possible about the river before you plan a trip or outing. Knowledge of such factors as the speed of the current, the depth of the river, rocks that might be obstacles, overhanging trees and brush, and sections of white water or rapids is extremely valuable to participants. Special tubing maps are available for a number of rivers across the country (for example, the Salt River and the Verde River in Arizona).

Table 12-5. Skin Diving Contract: Snorkel

Write the date when each performance objective is met.

_____ 1. Insert the mouthpiece by placing the wide flange between the lips and the teeth; hold the smaller flange lightly between the teeth. Breathe through the snorkel above the surface until you are comfortable with mouth breathing.

_____ 2. Squat down until mouth and nose are submerged, and breathe cautiously through the mouth. Repeat five times.

_____ 3. Squat under water until the snorkel floods. Rise until the eyes are above the water, and puff forcefully through the mouth to clear the snorkel in four out of five attempts.

_____ 4. In shallow water, attach the snorkel to a mask and submerge with a clear mask and snorkel. Flood and clear the snorkel in four out of five attempts.

_____ 5. Breathe with the face submerged (snorkel above the surface), flood the mask and snorkel by submerging, and surface with mask and snorkel clear in four out of five attempts.

_____ 6. Repeat objective 4 in six feet of water.

_____ 7. Repeat objective 4 in nine feet of water.

_____ 8. Repeat objective 5 in six feet of water.

_____ 9. Repeat objective 5 in nine feet of water.

Surface Dives

_____ 1. Swim at the surface with the face in the water, pike at the waist, and dive to the bottom. As you surface, clear the snorkel in four out of five attempts.

_____ 2. Start at the shallow end of the pool, begin on the surface of the water, and complete three surface dives before you reach the deep end. The snorkel should be cleared after each dive. Complete three lengths.

Skills

No sophisticated skills are needed to ensure a successful tubing experience. The arms and legs can be used in a variety of ways to guide, steer, and propel your craft. Navigating your tube gives you an opportunity to "do your own thing." Some people prefer to lie on their stomach and use a flutter or dolphin kick with their legs and a modified breast stroke or overhand stroke with their arms. Some prefer to sit in the tube and use these same strokes and kicks, and others enjoy putting themselves in the center of the tube for navigation. People obviously enjoy a variety of methods for steering and propulsion; this is one reason why tubing is so much fun.

Safety Procedures

Tubing can be a very enjoyable experience for all ages if a few safety procedures are followed:

1. Fill your inner tube with air a day or two before your planned excursion begins. Make sure that there are no leaks. If you have a slow leak and are not able to find it, place the inner tube in a bathtub full of water; bubbles will appear at the leakage site. These leaks can be patched quickly with a simple patch kit, which you can purchase for less than a dollar at most hardware stores or tire dealers. It is a good idea to take a patch kit along on a tubing trip in case of an unexpected blowout.

2. Trips should be thoroughly planned ahead of time. Transportation to the beginning site of a trip and from the ending site of a trip should be considered. Always let someone not on the trip know where you are going and how long you will be gone. Food, drinking water, and first aid equipment should be considered according to the length of the trip and the hazards on the river. Do not attempt a river trip unless you have all relevant information about the nature of the river.

3. The sun can provide the unprepared tuber with an extremely painful sunburn. Reflection from the water can intensify the amount of sun received. Be prepared with long-sleeved shirts and pants, sunglasses, and a hat if necessary. Some people like to carry a small nylon day pack for these extra clothes and materials. A sun lotion might also be a good idea.

4. Tennis shoes or some other type of footwear is a must for all tubers. River bottom and banks are always loaded with sharp rocks, branches, and brush that could open up a cut or puncture wound. This is a very quick and effective way to ruin a fun experience.

5. Many tubers enjoy tying a number of tubes together to produce a more stable craft over a rough section of a river. Some people tie themselves to the tube in order to prevent falling into the river. We advise against this practice because of the chance that the tube can be flipped over so that the person would become trapped beneath the tube. If the river is so rough that you cannot

Table 12-6. Skin Diving Contract: Combined Skills

Write the date when each performance objective is met.

_____ 1. In shallow water, don all equipment and come to the surface with mask and snorkel cleared. Complete in four out of five attempts.

_____ 2. Complete objective 1 in deep water.

_____ 3. In deep water, don all equipment, come to the surface, and swim two lengths of the pool. At least three surface dives are to be taken within the two lengths.

_____ 4. From three objects placed on the bottom of the pool in the deep area, pick one indicated by the instructor in two out of three attempts.

5. Do the following work underwater:

_____   a. Transfer different objects to an area indicated by the instructor.

_____   b. With three breaths or fewer, place a nut on a bolt in two out of three attempts.

_____   c. With three breaths or fewer, tie a regular shoe knot in two out of three attempts.

_____ 6. Complete the obstacle course set up by the instructor, and meet the standards set. The instructor will explain all standards before you start the obstacle course.

stay on your tube, then we suggest that you get off the river immediately and walk downstream to a safe section.

6. Many tubers include a variety of alcoholic beverages on the menu of their trips. We urge you to exercise moderation in this area. A number of tubers die every year, and the majority of these deaths are due in part to overindulgence.

7. Finally, and certainly not least important, all tubers must be adequate swimmers. If you have any doubts about your ability as a swimmer in the most dangerous section of the river, use some type of a life jacket or vest. It is not a bad idea for all tubers, regardless of their swimming ability, to use a life jacket. These jackets should carry the United States Coast Guard seal of approval.

Teaching Activities

Schools and recreational programs can provide students with opportunities for tubing outings. These outings can take place on weekends or during vacation periods and in conjunction with backpacking or camping trips. The programs can take the responsibility for all aspects of planning, including tubes, transportation, life jackets, instruction, and safety. The possibilities for tubing trips are only limited by the imagination of the people in charge of the programs.

Some programs hold tubing races and bestow awards for participation. The intramural programs at Appalachian State University and East Carolina University offer annual spring tubing races, which attract considerable attention from the student bodies and the local news media.[6] A Gold Inner Tube award is an example of an external motivator. The Appalachian State University race, which is 1.2 miles long, uses the following rules:

1. All entrants must be able to swim.
2. Only one person is allowed in a tube.
3. Tennis shoes must be worn.
4. No propelling devices—poles, paddles, swim fins, or other objects—are allowed.
5. Interfering with another tube to hinder its progress results in disqualification.
6. Propelling with hands, arms, legs, and feet is allowed.
7. Walking is permitted in areas too shallow for floating.
8. The first man and woman to cross the finish line in their tubes are declared winners of the Gold Inner Tube awards.

These programs stress the participation rather than competition in their annual tubing races.

RAFTING

Many people who have mastered their own special version of the art of tubing have become interested in running rivers that offer a bit more risk and challenge. Rafting is another form of river running that provides an opportunity to experience a wild river. It can be an exciting, breathtaking experience for those who respect the current and power of the river, but it can be a disastrous occasion for the inexperienced novice. Specific rafts enable river runners to cover rivers that a tuber, canoeist, or kayaker would never be able to navigate. However, rafters must learn to respect the strength of river rapids, since they are capable of breaking up even the strongest of rafts.

It seems that the birth of rafting can be traced to John Wesly Powell, who, in 1869, first explored the Green River and the Colorado River. Verne Huser, a professional river guide on several western rivers, points out that

---

[6] Paul Gunsten, "Coeducational Recreational Activities—Tubing Down the River," *JOPER* 47 (May 1976):18.

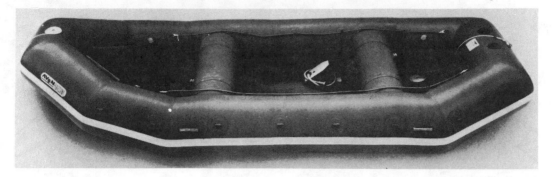

Figure 12-16. Basic river raft (Photo courtesy of Seagull Marine, Irvine, California)

Lewis and Clark and Powell were true pioneers. Their followers—Captain Gulicke on the Salmon; Nathaniel Galloway on the Green and the Yampa; the Kolb brothers and Norman Nevills in the Grand Canyon; Amos Burg, who pioneered inflatable boats on numerous rivers—were less explorers than adventurers. And in the 1930's and 1940's people began guiding trips down wild rivers, and commercial river running was basically born.[7]

Most rafting today is conducted by numerous professional river guides who work for commercial companies or groups. However, the number of private groups and individuals that are now running rivers on inflatable crafts is certainly on the rise. The popularity of running wild rivers has been fostered by popular literature, advertising, and movies such as *Deliverance*. It is extremely important for people to educate themselves on river running and then proceed cautiously into very mild rivers before they attempt to run a wild river.

We recommend that interested people should first experience a river trip with a professional river guide. Professionally guided trips are available on at least 30 rivers, ranging from gentle to raging currents. These river trips can last from 1 to 21 days and include from 3 to 20 people, depending on the type of craft and the company. The cost ranges from $30 to $70 daily, depending upon the type of trip and the services provided. Most trips include all meals and their preparation in addition to all raft equipment and accessories.

Equipment

Professional river outfitters provide most of the equipment necessary for a trip. Usually, they specify any additional equipment that you might need, such as a sleeping bag, blankets, clothing, flashlights, and sunglasses. The nature of your trip dictates the type of clothing and equipment needed.

Rafts

In selecting a river trip, you might have a choice of types of raft. Many types of rafts with many variations are being made; however, there are basically three common types:

1. Usually, the smallest rafts found on river trips are between 13 feet and 20 feet long and hold from four to eight people. They are either rowed or paddled. Numerous models are available on the market, with an extensive price range.

[7] Verne Huser, *River Running* (Chicago: Henry Regnery Company, 1975), pp. 1-2.

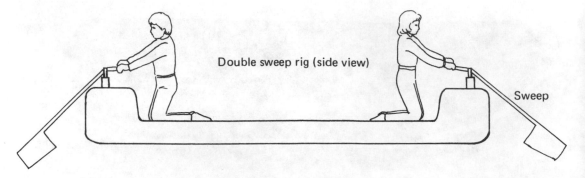

Figure 12-17. Pontoon sweep rig

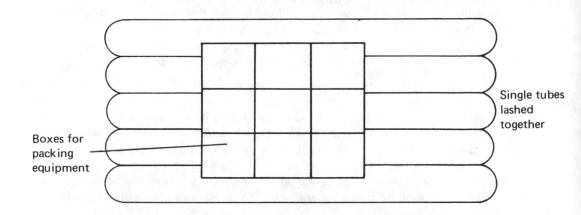

Figure 12-18. J-rig

2. The next size of raft, called a pontoon sweep rig, is between 22 feet and 32 feet long. These sometimes have an outrigging on the side and can be rowed or powered by a motor.
3. The third and largest rafts are J-rigs, which are between 33 feet and 37 feet long. These usually consist of five cylinder pontoons secured with a deck and an outrigging on each side. These crafts are very stable, can carry as many as 20 people, and are usually powered by a motor.

Additional equipment for river running can be quite extensive depending on your personal preferences and the specific type of trip. If you are going to make a private trip of some kind, make sure that you include an experienced person in order to provide you with the information on the type of equipment that will be needed. Check the references in this chapter and the chapter on back-packing and camping.

Figure 12-19. River running (Photo courtesy of Seagull Marine, Irvine, California)

Safety Procedures

River guides provide life jackets and teach safety procedures for rafting. Pretrip discussions should focus on procedures for rough waters and for emergencies that might occur, such as overturning a raft or getting stuck in a suck-hole or hydraulic. Individual guides give different directions to follow in case of an emergency. Be sure that you know what you are going to do if an emergency does occur.

After you have gained some experience with a professionally guided river trip, you might wish to purchase a raft and develop your own river running skills. We suggest that you follow these basic guidelines:

1. Read all available information on river running.
2. Get involved with local outing clubs or groups that have experienced river runners. Find out as much information as possible about nearby streams and rivers and about the techniques for river running.
3. Try out several types of rafts on a gentle body of water before you purchase your own. Many dealers have demonstration models available for this purpose.
4. Plan a short (half-day) river trip with a group of people on a nearby river. Make sure that at least one person has traveled the river previously.
5. Continue slowly and carefully gaining experience in handling a raft in various types of rapids and around specific obstacles.
6. Finally, after you have enough experience to successfully navigate a river, begin to teach your students and begin planning short trips for them.

River Running Information

The following list includes just a few of the commercial river outfitters that run major rivers in the United States. We suggest that you contact a group in your area for additional information.

American Canoe Association
4260 East Evans Avenue
Denver, Colorado 80222

American River Touring Association
1016 Jackson Street
Oakland, California 94607

American Whitewater Affiliation
P.O. Box 1584
San Bruno, California 94066

Pacific River Outfitters Association
c/o George Wendt
Oars Incorporated
Box 67
Angels Camp, California 95222

Rogue River Guides Association
(for current address, write
Oregon State Recreation Department or
Travel Information,
Salem, Oregon 97310)

Western River Guides Association, Inc.
994 Denver Street
Salt Lake City, Utah 84111

Eastern River Guides Association
P.O. Box 33
Ohiopyle, Pennsylvania 15470

QUESTIONS FOR REVIEW AND DISCUSSION

1. Explain and demonstrate the five phases of survival floating.
2. How does a person's body composition affect his or her ability to float?
3. What are survival flotation devices and how do they work?
4. If a person gets caught in a fast moving current, what procedures should they take in order to free themselves from the current?
5. What are the basic procedures to follow in performing any type of rescue?
6. What is the basic equipment for skin diving?
7. Compare open-heeled and closed-heeled fins' relation to a swimmer's strength and ability.
8. Explain middle ear squeeze, sinus squeeze, thoracic lung squeeze, and mask squeeze.
9. What are the symptoms of shallow-water blackout?
10. What specific swimming skills are important to a skin diver?
11. How should a diver clear a face mask?
12. What key points should a diver consider in entering the water with skin diving equipment?
13. What procedures should a diver follow to surface?
14. How can a diver avoid contact with a shark beneath the water?
15. What safety procedures should a tuber follow?
16. What are some specific "fun" activities based on tubing?
17. Why is rafting becoming such a popular activity?
18. What are the three major types of rafts?
19. What safety procedures should a rafter follow?
20. What steps should a beginning rafter follow in order to improve his or her abilities?

REFERENCES

Books

American National Red Cross. *Lifesaving—Rescue and Water Safety*. Garden City, N.Y.: Doubleday and Company, 1974.
Council for National Cooperation in Aquatics. *The New Science of Skin and Scuba Diving*. New York: Association Press, 1970.
Gilbert, Perry W., ed. *Shark and Survival*. Lexington, Mass.: D. C. Heath Company, 1963.

Huser, Verne. *River Running*. Chicago: Henry Regnery Company, 1975.

Ketels, Henry, and Jack McDowell. *Safe Skin and Scuba Diving: Adventure in the Underwater World*. Boston: Educational Associates—Little, Brown and Company, 1975.

Article

Gunsten, Paul. "Coeducational Recreational Activities—Tubing down the River." *JOPER* 47 (May 1976).

SUGGESTED READINGS

Dablemont, Larry. "How to Take a Float Trip." *Outdoor Life* 156, no. 1 (July 1975):52-55.

Forester, John W. "Run the Cheat." *American Forests* 81, no. 9 (September 1975):10-11.

Martin, Steve. "Dilemma in Grand Canyon." *National Parks and Conservation* 50, no. 10 (October 1976):16-17.

Nichols, Margaret G. "Riding Wild." *Field and Stream* 80, no. 1 (May 1975):54-55.

Rivers of the West. Menlo Park, Calif. Lane Publishing Company, 1974.

Sumner, David. "What Fate for the Beleaguered Dolores?" *The Living Wilderness* 39, no. 131 (October/December 1975):6-17.

"The Quiet and the Roar." *Sunset,* April 1975, pp. 78-85.

thirteen

basic canoeing

During the past century, the canoe has become a very popular recreational water craft. The canoe, which at one time was nothing more than a floating log, has evolved into a highly maneuverable craft made out of wood, aluminum, fiberglass, or plastic. The canoe that most people are familiar with is the birchbark, designed by the North American Indians. Those canoes were built to meet special needs, and had a great range of lengths and beam widths. They were light, fast, and maneuverable in all types of water. The only drawback to the original birchbark was that it was difficult to repair.

In 1879 the Peter Borough Canoe Company, in Ontario, Canada, started to develop an all-wood canoe of rib-and-plank construction. A few years later, a company in Old Town, Maine, started building wood and canvas canoes. Today, the Old Town Canoe Company is one of the leading manufacturers of canoes constructed out of fiberglass and plastic. Aluminum canoes were introduced to the public shortly after World War II because of their light weight, toughness, and minimal maintenance requirements.

In today's market, canoes range in price from $250 to $1,000, depending on the size and the materials used for construction.

PARTS OF THE CANOE AND TERMINOLOGY

Aft—toward the stern
Beam—center width
Bow—the extreme end of the forward part
Bow thwart—front braces from gunwale to gunwale
Forward—toward the bow
Freeboard—side from gunwale to waterline
Gunwale—the topside running from bow to stern
Keel—a projecting strip on the bottom outside part of the canoe, which cuts down sideslipping and thus helps the canoe trace a straight line in the water
Midship thwart—center braces from gunwale to gunwale
Portside—left side
Starboard—right side
Stern—the extreme end of the back part
Stern thwart—back braces from gunwale to gunwale

Modern canoes are made in various lengths. The buyer should select one that fits his or her needs.

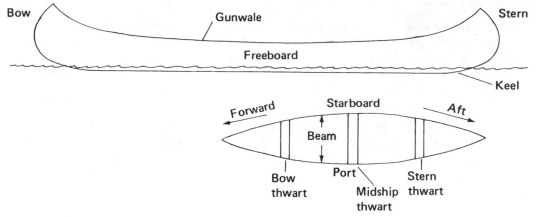

Figure 13-1. Parts of a canoe

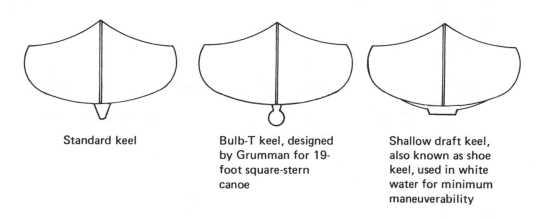

Standard keel

Bulb-T keel, designed by Grumman for 19-foot square-stern canoe

Shallow draft keel, also known as shoe keel, used in white water for minimum maneuverability

Figure 13-2. Keels

Table 13-1. Canoe Lengths

LENGTH	USES
15 feet	Lightweight. Good for beginners. Relatively slow-moving because of the beam-length ratio. Good for a strong canoeist looking for a high degree of maneuverability.
16 feet	Good for recreational use. Can carry an extra person or duffel.
17 feet	Relatively stable in white water. Heavier, but with greater carrying capacity, than the 16-foot canoe.
18 to 20 feet	Good as a white-water and cruising canoe. Can carry as many as four people or large duffel loads.

Construction Materials

1. *Aluminum.* General construction of 6061-T6 Maine aluminum alloy. The T6 represents the temper process by heating the aluminum.
2. *Fiberglass.* A woven cloth cover with a polyester resin.
3. *Royalex®.* Developed by UniRoyal, composed of a cross-linked vinyl, and A.B.S. plastic (acrylo-nitrite-butaliene-styrene).
4. *Kevlar®.* Developed by Dupont, of a high-modulus organic fiber.

Many canoeists disagree on the advantages and disadvantages of the various types of construction materials. From the authors' point of view, Royalex and Kevlar canoes have proved to be the strongest and most durable under all conditions.

PADDLES

Canoes paddles are either single-bladed or double-bladed. The single-bladed type is most commonly used; however, double-bladed paddles are good for solo canoeists and are espcially good for paddling against wind or waves.

A good paddle is constructed from several pieces of wood, generally spruce. Other softwoods, such as cedar, basswood, and fir, are also used. Hardwoods, such as ash or maple, are much heavier but can stand greater abuse from contact with rocks in shallow water. A single wood piece construction is heavier than the laminated type.

The proper length of a paddle is based on the size and strength of the paddler. As a general rule, the paddle should span the outstretched arms of the paddler with the fingers curled over the tip of the blade and the end of the grip.

Today, many canoeists use paddles constructed of wood together with fiberglass or paddles with aluminum shafts and plastic blades. Both combinations have proven to be durable and efficient.

LIFE JACKETS AND ACCESSORIES

Great swimming ability is no excuse for not wearing a life jacket in a canoe. All life jackets used for any boating activities should be approved by the United States Coast Guard. The Federal Boat Safety Act of 1971 requires that all canoes must have on board for each occupant an approved personal flotation device. The life jacket should be a full-flotation preserver and be capable of supporting the neck and face above the water even if the victim is unconscious. For general flatwater canoeing, a horse-collar type is satisfactory; however, a full jacket type is more comfortable during activities and is recommended for white-water canoeing. Flotation cushions can serve as a backup to a life jacket, but should not be relied upon solely. The only real benefit of flotation cushions is to make the kneeling position a bit more comfortable on long trips.

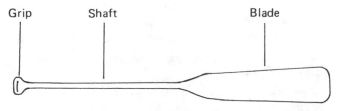

Grip   Shaft   Blade

Figure 13-3. Parts of a canoe paddle

Figure 13-4. Proper paddle length

A lightweight canvas shoe is also recommended for protection of the feet when getting in and out of the canoe in shallow water or rocky beaches.

Additional equipment and accessories will depend on the area where you will be canoeing, the types of water you will encounter, and the number of days you plan to be out. A list of the types of equipment usually needed for canoe trips is given below. Check the list, and remember to take only what you need on your trip.

All equipment should be packed in a dry storage bag made of polyethylene or 20-mil vinyl and should be tied into the canoe. The early trappers and fur traders developed a large water-repellent canvas bag called the Duluth pack, which is still popular today. The big advantage of a Duluth pack is that it has shoulder straps, which makes transportation of equipment easier if portaging is required along the way.

TRIMMING

The term *trimming* refers to the angle plane of the water at which the canoe rests. For example, *bow trim* means that the canoe is tilting down in the water in front of the canoe, and *stern trim* means it is tilting down in the back of the canoe. The canoe is a shallow-draft boat, which requires an even trim (proper weight distribution) to ensure maximum performance and safety. An improper arrangement of weight makes the canoe difficult to maneuver and decreases stability. A canoe should always be evenly trimmed; this is achieved by distributing the weight of equipment and people throughout the entire hull of the craft.

All canoes have a maximum weight capacity, which is established by the manufacturer, and these limits should never be exceeded.

Table 13-2. Equipment Checklist

Required

Canoe	First aid kit
Canteen	Large sponge (for bailing)
Bow & stern painters (18'–20' of rope	Life jackets
tied to the bow & stern)	Three paddles
Flotation cushions or knee pads	

Overnight

Bathing suit	Fuel bottles
Camera	Insect repellent
Clothing (wool is best)	Maps of the area
Compass	Rain gear (or poncho)
Cooking gear & utensils	Sleeping bag
Ensolite pad (or air mattress)	Stove
Extra matches	Sun cream
Extra rope	Sunglasses
Fishing tackle	Tarpaulin
Flashlight & extra batteries	Tent
Folding camp saw	Twine
Food	

TRANSPORTING AND LAUNCHING

Various methods can be used to carry and launch a canoe, depending on its size and the number of people involved (see Figure 13-5).

Single-Person

In the single-person lift and carry, the canoeist grips the gunwales with both hands in the center of the canoe, bends slightly at the knees, and lifts the canoe to his or her hips, with the side of the canoe resting on the thighs. To launch from this carry, simply place the side of the canoe in the water, let the buoyant force of the water push upward, and slide the opposite side down into the water.

Two-Person

The two-person carry is the most efficient method for carrying a canoe. The person at the bow turns his or her palms outward. The bow is placed in the water first; the person at that end gets into the canoe, and the other person lifts and slowly pushes the canoe into the water. Once it is completely buoyant, the stern person gets in. To launch from a deck, both canoeists should hold the canoe by the gunwale at the center; then they tilt the bow down and slowly feed the canoe into the water.

Four-Person

The four-person carry is recommended for children. Each person stands by the sides, two at the bow and two at the stern. The canoe is lifted by the bow thwart and the stern thwart.

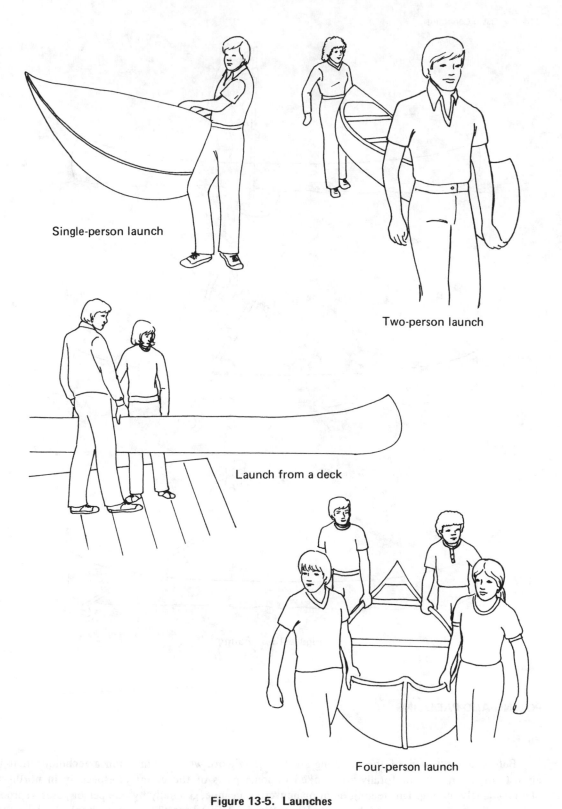

Single-person launch

Two-person launch

Launch from a deck

Four-person launch

Figure 13-5. Launches

Figure 13-6. Poling

POLING AND PADDLING

Poling

    Before a discussion of the paddling strokes, it is worthwhile to mention a technique that is almost forgotten but not totally overlooked in some parts of the country, especially in northern Maine—namely, poling. This technique of maneuvering a canoe, generally by one person, uses a spruce pole one inch in diameter and between 10 feet and 12 feet long. The canoe should be trimmed slightly downward with duffeled equipment. If equipment is not being carried, a log can be used to achieve the proper trim. The canoeist stands in the stern with body weight evenly balanced over both feet and grips the pole in both hands with a comfortable spread between the hands. A downward push on the pole causes the canoe to gain momentum. The downward force is continued until the angle is increased and the pole starts to lift from the water naturally. As the canoe continues moving forward, the canoeist slides a hand down the pole and brings the pole out of the water. Then the hand is slid up the pole and the pole is placed back in the water. Poling is a skill that must be practiced before it can be completely analyzed.

Paddling Strokes

Bow Stroke

The bow stroke is the basic propelling stroke, from which all other strokes originate. This is the correct stroke for propelling the canoe forward and backward. The paddle is held with the palm of the upper hand on the grip and the other hand several inches above the blade. The distance from the paddler's armpit to the tips of the fingers is about the right distance to maintain between the upper and lower handholds.[1] To start the stroke, the lower arm pushes straight out and swings the blade forward, flat and close to the water (see Figure 13-7). When the blade makes contact with the water, the upper arm pushes forward and crosses the body, and the lower arm pulls backward (see Figure 13-8). As the canoe moves forward, the upper arm stops its pull at the midpoint of the hip (see Figure 13-9). Then the blade of the paddle is lifted and turned parallel to the water's surface to be returned forward for the next stroke.

An important point to remember is that the stroke should be made parallel to the keel. If the stroke is made parallel to the gunwale, the force is wasted and pushes the canoe sideways. Also, do not lift the paddle out of the water; let it ride up naturally.

Backwater Stroke

The backwater stroke is the reverse of the bow stroke with respect to arm movement.

J-Stroke

The J-stroke is a forward steering stroke used by the stern person to keep the canoe on a determined line of travel. The proper use of the J-stroke makes it unnecessary for the stern person to use

[1] Joseph L. Hasenfus, *Basic Canoeing* (Washington, D.C.: American National Red Cross, 1965).

Figure 13-7. Bow stroke, starting position (Photo courtesy of The Coleman Company, Wichita, Kansas)

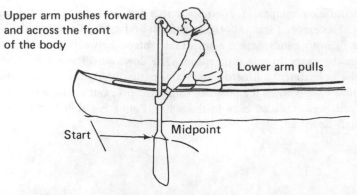

Upper arm pushes forward
and across the front
of the body

Lower arm pulls

Start

Midpoint

Figure 13-8. Bow stroke, second phase

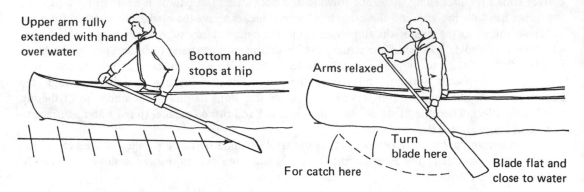

Upper arm fully
extended with hand
over water

Bottom hand
stops at hip

Arms relaxed

Turn
blade here

For catch here

Blade flat and
close to water

Figure 13-9. Bow stroke, final phase

Pull with upper arm

Push forward
with lower arm

Keep stroke
parallel to keel

Allow the paddle
to rise out of the water

Figure 13-10. Backwater stroke

the paddle for a rudder, as many beginning canoeists do. The J-stroke starts with the same technique as the bow stroke and ends with an outward hook. The length of the hook is determined by the amount of course correction needed.

When the lower hand on the paddle is just about at the mid-point of the hip (or stroke), both hands turn, forcing the paddle blade outward. The J-stroke is most effective when the paddle is turned out as close to a right angle as possible from the original line of the stroke. The J-stroke is used only as needed for correcting a course.

Draw Stroke

The draw stroke is used to move the canoe laterally, either left or right (for example, to avoid an obstacle). The draw starts with the canoeist turning the paddle blade parallel to the freeboard and gunwale. The lower hand tilts the blade slightly upward and both hands place the paddle deep in the water. The paddle is then pulled toward the paddler, the pull stopping a few inches from the canoe. To recover the paddle, turn the blade and slice it back through the water.

Pushaway

The pushaway is the opposite of the draw. It is used to move the canoe away from the side of the paddler. The techniques are the same, but in reverse from the draw.

Pryaway

The pryaway is the same technique as the pushaway, but it is a deeper, more powerful stroke, used in white water.

Sweep

The sweep is used for a major turn of the bow or a complete pivot originating from the stern. Again, the stroke starts with the technique of the bow stroke, but the paddle is extended farther from the gunwale and with a decreasing angle to the water.

Sculling Stroke

The sculling stroke is an alternative to the draw for sideways movement. The paddle is held in a vertical position away from the canoe, similar to the draw. The movement of the paddle is fore and aft of the keel with the edge of the paddle held at more of a cutting angle.

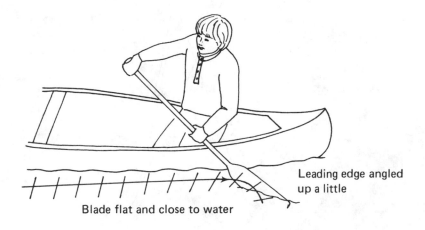

Leading edge angled
up a little

Blade flat and close to water

Figure 13-11. J-stroke

Figure 13-12. Draw stroke (Photo courtesy of OLD TOWN Canoe Company, Old Town, Maine)

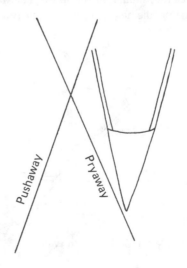

Figure 13-13. Pushaway and pryaway strokes

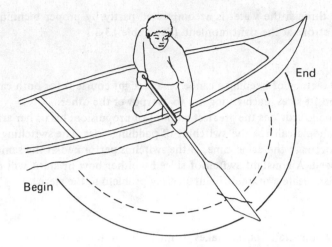

Figure 13-14. Sweep stroke

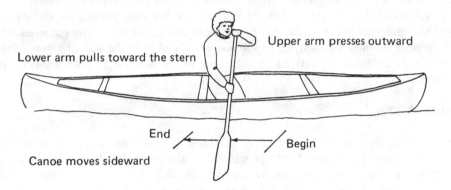

Lower arm pulls toward the stern

Upper arm presses outward

End

Begin

Canoe moves sideward

Figure 13-15. Sculling stroke

The American National Red Cross text, *Basic Canoeing,* describes the paddle movement as follows:

> When the paddle is moved forward, the forward edge of the blade is turned away from the canoe. When the paddle moves aft, it is the after edge of the blade that is turned away. The action places pressure always on the face of the blade that is next to the canoe. This pressure draws the canoe toward the paddle. The action is reversed to move the canoe away from the paddling side.[2]

Rudder Strokes

Rudder strokes include the bow rudder and the stern rudder. The paddle is placed edgewise in the water against the gunwale. It should be braced against the gunwale to help resist the force of the water on the paddle blade. The bow rudder is used to make a sharp turn toward the paddling side; the stern rudder, to make a sharp turn away from the paddling side.

[2]*Ibid.,* p. 38.

Propelling a canoe through the water is accomplished partly by proper technique and partly by application of the right stroke at the right moment. (See Table 13-3.)

Paddling Sides

The most effective method of keeping a canoe on a straight course is for both canoeists to paddle at the same rate on opposite sides, each trying not to overpower the other.

Since the bow canoeist provides the greatest amount of propulsion, his or her arm will tire faster. Thus, the bow person should call for the switching of paddling sides. The switching of sides between bow and stern should occur at the same time. If the switch is performed at the same time, the canoe will not decrease its speed. A constant switch of sides by either bow or stern will cause loss of forward momentum and also create a more difficult steering problem in the stern.

Exchanging Positions

On long canoe trips, especially on big lakes, it might be desirable for the bow and stern persons to exchange paddling positions. The bow person places the paddle behind the bow thwart, then slides his or her body over the bow thwart and takes a sitting position while keeping the canoe trimmed. The stern person slides his or her paddle forward on the opposite side, places both hands on the gunwale, and moves forward, stepping to the side of or over the bow person. As the stern person proceeds forward, the bow person tucks his or her head and ducks below the gunwales. Once the stern person assumes the new position, he or she places the paddle in the water to steady the canoe, and the bow person continues to walk backward to the new position with both hands on the gunwales at all times.

ENTRY FROM WATER

To enter a canoe from water, the swimmer places both hands over the gunwale in the center (amidship) of the canoe. The hands should be out flat on the bottom and pushing downward. The swimmer then flutter kicks until the hips are over the gunwale. Upon acheiving this position, the swimmer turns the hips to the side and slides into a sitting position in the bottom of the canoe.

Table 13-3. Actions Caused by Paddling Strokes

ACTION	STROKE
Propulsion and foundation of all strokes	Bow
Backward propulsion	Backward
Sideways movement toward the paddling side	Draw
Sideways movement away from paddling side	Pushaway
Sideways movement away from paddling side in whitewater	Pryaway
Small forward corrective steering	J-stroke
Major turn, or complete pivot	Sweep
Alternative to draw stroke	Sculling
Stop	Backward

Figure 13-16. Exchanging positions

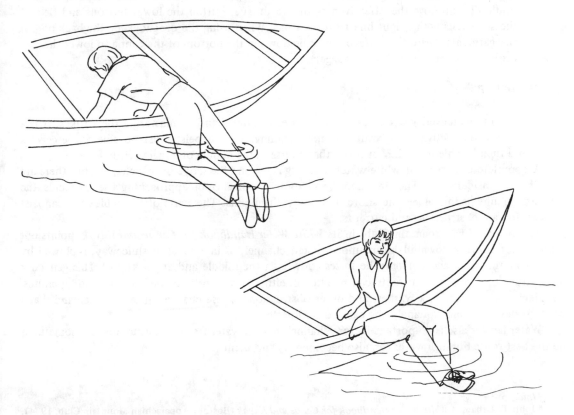

Figure 13-17. Entry from the water

CAPSIZING

The canoeist should stay with a capsized or swamped canoe and use it as a life raft. A canoe totally filled with water will still have buoyancy in the water and be able to support the canoeist. Enter the canoe in the same fashion as just mentioned. If paddles have been lost, the canoe can be paddled with both hands.

FLATWATER (STILL WATER) CANOEING

In still water, the stern paddler is responsible for steering the canoe. Once the steering strokes have been mastered, this is a relatively easy task under normal conditions. Under adverse conditions, such as high winds or surf, the following rules should be adhered to for greatest possible safety:

1. Always stay in the kneeling position with the weight concentrated in the middle of the canoe.
2. Never venture into the middle of a wide lake or river in high winds and surf.
3. Tack a canoe back and forth when canoeing directly windward.
4. Approach a lee shore (away from the wind) carefully, because surf and wind are difficult to judge coming off shore.
5. In extremely high winds and surf, the American National Red Cross recommends the following:

> In extreme conditions, when paddling is no longer possible, improvise a drogue, with a paddle and a long-sleeved shirt, a coat, or a jacket. Thread the paddle through the sleeves and attach a short bridle over the cuffs. Secure the bowline to the center of the bridle. To improve the effectiveness of the drogue, button the lower buttons and tie the shirt tails with a light line to form a bag. When using the drogue, keep the back of the garment toward the surface. Sit or lie down in the bottom of the canoe to lower the center of gravity and reduce windage.[3]

WHITE WATER

The art of maneuvering a canoe in white water is more than just mastering the strokes. It is a highly adventurous activity, requiring specific planning. The canoeist must be able to perceive a course and then be able to modify or revise that course in the middle of a raging river.

A complete discussion of white-water canoeing is beyond the scope of this chapter, but there are some basic considerations. The first step is to choose a course. Upon approaching a set of rapids, the canoeist should paddle along the shore and study the rapids. The parts of the rapids the canoeist notices first are obstructions and currents.

The Appalachian Mountain Club, in its *White Water Handbook for Canoe and Kayak,* points out that "water flowing downhill in an unobstructed channel, as in a canal or sluiceway, is slowed by friction at the sides and bottom; the fastest flow is in the middle and at the top."[4] This generally holds true for rivers, but currents can be altered, either slowed or increased by descending chutes, boulders, rock ledges, back washes, and other obstructions. These changes in current demand that a canoeist develop a plan for analyzing each current pattern.

Water level is also an important factor. Channels in high water free of obstructions can sometimes be the best route but high water can also become very turbulent.

---

[3]*Ibid.,* p. 59.
[4]John T. Urban, *A White Water Handbook for Canoe and Kayak* (Boston: Appalachian Mountain Club, 1974), p. 30.

Figure 13-18. Paddling a capsized canoe

In fast water, river bends can also present tricky maneuvering problems. The deep water in a bend is always to the outside, with sand and rocks settling to the inside. The safest route to negotiate a bend is to the outside, staying in the deeper water.

To maneuver around an obstruction, plan each maneuver far in advance. Always consider the bow of the canoe first; remember that where the bow goes, the stern will follow on the same line. It is the responsibility of both the bow paddler and the stern person to steer so that the canoe follows the determined line.

To help the canoeist plan a white-water trip, river maps or guidebooks are available for most rivers throughout the country. The maps and books will describe each set of rapids and tell the classifications and obstructions (see Table 13-4). Water level affects the rating. Rivers are rated when their water is at the best height for paddling, but the height can change from season to season, so that the river can become less canoeable or more dangerous. For example, a Class 2 (medium) set of rapids might become more turbulent after a hard rain and so be regarded as Class 3 (difficult).

TEACHING ACTIVITIES AND SAFETY

To teach basic canoeing skills, dry land drills are extremely beneficial. A low deck (pool deck) is also useful for teaching stroke action. By kneeling on the edge of the deck with the paddle in the water, individual students can practice proper stroke technique without entering the canoe. The teaching of drownproofing is also important before students are allowed to venture out in a canoe (see Chapter 12). To practice maneuvering a canoe around obstructions, inner tubes or other buoyant objects can be placed in the water to represent the obstructions.

TRIP PLANNING

In preparation for a canoe trip the following points should be considered:

1. *Skill level.* Select a body of water that is challenging but within the skill of the average student.
2. *Length of trip.* An average canoeist can paddle about 3 mph in flatwater, but always allow for any adverse conditions or storms.

Table 13-4. International Scale of River Difficulty

RATING	CHARACTERISTICS	SKILL LEVEL
1	Sand-banks, bends without difficulty, occasional small rapids with waves regular and low. Correct course easy to to find, but care is needed with minor obstacles like pebble banks, fallen trees, etc., especially on narrow rivers. River speed less than hard back paddling speed.	Practiced beginner
2	Fairly frequent but unobstructed rapids usually with regular waves, easy eddies and easy bends. Course generally easy to recognize. River speeds occasionally exceeding hard back paddling speed.	Intermediate
3	Maneuvering in rapids necessary. Small falls, large regular waves covering boat, numerous rapids. Main current may swing under bushes, branches or overhangs. Course not always easily recognizable. Current speed usually less than fast forward paddling speed.	Experienced
4	Long extended stretches of rapids, high irregular waves boulders directly in current. Difficult broken water, eddies, and abrupt bends. Course often difficult to recognize and inspection from the bank frequently necessary. Swift current. Rough water experience indispensable.	Highly skilled (several years experience with organized group)
5	Long rocky rapids with difficult and completely irregular broken water which must be run head on. Very fast eddies, abrupt bends and vigorous cross currents. Difficult landings increase hazard. Frequent inspections necessary. Extensive experience necessary.	Team of experts
6	All previously mentioned difficulties increased to the limit. Only negotiable at favorable water levels. Cannot be attempted without risk of life.	Team of experts (taking every precaution)

Source: Robert E. McNair, *Basic River Canoeing* (Martinsville, Ind.: American Camping Association, 1972), Appendix III. Reprinted by permission of the author.

3. *Permits and fees.* State forest services may require camp permits and may charge fees to put in or take out canoes.
4. *Map and guidebooks.* The instructor should always carry a complete set of maps and guidebooks of the river.
5. *Swimming ability.* Each student's swimming ability should be checked out before starting on the trip, and life jackets should always be worn in the canoe.

The authors recommend that instructors and students study the safety code developed by the American Whitewater Affiliation:[5]

    I. Personal preparedness and responsibility
        1. *Never boat alone.* The preferred minimum is three per craft.

[5]Quoted in Robert E. McNair, *Basic River Canoeing* (Martinsville, Ind.: American Camping Association, 1972), pp. 56-57.

2. *Be a competent swimmer* with ability to handle yourself underwater.
3. *Wear your life jacket* wherever upsets may occur. The life jacket must be capable of supporting your face up if unconscious. A crash helmet is recommended in rivers of Grade IV and over.
4. *Have a frank knowledge of your boating ability*, and don't attempt waters beyond your ability.
5. *Know and respect river classification.*
6. *Beware of cold water and of weather extremes;* dress accordingly. Rubber wet suits or long woolen underwear may be essential for safety as well as comfort.
7. *Be suitably prepared and equipped;* carry a knife, secure your glasses, and equip yourself with such special footgear, skin protection, raincoat, etc., as the situation requires.
8. *Be practiced* in escape from spray cover, in rescue and self-rescue, and in first aid.
9. *Support your leader* and respect his authority.

II. Boat preparedness and equipment (changes or deletions at the discretion of the leader only)
1. *Test new and unfamiliar equipment* before taking hazardous situations.
2. *Be sure craft is in good repair* before starting a trip.
3. *Have a spare paddle,* affixed for immediate use.
4. *Install flotation devices,* securely fixed and designed to displace from the craft as much water as possible. A minimum of 1 cubic foot at each end is recommended.
5. *Have bow and stern lines,* optional for kayaks depending on local club regulations. Use ¼" or ⅜" diameter and 8 to 15 ft. long rope. Fasten securely to the boat at one end and other end must release only if tugged. Floats and knots at the ends are not recommended.
6. *Use spray cover wherever required;* cover release must be instant and foolproof.
7. *Carry repair kit,* flashlight, map and compass for wilderness trips; survival gear as necessary.

III. Group's equipment (The leader may supplement this list, at his discretion)
1. *Throwing line,* 50' to 100' of ¼" rope.
2. *First aid kit* with fresh and adequate supplies; waterproof matches.

IV. Leader's responsibility
1. *He must have full knowledge of the river.* He determines the river classification on the spot and adapts plans to suit.
2. *He does not allow anyone to participate beyond his proven ability.* Exceptions: (a) when the trip is an adequately supported training trip, or (b) when difficult stretches can be portaged.
3. *He must know what conditions in weather, visibility and water to expect;* he should instruct the group relative to these conditions and must make decisions on the basis of the related dangers.
4. *His decisions in the interest of safety are final.*
5. *He designates the necessary support personnel,* and if appropriate, the order and spacing of boats.

V. On the river
1. *All must know group plans, on-river organization, hazards expected, location of special equipment, signals to be used.*
2. *Lead boat knows the river, sets the course, is never passed.*
3. *Rear-guard is equipped and trained for rescue, always in rear.*

     4. *Each boat is responsible for boat behind;* passes on signals, indicates obstacles, sees it through bad spots.

     5. *Keep party compact.* Divide into independent teams if party is too big.

VI. On lake or ocean

     1. *Do not travel beyond a returnable distance from shore.*

     2. *Know the weather.* Conditions can change drastically.

     3. *Secure complete tide information* for trips involving tidal currents.

     4. *Lead rear-guard and side-guard boats are strongly recommended* to prevent large groups from becoming dangerously spread out.

     5. *Eskimo roll* mastering should be seriously considered by Kayakists on tidal or large lake waters. Canoeists should learn to right, empty out water and board a swamped canoe.

VII. If you spill

     1. *Be aware of your responsibility to assist your partner.*

     2. *Hold on to your boat;* it has much flotation and is easy for rescuers to spot. Get to upstream end so boat cannot crush you on rocks. Follow rescuer's instructions.

     3. *Leave your boat if this improves your safety;* your personal safety must come first. If rescue is not imminent and water is numbing cold or worse rapids follow, then strike for the nearest shore.

     4. *Stay on the upstream end of your boat;* otherwise you risk being pinned against obstacles, or, in waves, may swallow water.

     5. *Be calm,* but don't be complacent.

VIII. If others spill

     1. *Go after the boater;* rescue his boat only if this can be done safely.

QUESTIONS FOR REVIEW AND DISCUSSION

1. What are the basic parts of a canoe?
2. What lengths are canoes made?
3. What are the advantages and disadvantages of the various construction materials of canoes?
4. How long should a canoe paddle be?
5. What materials are necessary on a canoe trip?
6. What does it mean to trim a canoe?
7. What are the basic propelling strokes for canoeing?
8. Explain the techniques for entering a canoe from the water.
9. What are some basic safety rules for canoeing?
10. What are some key points in white-water canoeing?
11. What is the International Scale of River Difficulty?
12. What factors should be considered in the planning of a canoeing trip?

REFERENCES

Hasenfus, Joseph L. *Basic Canoeing.* Washington, D.C.: American National Red Cross, 1965.

McNair, Robert E. *Basic River Canoeing.* Martinsville, Ind.: American Camping Association, 1972.

Urban, John T. *A White Water Handbook for Canoe and Kayak.* Boston: Appalachian Mountain Club, 1974.

SUGGESTED READINGS

Esslen, Rainer. *Back to Nature in Canoes: A Guide to American Waters*. Frenchtown, N.J.: Columbia Publishing Company, 1976.

Huser, Verne. *River Running*. Chicago: Henry Regnery Company, 1975.

Michaelson, Mike, and Keith Ray. *Canoeing: An Outdoor Encounter Resource Book*. Chicago: Henry Regnery Company, 1975.

Norman, Dean. *The All-Purpose Guide to Paddling, Canoe, Raft, Kayak*. Matteson, Ill.: Greatlakes Living Press Publisher, 1976.

fourteen

sailing

During the past decade, sailing has become one of the most popular outdoor recreation activities. It seems that Americans now flock to the water—to the lakes, bays, and shores—to spend a few hours, a few days, or a few weeks.

The thrill of sailing cannot be expressed by mere words. It is a feeling not only of power but of awe; it is a test in which you pit yourself—and your fear—against the demands of wind and water. And there is also the aesthetic appeal of hull and sail seen against the far-reaching blue water.

Sailing demands many skills, including the mastery of sailing techniques, the understanding of boat-to-wind relationships, and a practical grasp of nautical terminology. A firm knowledge of a boat's nomenclature and the theory behind sailing will enhance not only one's pleasure on the water but also one's safety.

Sailing is one way in which a person can interact in a totally natural way with the environment. It has not changed radically over the years. The first "sailors" probably took to the water in dug-out logs or rafts. Boats were made from trees, sails from branches and skins of animals or woven reeds, and the power to move came from the wind. Today, sailing can still be a vital way to experience the out-of-doors. It is no longer necessary to build boats from scratch, but the wind is still a sailboat's source of power.

Sailing is not a threat to the aquatic environment. Most small sailboats do not use motors, and thus do not pollute the water with leaking oil or gas. Recreation or race class boats that do have motors use them mostly for entering or leaving morrings.

Noise pollution primarily affects humans, because it occurs mainly in urban areas. But it can also have an adverse effect on wildlife. The tranquility of remote places can be upset by the harsh noise often associated with water recreation. The more peaceful the setting, the more aesthetically pleasing sailing becomes. Sailing does not contribute to the overall level of noise in any environment.

EQUIPMENT AND CLOTHING

There are many types of sailboats afloat today. The most important factor to consider when you select a boat is how it will be used. Will it be used only for teaching? For competition or recreation? Will it be moored in the water or docked or must it be towed to the water each time you use it? Large boats look nice, but often they are harder to sail and need more upkeep. Small boats respond

Special thanks to our colleague, Dr. Diane Spitler, of the University of California at Santa Barbara, for help in the preparation of this chapter.

more easily to changes in the wind and are generally easier to steer and harder to damage. The sailor who learns in a small boat will know more about sailing, the wind, and seamanship than one who starts in a large boat.

The most practical boat for beginners is an 8-foot to 12-foot dinghy, catboat, or sloop. There are hundreds of one-design boats in this size. A one-design boat is built to the same design and specifications as all other boats in its classification. If budget considerations limit the number of boats initially purchased, the choice of a standard class or one-design boat has the advantage of allowing additional purchases to match the original fleet. Final selection should be based on the facilities available, the desired expenditure, the projected class size, and the durability of the boat.

The hull is the main body of the boat. There are two basic types of hull design. The displacement hull displaces a volume of water equal to its total weight as it floats or moves through the water. Planing hulls are designed to plane or skim on the surface, under optimum conditions. Hulls are made of various materials, wood and fiberglass being the most common. Wood boats require a great deal more care and upkeep than fiberglass boats. Although plastic and fiberglass hulls need less painting, are lighter, and tend to be rotproof, they are a disadvantage when fittings must be repaired or replaced. Depending upon the design of the craft, for the money, a fiberglass hull is a practical sailboat for instructional purposes.

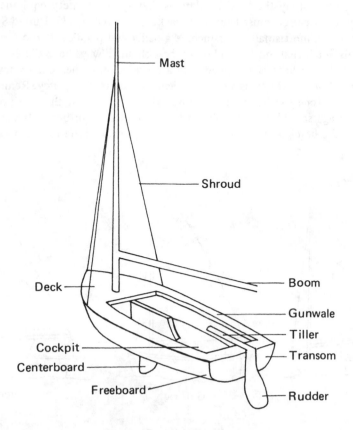

Figure 14-1. Parts of a boat

While it is not absolutely necessary to be able to name every part of the boat, the use of correct names facilitates learning about and handling the gear and thus reduces confusion (see Figure 14-1).

The simplest boat, often called a cat-rigged sloop or a catboat, is rigged with one mast, one boom, and one sail. The term *rig* refers to the number of masts, booms, sails, and supporting wires on a boat. A few of the more commonly known rigs are illustrated in Figure 14-2. Additional working sails are found in the larger boats and include the jib—a second, smaller sail up front—and sometimes a specialty sail such as a spinnaker, which is used only when sailing off the wind.

Almost all boats have wire guys or supports for the mast, called the standing rigging. They "stand" permanently, as long as the mast is up, holding it securely in place. The wires that support the mast sideways are called shrouds; those that support it the length of the boat are called stays.

Running rigging is the lines (ropes) that "run" (move) to raise and control the sails. Halyards are lines used to hoist the sails up and down. Sheets are lines that move the sails in and out. Each sail has its own halyard and sheet.

The helm is the steering mechanism of the boat. The tiller is the part you hold in your hand, and the rudder is the section in the water.

To provide stability, to keep from tipping over, and to keep sailing straight, all boats need a centerboard, dagger board, or keel. This flat plate of metal or wood extends down through the middle of the boat into the water.

The parts of the sail also have proper names, primarily the corners and edges. These are shown in Figure 14-4. Another term used in connection with sails is *roach,* which is the curve in the leech (the trailing edge of the sail). Roach can be adjusted to sailing conditions.

Before using a boat, study the local regulations that apply to safety equipment and running of the boat. Basically, each person must have a life jacket approved by the United States Coast Guard. Other safety features on most small boats include a bailer and paddles. If room permits, it is handy to keep repair tools and a first aid kit on board; these should always be available from the instructor in a class situation. If your boat is equipped with a power motor, then emergency fire equipment is necessary. Finally, a horn or whistle is needed to signal in case of emergency. Remember, safety regulations may vary from one locality to another, so take care to know those in your particular area.

Mooring or storage should be considered when you select your boats. If you plan to keep the boats in the water, the best place to secure them is at a mooring. Here they can swing with the wind

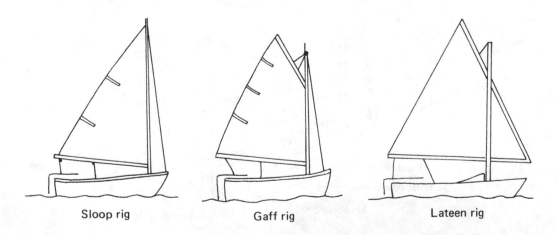

Sloop rig   Gaff rig   Lateen rig

Figure 14-2. Rigs

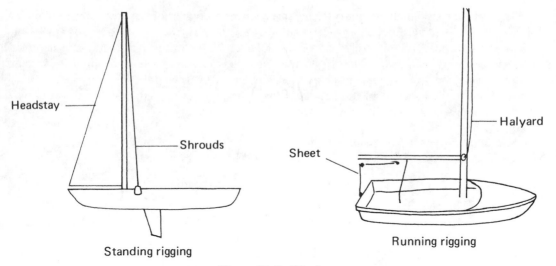

Figure 14-3. Rigging

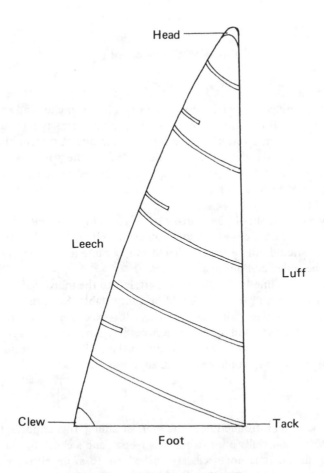

Figure 14-4. Parts of a sail

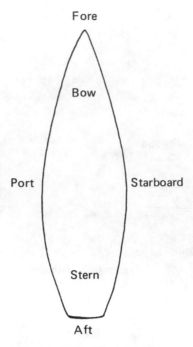

Figure 14-5. Directions

and not hit other boats. Moorings are usually made by using a heavy anchor and some kind of float to keep the lines near the surface. If docking space is available, suitable crosstying is necessary to prevent the boat from hitting the dock as a result of wave action or the tide. A system of fore and aft lines is usually effective. Perhaps you will prefer to remove the boats from the water entirely. If so, care must be taken to prevent scraping and unnecessary damage. Boats stored upside down do not accumulate rainwater. It is probably a good idea to secure the boats to rails or trees to protect them from high rising waters and from theft.

All running rigging and sails should be stored carefully out of the elements. Sails should be kept in sail bags and hung in a locker, a closet, or some other dry place. If folded, they will take up less room in the sail bag. Sails should not be stored when damp, because moisture hastens mildew and rot. Running rigging should be coiled and put in a dry place.

The choice of attire for sailing is, for the most part, left to the individual. A great deal of agility is often necessary when sailing, so garments should be comfortable. Swimsuits, shorts, and shirts are popular small-boating attire. A wise sailor also prepares for excessive exposure to the sun and for sudden drops in temperature. Nonskid shoes are a necessity. Since there is apt to be water on the decks of the sailing boat, a sailor's safety may depend on the ability to get around without slipping. Of course, no true sailing enthusiast would neglect an approved life jacket.

BASIC SKILLS

A sailing class can be a fun introduction to the sport of sailing. It is important that each member of the class demonstrate certain skills prior to entering a boat, and a check of swimming skills should be the first order of business. It is not necessary to be able to swim all the strokes listed by the American Red Cross, but persons in the class should be competent swimming both in a prone position and on their backs for at least 200 yards and they should be able to tread water or keep afloat for at least 15 minutes without support. In addition, they should appear relaxed when working in and about the water while wearing a life jacket. Responsibility for the safety of the class lies with the instructor, so persons who cannot handle themselves in the water should not be admitted.

Most novices find sailing confusing at first. It is important that each member of the class learn the correct sequential pattern for rigging and caring for the boats.

Entering a Boat

Knowing how to enter and leave the boat safely is basic to sailing. A boat should be balanced at all times. When you enter a boat, support your weight before stepping into the center of the craft. If you enter from the water, reach across to the opposite side as you lift yourself aboard, and then swing your legs over. Always place your hands so that no fingers or thumbs hang over the gunwale, because the boat might bump against the pier or dock.

Rigging

If the students have had no experience with boats, it is a good idea to rig a boat with just the rudder and tiller. By means of a long line, the boat can be pulled for short distances along shore, giving students a chance to practice turning or steering the boat. Many novices find it confusing that the tiller moves in the opposite direction from the bow.

The actual rigging of the boat will depend on the type of boat being used. A general pattern should be established, and it should be followed each time the boats are rigged. The standard first step in rigging is to lower the centerboard or dagger board and turn the bow into the wind. The lowered centerboard provides stability so one can move about the boat more freely. With the boat's bow facing into the wind, there will be less resistance when the sails are hoisted.

The rudder and tiller should be attached next. Then check to see that the sheets and halyards are not tangled. Check the mainsail to see that there are not twists along the foot or luff. Attach the halyard and bend on the sail. Bending a sail on the boat means attaching it. Begin to feed the luff along the slot of the mast for a short distance. Feed the foot of the sail along the boom while securing the tack and the clew by stretching the sail. Again, check for twists and see if the halyard and sheet are clear. You are now ready to hoist the mainsail to the top of the mast. Adjust any slack in the sail by pulling down on the downhaul and securing it. With the main sheet free, the sail will not power the boat. It is important to secure the halyards and stow any excess line in an orderly fashion— you never know when you'll have to let the sails down fast. You are now ready to trim the sheets and begin sailing.

Knots

Obviously, becoming a seasoned skipper takes more than studying a book. One must sail in order to learn how to sail. Along with the proper rigging to the boat, every sailor needs to know some of the most common and useful knots. Correct securing of lines is a safety habit that can never be over-emphasized.

The overhand knot is used to keep the end of a line from unraveling. This knot often jams and becomes impossible to release.

The figure eight or stopper knot is used to prevent a line from slipping through a sheave or pulley. It does not jam and can be released quite easily.

The square, reef, or right knot is used for tying lines of the same size together. It can jam when stressed or when it gets wet and will not release easily.

The bowline, along with the square knot, is one of the most useful knots used for sailing. It will not slip, jam, or become difficult to release. It is used wherever a secure loop or running noose is needed. It is often used to secure lines to anchors or to secure a line to a cleat or bit on the dock.

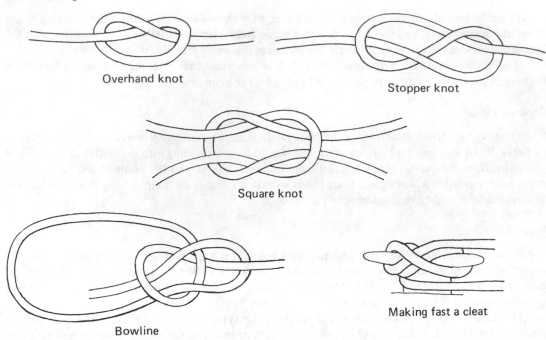

Figure 14-6. Knots

The correct method of making fast to a cleat is completed with a half hitch. This must be taken with the free part of the line, so that the line can be released without taking up slack in the standing part.

Righting a Capsized Boat

One of the most exciting elements of sailing a small, centerboard boat is the chance of capsizing. While this is nothing to fear, it is important to follow a set procedure when it does occur, to minimize the problems. Class practice of this procedure should be done in quiet waters or in a pool before the boats are taken out for the first sail.

After capsizing, the first act upon surfacing is to locate all persons who were aboard. When everyone has been accounted for, turn the bow into the wind, trying not to turtle, or completely overturn, the boat (most capsized boats rest on their sides). After making sure the sheets are clear and the halyards are still secure, grasp the centerboard, pulling down with all your weight. Sometimes it may be necessary to lift yourself up on the board. The boat will right itself. After everyone has re-entered the boat, check the lines, trim the sheets, and you are ready to sail once again.

Sailing Theory

When running downwind, a sailboat is pushed along by the pressure of the wind on its sail. When sailing across the wind, however, other factors come into play. As the wind flows past the sail, part of it changes direction when flowing around the shape of the sail. The difference between the two streams of air causes a decrease in pressure behind the sail, and the boat tends to move toward this area. The centerboard provides lateral resistance to keep the boat from blowing sideways, while the rudder provides the steering direction. Together, these forces exert a squeezing action on the hull, and the boat moves through the water in the direction that offers the least resistance.

To sail a desired course no matter what direction the wind is coming from requires knowledge of the points of sail (see Figure 14-8). A boat cannot sail into the wind at an angle of less than 45°, but it is capable of sailing close to the wind (beating), sailing at right angles to the wind (reaching), and sailing with the wind (running). These three points of sail, with their variations, can be done on either tack.

For the beginning sailor, beating is the most difficult point of sail to understand. It is important when sailing on a beat or to windward to "feel" when you have the sails properly trimmed—not too far out and not too tight. When beating, you will experience the greatest angle of heel, and in a stiff breeze the leeward rail will probably be under water. It may be necessary to move yourself and your crew to the windward rail to help balance this heel, especially if you are racing.

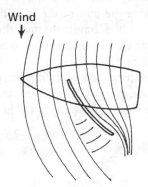

Figure 14-7. How a boat sails

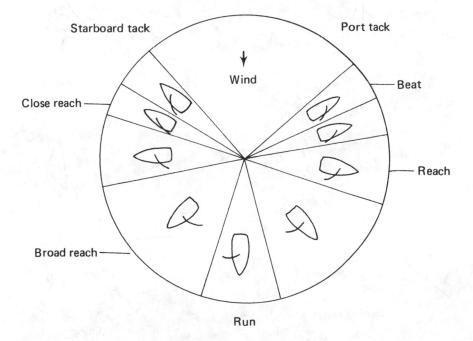

Figure 14-8. Points of sail

Reaching is the course between beating and running. It is the fastest and easiest angle of sail. A close reach is approximately 80° off the wind, a beam reach is 90° off the wind, and a broad reach is 90° and 180° off the wind. Reaching is usually a trouble-free point of sail as long as the wind is not too strong. This angle of sail is probably the best for the beginner.

Sailing in the same direction as the wind is called running. The idea is to expose as much of the sails' surface to the wind as possible. In this position, the boat is traveling as fast as the wind is pushing it. Running is an easy angle of sail except when the wind is up. If the wind should change or a sea roll should swing the stern around, an uncontrollable jibe (called a "flying jibe") could take place. This is a very dangerous situation. The novice should practice sailing on a broad reach before running under strong wind.

Tacking means changing the sail from one side of the boat to the other. Coming about is changing to the opposite tack while sailing windward. Jibing is changing to the opposite tack while sailing downwind. To come about, swing the bow of the boat through the wind, pushing the tiller toward the boom or leeward side. As the bow travels through the eye of the wind, the sails will lose all of their wind power. Be sure to have enough momentum to coast through this luffing period and reach the desired tack. If the boat gets caught halfway between tacks so that it cannot go to either tack, it is said to be "in irons." When preparing to tack, notify all hands. A command of "ready about" warns them of the intended maneuver, while the command "hard-to-lee" indicates the action of the tiller being moved hard to the lee side (downwind) of the boat.

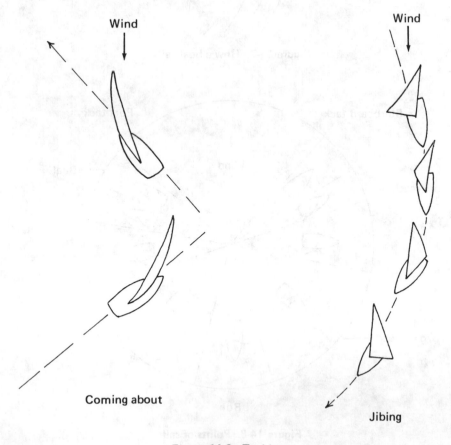

Wind

Wind

Coming about

Jibing

Figure 14-9. Tacking

Turning the bow of the boat away from the wind when changing tacks is called jibing. As the wind catches the back side of the sail, the boom and sail will swing across the cockpit to the opposite side of the boat. This movement is much faster and generally more forceful than coming about. The initial command given by the skipper to the crew is "prepare to jibe." As the tiller is moved to the windward side, the command is "jibe ho." As the bow falls off the wind, the mainsail is hauled in as fast as possible to control the crossover. Then, as the wind catches the sail on the new tack, the sheet is quickly let out to the desired trim.

One of the best ways to get out of irons is to redistribute the boat's balance until it is heeling in the desired direction. Be prepared to trim the sail carefully as the boat moves off the wind, or the bow will again swing into irons.

Person Overboard

When a person falls over the side of the boat, immediate action is necessary for a rescue. Since a jibe is the fastest turn, make one immediately, while keeping your eyes on the person in the water. Then steer a course toward the victim. As you approach, shoot the boat up into the wind to lose all wind power. This will allow you to come alongside the victim with no momentum. It is almost impossible to pick up someone in the water by snatching the person up while you are sailing by.

Rules of the Road

Some basic rules of the road or the right-of-way will add to the enjoyment and safety of any sailing experience. A sailboat has the right-of-way over any boat under power, including a canoe. Common sense should rule in certain situations, such as a trolling fishing boat, large barges, and, in most cases, crew boats. An overtaking boat must give way to the boat being overtaken regardless of its source of power. When two sailboats converge, the boat on the port tack must give way to the boat on the starboard tack, or, if both boats are on the same tack, the leeward boat has right-of-way over the windward boat. While the rules may be confusing at first, they are basically simple and it is very important to follow them. Remember, too, it is better to give up your right-of-way than to risk damage or injury.

Landing

When you launch or land a boat, always remember to head into the wind when raising or lowering the sails. The approach to landing your boat will depend upon the landing facilities and the direction of the wind. It is always better to come up into the wind and drift toward the dock or beach than to risk damage to the boat or crew by sailing forcefully into the dock. When leaving the boat for the night, make sure that all lines are secured and coiled and that all the gear to be protected has been removed and stored in a dry place. Raise the centerboard after making sure the rudder and tiller have been removed. If you have a cover, use it to protect the boat. Finally, make sure the boat is secured safely and will not drift or be damaged by the water's motion.

SAFETY PROCEDURES

Learning to sail is fun, but it takes time to master the necessary skills. It is important that all classes be conducted so as to ensure maximum safety for all participants. Safety is an integral part of sailing, not just an added dimension.

Any person entering a boat should be able to swim. When one is sailing, events sometimes occur so fast that it becomes impossible to keep an eye on the nonswimmer.

The proper care and maintenance of the boat and its gear also contributes to the general safety of a cruise. Repairs should be made as soon as possible and defective parts should be replaced. The rigging ought to be checked carefully and the halyards should be secured with appropriate knots correctly tied.

The ability to right a boat after it capsizes and to rescue a person overboard are skills basic to the safety of everyone sailing. The rules of the road provide protection from overenthusiastic boaters.

In spite of all the best-laid plans, you may be caught out in bad weather. A few commonsense rules can help you reach safety. If caught in very heavy winds, lower the sail and reef it if it has reef lines. Keep a large luff in the mainsail. Do not try to run with the wind. If there is no wind, a paddle will come in handy. If lightning threatens, lower your sails, and, if possible, lower the mast. If you get into very high seas or high winds, create a sea anchor by dragging the sail or an anchor from the stern. At all other times, try to make it to the nearest shore to wait out the weather. Then return to your landing.

TEACHING ACTIVITIES

Sailing can be a challenging part of a school or recreation program. It is a lifetime activity that brings pleasure and satisfaction to young and old alike. A school need not have a private lake or ocean in its backyard in order to have a sailing program; however, a lake or quiet, protected waters must be near enough so that travel time is not excessive. For most programs it is best to own a certain class of boat, because this makes it easier to add new boats.

The size of the sailing class will be limited by the equipment available and by the instructor's ability to maintain safety procedures. Most small boats can be sailed by two people—a skipper and the crew. This permits maximum participation by students. Time is an important factor in the learning process; long periods of uninterrupted practice are most beneficial for the beginner.

The plans for a sailing program must allow time for travel to and from the sailing site, for rigging the boats, and for stowing the gear when the day's sail is over.

Requirements for entering the sailing class should be stated clearly before the course begins. It is wise to let the instructor have the final say about who shall be admitted to the class. Possibly a mixture of beginners and persons with limited sailing experience would be most conducive to a pleasant learning experience for all concerned.

Sailing is a competency-based activity. There are certain basic skills that have to be mastered if one is to become a competent sailor. These skills should be taught in a logical sequence. If a student has trouble learning a particular skill, the instructor can make adjustments for that person.

Sailing in a school or recreational setting should not be limited to instructional situations. Once they have developed their skills, students should be encouraged to sail outside of class. With an organized system for clearing potential sailors to check out boats and care for equipment, the school or the recreation department can offer students a chance to improve their sailing skills or simply to enjoy some very pleasurable moments on the water.

Competitive sailing can also be included in a well-rounded sailing program. All that is needed to set up intramural and interschool regattas are several one-design boats and a sailing area large enough to accommodate a course.

QUESTIONS FOR REVIEW AND DISCUSSION

1. Why is sailing becoming so popular?
2. What type of sailboat is best for beginners?
3. What are the basic parts of a sailboat?
4. What is the difference between the running rigging and the standing rigging?
5. What are the basic parts of a sail?
6. What safety equipment should be stored in a sailboat?

7. What are the procedures for storing a boat and its sails?
8. What specific knots are important to a sailor?
9. Explain the key points of sailing theory, i.e., *tack, reach, beat, run.*
10. What are jibing and coming about?
11. What are some basic safety rules for sailing?
12. What procedure should be followed if you get caught on the water without any wind?

SUGGESTED READINGS

American National Red Cross. *Basic Sailing.* Washington, D.C.: American National Red Cross, 1969.
Bottomley, T., ed. *Boat Man's Hand Book.* New York: Motor Boating and Sailing Books, 1975.
Brown, A. *Invitation to Sailing.* New York: Simon and Schuster, 1968.
Vaughan, L. K., and R. H. Stratton. *Canoeing and Sailing.* Dubuque, Iowa: William C. Brown Company, 1970.

fifteen

cross-country ski touring

Cross-country ski touring should be distinguished from cross-country skiing, which includes both racing and touring. Although the various techniques and equipment discussed in this chapter could be adapted for racing, there is no specific focus on racing. If you are interested in racing, you should refer to the Suggested Readings at the end of the chapter for information about specific racing techniques and conditioning programs.

To most people, cross-country ski touring means skiing across the countryside at one's own pace while enjoying the fresh air and the beauty of snow, trees, and hills. Touring is usually done at a leisurely pace on a marked or unmarked trail and may take a full day, half a day, or just two or three hours. It can be a means of experiencing companionship, solitude, vigorous activity, beautiful surroundings, quiet, speed, and excitement. Some people enjoy touring because they can get away from people, while others tour in order to be around people with similar interests.

Cross-country ski touring is usually referred to as Nordic Skiing, in contrast to Alpine or downhill skiing. It was developed and used in the Scandinavian countries primarily as a means of getting around in the harsh winter weather. Even though Nordic skiing is thought to be the older of the two types of skiing, at present it can be considered a counter movement to Alpine skiing. Not only is Nordic skiing much easier to learn, but it offers more freedom. For example, there are no nine-dollar lift tickets, no lift lines, and no cafeteria lines back in the lodge. Nordic equipment is also considerably less expensive than downhill equipment. Owing to all of these factors, the growth rate for cross-country ski touring has been tremendous, even though downhill skiers still outnumber tourers.

Touring gives you opportunities to explore new areas of the wilderness with all members of your family, regardless of ability, age, or sex. Very little practice time and mastery of only a few specific techniques are necessary in order for you to enjoy a leisurely tour across the countryside on skis. Beginners at ski touring experience success much more quickly than beginners at Alpine skiing.

Ski touring is also very good exercise, depending upon how fast you are traveling. All of the major parts of the body are involved (legs, arms, shoulders, stomach, lower back, and neck). The caloric expenditure is tremendous, and a certain degree of stretching and flexibility is required of all tourers.

Injuries incurred in cross-country touring are very minimal, especially in comparison to injuries resulting from downhill skiing. Margaret Bennett points out that studies show that out of 100,000 ski tourers, one or two probably suffer a broken bone or a severe sprain, whereas about 50 out of 100,000 downhill skiers will be injured.[1] In cross-country touring, there is no continual pressure to

---

[1] Margaret Bennett, *Cross-Country Skiing for the Fun of It* (New York: Ballantine Books, 1973), p. 6.·

try a steeper and more difficult slope. It is a much more relaxed activity than downhill skiing, and people can help others to enjoy the activity without the constant push to go faster, higher, or longer. There is little extrinsic pressure on the cross-country tourer unless she or he gets involved in a group of skiers who are trying to meet some self-imposed goal. Obviously, beginners should avoid this type of situation.

Touring can be a great addition to your winter sports repertoire. It is a simple way to hike through the woods and the great outdoors. It gives one a new excuse for observing and using our outdoor resources, and it can be a relaxing change from the madness of overcrowded downhill skiing. The combination of peacefulness and physical activity is one of its major attractions.

Ski touring does not have to preclude downhill skiing. You can certainly do both. Touring can serve as a conditioner, and you can tour when you just cannot make it to the lifts or when you know the lifts will be tremendously crowded. Touring is also possible when the snow conditions for downhill skiing are poor.

John Caldwell summarizes the scope of cross-country ski touring and the flexibility it allows:

> Cross-country skiing should be fun for everyone. The range of possibilities for enjoyment is unlimited. You can ski anywhere there's snow, you can use a wide variety of equipment, you can ski alone or with a group, you can use the very best techniques while wearing the clothes you just picked up from the local rummage sale, or you can wear the latest styles and invent your own technique.[2]

EQUIPMENT AND CLOTHING

Selecting the right ski equipment is very important. It is our opinion that everyone should rent equipment at first, because this will provide a basis for knowledgeable choices. It is also helpful to get the opinions of persons with ski touring experience. Remember that there are many high-quality brands of equipment on the market, and be sure to consider your own abilities and desires when purchasing equipment. Always deal with reputable people; that is more important than buying a particular brand.

Skis

Ski touring seems to be following the trends of downhill skiing as regards skis themselves. Wooden skies are slowly being replaced by synthetic skis, some of which have a wooden interior or a mixture of wood and fiberglass. Many of the skis with synthetic bottoms include fiberglass which has some pitch or pine tar added and a teflon-like material.

Many of the no-wax skis are becoming popular because people do not enjoy waxing and they are not concerned if their skis do not respond perfectly. The no-wax skis include fish-scale-type bottoms, variations of the fish scale, and mohair strips (see Figure 15-1). There have been several problems with some of the no-wax skis, for example, the mohair strips have slipped under certain conditions. However, many people enjoy this type of ski anyway. Be sure to try no-wax skis before you buy them.

There are three primary categories of cross-country skis:

1. *Touring ski.* This ski is wide, stable, heavy, durable and weighs about five or six pounds. Touring skis are easy to learn on and will sink very little in powder snow.
2. *Light touring ski.* This ski is narrower, less stable, lighter, more flexible, and less durable than the

[2]John Caldwell. *The New Cross-Country Ski Book,* 4th ed. (Brattleboro, Vt.: Stephen Greene Press, 1973), p. 7.

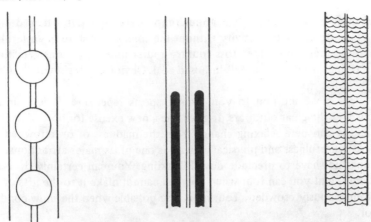

Figure 15-1. Synthetic ski bottoms

touring ski. Since the sport is emphasizing lightness and freedom, many people are learning on this ski. It weighs three or four pounds and is 2¼ inches wide.

3. *Racing ski.* This ski is two inches wide, weighs about two or three pounds, and is obviously very light, narrow, flexible, and less durable than the other two skis. Racing skis are made for racing and for well-groomed tracks. They might last one season or less. They are not for beginning skiers.

The flexibility and length of the ski are also important variables that should be considered. As a general rule, stiff skis work better on ice or hard-packed snow, while softer skis work better on soft or powder snow. If you are fairly sure about the usual snow conditions in your area, you may want to make a decision on the flexibility of your skis. Remember that if your skis are too stiff the wax will not reach the snow, and this can cause some problems.

The trend in downhill skiing is toward a shorter ski for more control and easier handling. In cross-country touring, however, most people believe that the better you get, the longer your ski should be. Some believe that your ski should be four inches taller than you are. The old rule of thumb is to stand with your arm extended overhead and then buy a ski that comes up to your wrist. Weight is usually considered a factor, the idea being that a little less weight should require a shorter ski and a little more weight would require a longer ski.

Ski bottoms are primarily wood, plastic impregnated or treated, or a no-wax surface. The wooden bottoms must go through the entire waxing process, which will be discussed later. The plastic bottoms are more durable and do not need the running wax. The no-wax ski is very durable and fast but does not respond perfectly under all snow conditions. Be sure to consider all of these variables.

Bindings

There are two major types of touring bindings—toe-clamp styles, and heel-cable styles that force the toe of the boot into a toe piece.

1. *Toe-clamp style.* This binding is much lighter than the heel cable and allows for a free-moving stride; however, it takes a bit more skill to control the ski with this style of binding. There are many toe-clamp styles available ranging from pins that attach to the boot sole, to step-in bindings that snap shut when you step into them. Most people prefer the toe-clamp binding because it permits the heel to move up and down.

2. *Heel-cable style.* This bindings is heavier than the toe clamp and restricts the total movement of the foot. With a heel-clamp binding it is easier to control the ski, especially for downhill

travel. This binding is much more durable and will probably last longer than a clamp binding. Regular hiking boots can be used as long as the boots actually fit the bindings.

Tourers also need a heel plate or another device called a pop-up. These are usually made of metal or rubber and are attached on the ski directly beneath the heel of the boot. They act as a de-icer and prevent snow from collecting under your boot. The edges of the heel plate are serrated and will help to keep your heel from slipping off the ski when you turn. Most skiers also place a pop-up under the ball of the foot up near the binding. This also prevents snow buildup and aids in the handling of the ski.

Boots

Touring boots are usually categorized similarly to touring skis—regular touring, light touring, and racing boots. Hiking boots can sometimes be adapted to certain bindings, but the soles are usually too stiff for ski touring. Touring boots need to have a flexible sole. Each boot has advantages and disadvantages.

1. *Regular touring boot.* This boot is usually higher, heavier, more durable, and has a heel groove for cable bindings. Regular touring boots are usually stiffer and provide additional warmth. Beginners are usually more comfortable with this type of boot, but someone with the time to work on technique may want to start with a lighter boot.
2. *Light touring boot.* This boot is about one-half pound lighter than the regular touring boot and is more flexible. It can be purchased with a high top or a top that comes just below the ankle.
3. *Racing boot.* This is a very light, flexible boot that provides very little warmth and is used only for racing.

Most boot soles are a molded or foam type. These are waterproof and are made to fit the specific bindings quite nicely. Leather soles are becoming a thing of the past.

It is important that boots fit well. Try the boot on with the type of sock that you will wear for skiing. We recommend wearing at least one pair of wool socks, and sometimes two pairs are preferable. A poorly fitted touring boot can be quite painful and cause blisters.

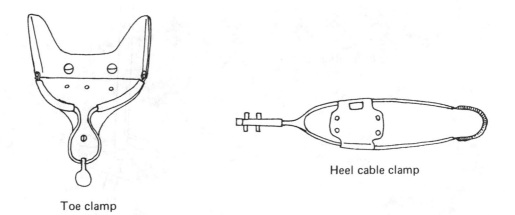

Toe clamp

Heel cable clamp

Figure 15-2. Bindings

Poles

The poles used in ski touring are lighter and longer than normal downhill poles. They also have a curved tip, which enables them to slip out of the snow easier once the skier has glided past that point. The baskets are larger, and some are being made slightly canted, as an aid in poling. The common materials for poles are bamboo, tonkin (strong bamboo), metal, fiberglass, and aluminum. Most people like to have an adjustable hand strap to accommodate changes in gloves or mittens. The pole should extend from the ground to the armpit or slightly beyond.

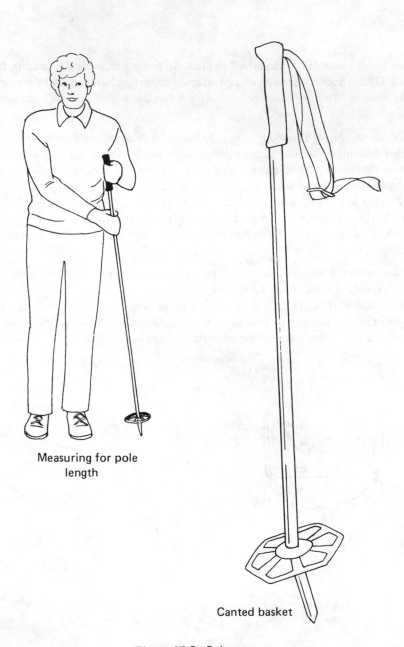

Measuring for pole
length

Canted basket

Figure 15-3. Poles

Table 15-1. Cost Analysis for Ski Touring Equipment

EQUIPMENT	LOW COST	HIGH COST
Skis	$ 30	$130
Boots	25	60
Bindings	12	35
Poles	8	30
Long underwear	12	25
Socks	2	4
Turtleneck	8	20
Knickers	18	30
Sweater	18	50
Mittens	8	25
Hat	8	15
Sunglasses	8	25
Backpack	10	50
Wax kit	15	30
Totals	$182	$529

Clothing

Dress for ski touring is strictly a matter of individual preference. There are many expensive, fancy ski clothes available—hats, parkas, knickers, warm-up pants, down jackets, sunglasses, sweaters, underwear, and backpacks. The choice depends on a person's interests and pocketbook. Here are a few basic suggestions that all beginning skiers should consider before venturing out into various kinds of weather:

1. Dress according to the weather. Be aware of the wind chill factor and the possibility of hypothermia. Many new skiers get themselves in trouble because they are not familiar with the actual weather conditions on the trails. Be sure to keep the extremities (hands, head, feet) covered adequately.
2. Avoid heavy perspiring. If you become extremely warm, start to ventilate by removing some excess clothing such as a hat, a jacket, or gloves. Wet underclothing can create problems as you cool down and the wind picks up.
3. Avoid tight-fitting or restrictive clothing, since touring requires a great deal of movement.
4. Avoid heavy clothing that will only slow you down and cause you to overheat. Remember, there are very few inactive periods during ski touring.
5. Try to keep your feet warm and dry. Wool socks and gaitors which fit snuggly over the top of the boot and the upper ankle will keep snow from getting into your boot.
6. Sunglasses or properly ventilated goggles can be used to protect the eyes on bright sunny days.
7. A variety of small backpacks are available for touring. They can be used to carry lunch, waxes, and first aid equipment.

Table 15-1 lists the usual ski touring equipment, with a cost breakdown for a low and a high price range.

WAXING

Waxing remains the mystical, ritualistic aspect of Nordic skiing. Many say that waxing is actually what separates lovers of Nordic skiing from lovers of Alpine skiing. There is no one method for all types of skis, skiers, or skiing conditions. Waxing can be the difference between a back-breaking, exhausting experience and a smooth, pleasant, exhilarating experience. Waxing enables the ski tourer to move effortlessly over a variety of terrains—gentle slopes or hills, flat lands, and downhill sections. Many tourers experience a great thrill of success after discovering the proper wax for specific conditions. Waxing becomes a tremendous challenge to many skiers. A constant debate or argument over waxing procedures seems to be inevitable.

There are three main reasons for waxing: (1) wax protects the ski, (2) it acts as a base for holding more wax, and (3) it facilitates the climbing and gliding of the ski. Wax works by providing a substance which the hexagonal crystals of snow can stick to during climbing. Then, during downhill or flat land motion, the wax permits the ski to slide forward over a small film of water that acts as a lubricant. If there is too little or too much penetration into the wax, the skier will slip backwards or have difficulty moving forward because of too much friction caused by excess wax.

To learn the art and science of waxing, one must first understand the terms. John Caldwell provides the following glossary:

> Running Waxes: These are the waxes you apply to your ski bottoms and actually ski on.
> Binders: Waxes that you apply to your ski for the purpose of holding the running waxes on better; therefore, all binders go on before running waxes, and then running waxes cover the binder.
> Base Waxes: Usually pine-tar compounds, used on wood-bottomed skis to help preserve them.
> Hard Waxes: Running waxes used primarily for powder snow. These waxes come in small tins or containers. Before application they give the appearance of being harder than klisters.
> Klister Waxes: Running waxes come in tubes, are very sticky, and if you get things messed up just right, can remind you of an underdone taffy-pull.
> Klister Snow: Snow that you use klister wax on—almost always snow that has melted and refrozen. There are two categories under this one—frozen granular snow, and corn snow.
> Frozen Granular Snow: Cold-dry, harsh snow that has melted at least once and refrozen. Westerners refer to it as "Eastern Powder Snow."
> Corn Snow: Granular snow which has started to melt and therefore is wet. It can be just a trifle moist or quite wet—depending on the temperature.
> Cork: A cork used to be a chunk of cork used for smoothing the wax after it's been daubed on the ski. However, nowadays a cork is a cork or something synthetic. But at least its use remains the same.[3]

The base or foundation wax is really only needed for wood bottoms. It is a pine-tar type of substance that protects the wood and makes it water repellent. It also serves as a binder for the running waxes. This wax can be painted, sprayed, or melted on the ski, depending on the type that you buy.

The binder wax is really not needed anymore because running waxes will usually stay on by themselves. However, a binder is sometimes necessary on a plastic ski bottom during certain conditions. Binders can be applied by heating the ski and then rubbing the wax on. A cork should be used with additional heat in order to smooth and thin out the wax. After the binder is dry, the running wax should be applied.

The running waxes include the hard waxes for snow that is in its original state and the soft klister waxes for snow that has melted and then refrozen. The running waxes are all color coded and there

---

[3]*Ibid.*, pp. 62-63.

are numerous types on the market. John Caldwell provides a wax equivalent table (see Table 15-2) and a waxing chart for Rex, Rode, and Swix brands of ski wax (see Table 15-3).

The best starting point for waxing is a look at the wax directions, the temperature chart, and the snow conditions chart. However, many skiers do not follow the chart exactly because of other variables such as height, weight, ski ability, strength, techniques, and waxing procedures. The ski waxer is not bound by one method; some skiers use a combination of waxes under various parts of the ski, such as the tips, the tails, or under the foot. Another general rule is that waxing is done in layers and the more uphill work involved, the more layers required.

All working waxes need to be removed before a new wax is applied. Waxing should be done when the ski is perfectly dry and preferably in a warm place, like a house. After you have completed waxing, the ski should be placed standing up in the outside temperature because if the wax is still warm, snow will collect on the wax in small balls. It is also common to rewax several times during the day as the snow conditions or terrains change. A wise skier will carry a variety of waxes to handle the varying conditions.

It seems important to select a wax that you have easy access to and are confident with. After trying a wax and finding out that it slips, then try thickening up the wax with another coat. Remember that you need a warmer or softer wax as the snow rounds off, collects moisture, and freezes. Some days, you may never find the correct wax for the existing conditions; this is part of the mystique of waxing. Another point to remember is that most skiers use a paraffin wax for the center groove of the ski in order to prevent icing and too much moisture.

It is impossible to develop a single waxing procedure to handle all situations. This is why experience in waxing becomes so important. Waxing is like selecting the correct golf club, baseball bat, or bait in fishing. Complete agreement will never occur and it becomes a matter of choice and personal experience.

TECHNIQUE

The techniques of ski-touring are relatively simple but they can produce some beautiful movements and accomplish some extraordinary things. Mark Heller points out the following:

> With these simple movements you can either produce a poetry of rhythm and motion with speeds in excess of a running man, which can be maintained for hours and countless miles, or a leisurely country walk through the winter landscape of sno-laden forest and windswept tundra.[4]

Some experts feel that specific techniques are not important and that moving across the countryside in any manner is certainly satisfactory as long as the individuals are having fun. We tend to agree with this point of view, but there are a few techniques that are valuable to all beginning tourers. In addition, many people want to improve specific techniques for a variety of reasons (speed, efficiency, distance, etc.).

Touring techniques can best be classified into flatland techniques, uphill techniques, and downhill techniques.

Diagonal Gait

The most common flatland technique is the diagonal gait or stride. The diagonal gait (Figure 15-4) starts with movement of the left leg and right arm working together in opposition to

[4]Mark Heller, *Ski* (London: Faber and Faber, 1969), p. 170.

Table 15-2. Wax Equivalents

	REX	RODE	SWIX	EX-ELIT	HOLMENKOL	TOKO	OSTBYE	BRATLIE
Hard waxes	Turquoise Special	Special Green	Special Green	Special Kold	Light Green	Olive	Mix	Silke
	Green	Green	Green	Green	Green	Green	Mix	Silke
	Blue	Blue	Blue	Blue	Blue	Blue	Medium	Blandingsfor
	Violet	Violet	Violet	Violet	Violet	Violet	Medium	Blandingsfor
	Red	Red	Red	Red	Red	Red	Mixolin	Klistervoks
	Yellow	Yellow	Yellow	Yellow	Klistervoks	Klistervoks	Klistervoks	Klistervoks
Klisters	Blue Klister	Blue Klister	Blue Klister	Skar Kristall	Blue Skare	Blue Klister	Skarevoks and Skare	Skarevoks and Green Klister
	Violet Klister	Violet Klister	Violet Klister	Skar Kristall To Kristall	Red Klister	Violet Klister	Mixolin Klister	Skare
	Red Klister	Red Klister	Red and Yellow Klisters	—	Yellow Klister	Red Klister	Klister	Vat Klister
	Silver Klister	Silver Klister	—	—	Silver Klister	—	—	—

Source: John Caldwell, *The New Cross-Country Ski Book*, 4th ed. (Brattleboro, Vt.: Stephen Greene Press, 1973), p. 64. Copyright © 1971, 1973 by John Caldwell.

Table 15-3. Waxing Chart for Rex, Rode, and Swix

AIR TEMP.	FINE NEW SNOW	OLD POWDER SNOW	GRANULAR SNOW (crusty or wet corn snow)
F.			
		Swix	Yellow Klister
40			
	Red	Red Klister	
35			Rex or Rode
32	Yellow	Red	Silver Klister
30	or	Purple	Purple Klister
28	Blue		
25		Blue	
20	Green		
15		Green	Blue
10			Klister
	Special	Green	
5			
0	Rex		
	Turquoise		
-5			

dry snow ———— increased moisture content ———→ wet snow

Source: John Caldwell, *The New Cross-Country Ski Book,* 4th ed. (Brattleboro, Vt.: Stephen Greene Press, 1973), p. 65. Copyright © 1971, 1973 by John Caldwell.

Note: Where no brand name is given, any may be used.

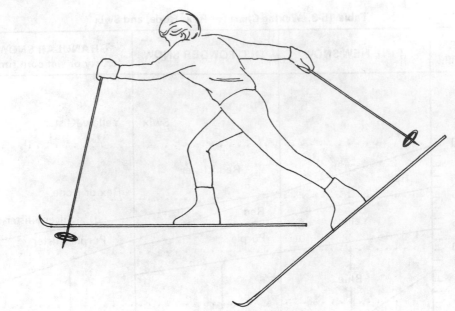

Figure 15-4. Diagonal gait

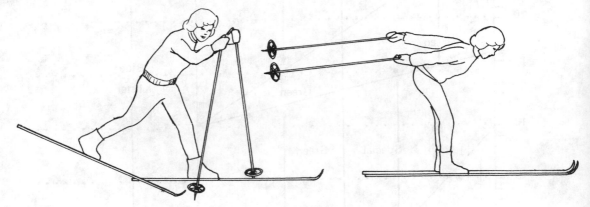

Figure 15-5. Double pole push

the right leg and left arm, similar to walking or running. There is a powerful forward driving motion with one leg and the opposite arm while the other arm and leg are extended backwards. While one set is moving forward, the opposite set is moving backward. There is a slide or glide in between movements and this helps to reduce fatigue. The forward leg drive is very important in being effective with this motion. Your body should have a slight forward lean or flex. The use of the arms and the poles is also very important. As your leg drive begins, the arm and pole on the same side should start to push forward. The arm and pole should be fairly close to the body to avoid wasted motion. Your hands should be placed correctly through the grips so that they will aid in your backward push on the poles. This gait should be learned without the poles and on flatland. It takes a great deal of practice in order to maintain proper balance, rhythm, and coordination. Some common errors include trying to use the arms too much, too much sideways or lateral motion, not enough knee drive, not enough backward extension, and hanging the back leg out too long.

Double Pole Push

The double pole push (Figure 15-5) is simply a forward movement with a push of both poles simultaneously. Both skis are parallel with the weight evenly distributed. The knees are slightly flexed with a slight forward body lean. A great deal of strength and balance is a necessity for this technique. You should try to swing your body weight into the motion to help you get more distance.

Tip Turns and Tail Turns

Tip turns and tail turns on flat areas (Figure 15-6) are made by keeping the ski tips (or tails) together and then moving the tails (or tips) around in a circle until the desired direction is obtained.

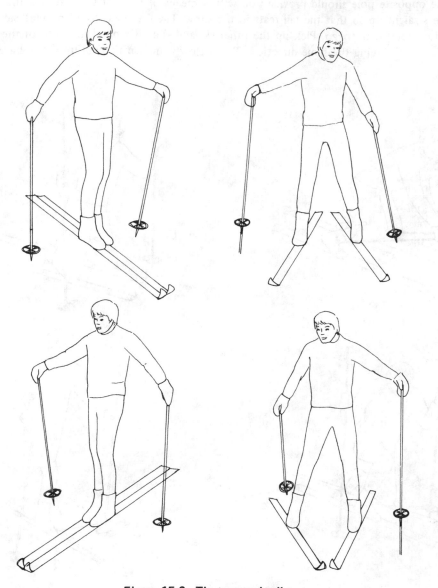

Figure 15-6. Tip turn and tail turn

Recovery from a Fall

Beginning skiers need to know the proper way to get up after a fall (Figure 15-7). Make sure that you get your skis going the same direction and that they are on the correct side of the body. Next, get up on one knee and use your poles, starting at about halfway up the poles. Then move to both knees or to one foot and then on up as you gain your balance. If you fall on a hill, make sure that you line your skis up across the hill and not up or down the hill.

Kick Turn

Another technique for turning is the kick turn (Figure 15-8). It is executed by turning the upper body slightly toward the turning direction. Place your pole on that side behind the tail of the opposite ski. The opposite pole should provide you with a means of balancing. Next, kick the ski on the turning side straight up so that the tail rests in the snow. Then, allow the ski tip to fall slowly in the new direction you want to go. Pick up the other ski and slide it around the boot of the other ski until they are both facing the same direction. Try it slowly and on flatland until you have the idea.

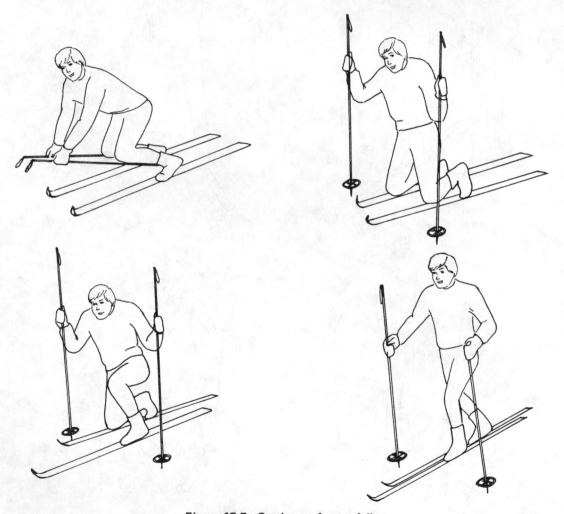

Figure 15-7. Getting up from a fall

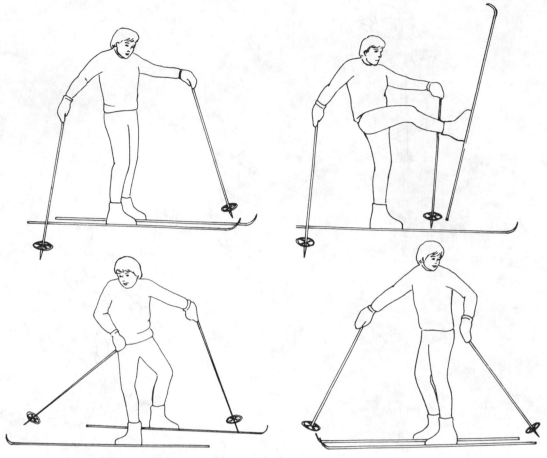

Figure 15-8. Kick turn

Skating Turn

The skating turn (Figure 15-9) is a very useful technique for rounding off corners while moving on flatland or down hill. This technique enables the skier to make turns without having to come to a complete stop. The skier begins by transferring his or her weight to the inside edge of the outside ski. The inside ski is then picked up and placed in the desired direction. Once the inside ski is placed on the snow, the weight is transferred to this ski and the outside ski is then moved parallel to the inside ski. The entire process is then repeated until the proper direction is acquired.

Diagonal Stride

Uphill techniques include the modified diagonal stride, the herringbone, and the sidestep. The modified diagonal stride is used for gentle slopes and areas that are slightly uphill. It cannot be used for climbing steep hills. In this technique the skier must use a bit more forward body lean, a slightly longer stride, and a much shorter glide period. The poles are placed in the snow right at the tip of the boot and are left in the snow slightly longer in order to avoid slipping backwards. As the hill gets steeper, the stride and glide will get shorter. Proper waxing will be quite beneficial for using this technique. Be sure to avoid attempting to muscle your way up the hill using only your arms. The arms are not nearly as strong as the legs.

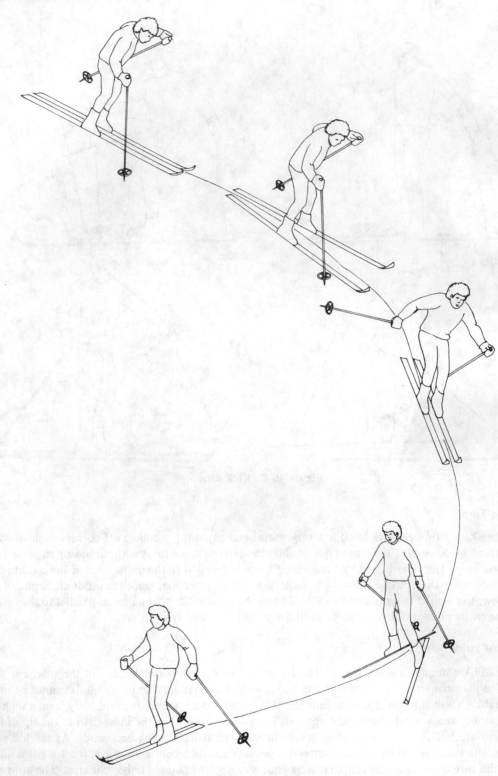

Figure 15-9. Skating turn

Figure 15-10. Herringbone

Herringbone

As the hills become steeper, you may want to change to a herringbone technique (Figure 15-10). The herringbone is a very quick, effective uphill technique, yet it is very tiring. The tips of the skis should be opened up very wide and the weight transferred to the inside edge of each ski. Alternate steps up the hill while keeping pressure on the inside edge of each ski. You need to grip the top of your poles and use them to push you forward. It is important to keep your skis wide apart in order to prevent the tails of your skis from crossing. The skis must remain in this *V* or herringbone pattern as you move up the hill.

Sidestep

The final uphill technique is the sidestep (Figure 15-11). In sidestepping, the skis must be turned across the hill or perpendicular to the fall line of the hill. The knees should be used to help bite the edges of the skis into the snow. The uphill ski is moved up the hill about a foot or so and then the downhill ski is brought up. The skis must be kept on their edges or they will slip back down the hill. The poles are used for pushing upwards and for balance. The sidestep is a very slow, tedious process that enables you to climb very steep areas. The sidestep can be combined with a forward slide in order to traverse a hill. These traverses can be linked to provide another uphill technique.

Snowplow Stop

Some additional downhill techniques that should be learned are the snowplow stop, the snow-plow turn, and the telemark position. The snowplow stop (Figure 15-12) is an important method for slowing down and stopping. It is executed by keeping the tips of the skis together and the tails far

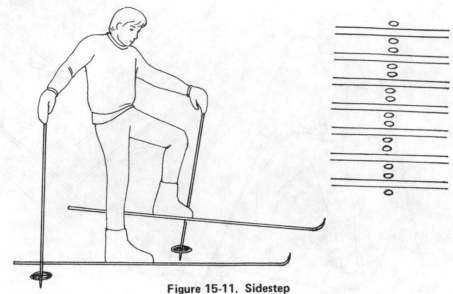

Figure 15-11. Sidestep

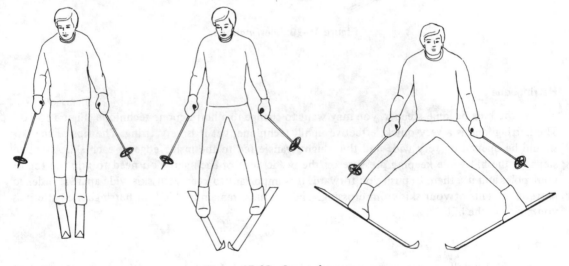

Figure 15-12. Snowplow stop

apart. The weight is transferred to the inside edge of both skis and pressure is exerted outward. This serves as a breaking action that can control the speed of the skier. The skier should remain in this position until he or she has gained control.

Snowplow Turn

The snowplow turn can be added to the snowplow stop by simply transferring the weight to the inside edge of the ski opposite the desired direction. For example, if you want to turn left, then put the weight on the inside edge of the right ski. This is an effective turning technique.

Telemark Position

The telemark position (Figure 15-13) can be used for turning, for traveling over rough or steep sections, or for handling bumps. In this position, either ski can be placed forward and the skier kneels slightly so that he or she is upon the toe of the rear foot. The front foot is relaxed and flat on the ski. The skis should be a comfortable distance apart (six to ten inches). The arms should be at the sides of the body and used for balance. You should be in a stable position. If you want to turn, stem the forward ski in the desired direction. It is easier if you put the opposite ski forward for turning; if you want to go left, place the right ski forward. The telemark is somewhat dated but can still be a very useful technique for certain ski conditions.

SAFETY PROCEDURES

Ski touring does include several inherent dangers that should be considered. Touring can be a vigorous activity and consequently should be attempted only in a moderate fashion by those who are in poor physical condition. If you are over thirty years old and have led a primarily sedentary life, then we encourage you to get a good physical examination. Please do not overdo a good thing like ski touring.

Hypothermia, the lowering of the body temperature, is a potential danger for skiers. Make sure that you understand the signs and methods of prevention. The spring can be a potential time of danger from hypothermia. Frostbite, which affects the body's extremities, can also be a problem in extremely cold weather.

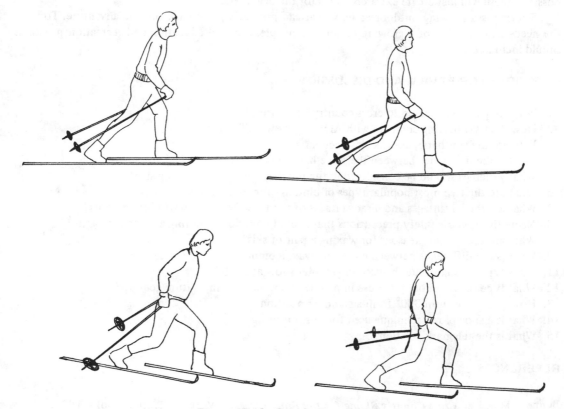

Figure 15-13. Telemark position

Some areas of the country are prone to avalanches. Make sure that you check with the park or forestry services before you enter an unknown area. It is also important for you to read available information on avalanches located in the reference section of this chapter.

It is also important to be careful in crossing small streams, bridges, roads, railroads, and fences. Each can provide its own unique challenge and danger. Use your own common sense and do not attempt foolish things that may end up in an accident or a broken ski.

TEACHING ACTIVITIES

Ski touring can easily be adapted to a school or recreation complex. The first step is to obtain the skiing equipment needed (skis, boots, bindings, and poles, etc.). A package deal may be available from your local dealer or you may be able to obtain some used equipment from a local ski area. Expensive and fancy equipment is not necessary to get a program started. You may be able to handle only a small group until you are able to build up a sufficient equipment base. Many fund-raising methods are available to you.

Ski paths can be made on the available grounds or in nearby woods. Remember, ski touring does not require any special terrain. It is best for beginners to learn on flatland and then slowly progress to uphill and downhill terrain. Make sure that you obtain the proper permission from various landowners. Local parks and recreation areas can usually be easily converted into ski touring paths.

Packed trails are easier to learn on, but, if you have enough people in a program, it will not be long until you have the trail well packed. Be careful to avoid bridges, roads, and creeks if at all possible; these will just create extra problems for the beginners.

Touring is a growing outdoor activity that can provide people with fun and adventure. To meet the needs and interests of a growing number of people, physical education and recreation programs should include this activity.

QUESTIONS FOR REVIEW AND DISCUSSION

1. Why are people attracted to cross-country ski touring?
2. How does ski touring compare with Alpine or downhill skiing?
3. Why are the synthetic, no-wax skis becoming so popular?
4. What is the difference between the three basic types of touring skis?
5. What variables should be considered in the purchase of a set of touring skis?
6. What are the two most popular types of bindings for touring skis?
7. What are the advantages and disadvantages of the three basic types of touring boots?
8. Name five specific safety precautions that should be followed during a ski touring trip.
9. What are the primary reasons for waxing a pair of skis?
10. What is the difference between a running wax, a binder wax, and a base wax?
11. What type of wax should be used in granular snow at 25°F?
12. What type of wax should you use in powder snow as the temperature goes up?
13. How can a skier turn 360° from a standing position?
14. What is a snowplow technique used for in ski touring?
15. What is the telemark position?

REFERENCES

Bennett, Margaret. *Cross-Country Skiing for the Fun of It.* New York: Ballantine Books, 1973.
Caldwell, John. *The New Cross-Country Ski Book.* 4th ed. Brattleboro, Vt.: Stephen Greene Press, 1973.
Heller, Mark. *Ski.* London: Faber and Faber, 1969.

SUGGESTED READINGS

Brady, Michael. *Nordic Touring and Cross-Country Skiing.* Oslo: Dreyers Forlag, 1966.

Brower, David, ed. *The Sierra Club Manual of Ski Mountaineering.* New York: Ballantine Books, 1969.

Caldwell, John. *Caldwell on Cross-Country.* Brattleboro, Vt.: Stephen Greene Press, 1975.

Lund, Martin. *The Pleasures of Cross-Country Skiing.* New York: E. P. Dutton & Co., 1972.

Nelson, Russell. "Touring Ski Repair." *Wilderness Camping,* February/March 1977.

Tejoda-Flores, Lito, and Allen Steck. *Wilderness Skiing.* San Francisco: Sierra Club Books, 1972.

U.S. Ski Association, Rocky Mountain Division, Ski Touring Instructors' Certification Subcommittee. *Ski Touring Instructor's Manual.* Denver, 1970.

sixteen

snowshoeing

Snowshoeing is a form of winter travel that can be considered a close approximation to cross-country ski touring. It began about 4000 BC in central Asia and has been important to all groups of people that have lived in areas covered by vast amounts of snow. Various groups of Indians have been given credit for designing and improving the early forms of snowshoes.[1] Hunters, trappers, fishermen, and explorers have made use of this mode of travel for many years. The popularity of the snowshoe began to dwindle in the early 1960s because of the rising interest in cross-country skiing. The skis offered a much faster means of travel. Skiing is still growing in popularity, but there are many people who still enjoy the ancient form of travel for a variety of reasons.

Most modern snowshoers enjoy the excitement and adventure of a snowy, wintry terrain. The quiet solitude of a snow-covered forest with various animals and their tracks is exciting to many snowshoers. Other snowshoers enjoy a relaxing trip into the outdoors to escape the tensions and pressures of modern living. Still others point to the physical benefits of snowshoeing, especially for cardiovascular and respiratory functioning. Snowshoeing can be very vigorous or quite moderate, depending on one's purpose. Osgood and Hurley point out that "those who have enjoyed the pleasures of slipping quietly through the snow covered forest aisles need not be reminded of the satisfaction that snowshoeing offers to all who claim an affinity with nature in winter.[2]

Snowshoes still provide certain groups of people such as telephone linesmen, electric power linesmen, surveyors, foresters, rangers, and game wardens with a useful mode of transportation. Snowmobile enthusiasts usually carry a pair of cross-country skis or snowshoes in case of a mechanical failure.

EQUIPMENT AND CLOTHING

Clothing for snowshoeing is similar to clothing for cross-country skiing (see Chapter 15). Individuals can dress more or less according to personal taste. It is important to be dressed properly for the prevailing weather conditions. If you are underdressed, the cold will possibly ruin a pleasant afternoon trip and, at worst, result in a case of hypothermia. If you are overdressed, the heat will make you uncomfortable and may cause you to perspire. It is best for beginners to ask those with experience in traveling during various weather conditions for specific advice. Be sure to read the sections on safety for winter traveling in the chapter on ski touring.

[1] William Osgood and Leslie Hurley, *The Snowshoe Book* (Brattleboro, Vt.: Stephen Greene Press, 1973), pp. 12-16.
[2] *Ibid.,* p. 11.

Snowshoes

A popular new snowshoe on the market today is the polypropylene plastic model, which is one entire unit with a plastic hinge. These models, called snowtreads, are a modified form of the bearpaw snowshoes . (See Figure 16-1). They are very light, durable, and inexpensive. They require very little maintenance and are useful for short distances. However, they are somewhat unstable and will tilt laterally in the snow. They also tend to pick up snow because of the short tail; this causes the snowshoer to collect snow on the back of the legs.

The round or oval-shaped bearpaw is very good for areas with many trees and dense vegetation. Turning and maneuvering are quite easy with this model. The disadvantages are similar to those of the plastic snowtread.

The bearpaw has been modified several times in order to produce a more efficient snowshoe. Proabably the most popular is the Green Mountain modified bearpaw.

Another snowshoe model that is useful for trails and open areas is the Maine style, which is also referred to as the Michigan style. It has a longer tail, which makes it easier to stay on a straight course. It also has a wide, up-turned nose.

Another popular model in the United States is the Alaskan style. These snowshoes are very long and narrow with an up-turned nose. They are very efficient in deep snow, but cumbersome in areas that require many turns. Because of their length, they are much more stable than the other snowshoes that have been described. They are easy to learn on in open areas, and many people recommend them for beginners.

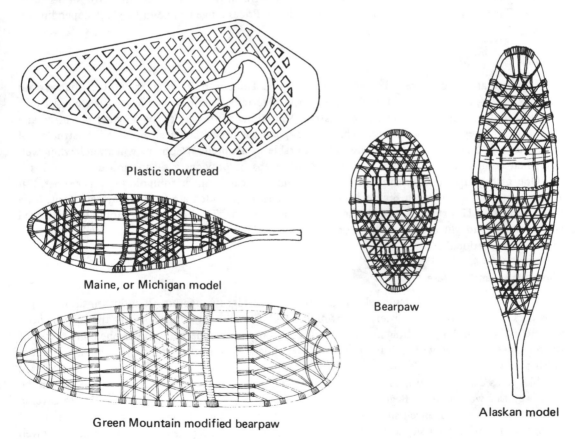

Plastic snowtread

Maine, or Michigan model

Green Mountain modified bearpaw

Bearpaw

Alaskan model

Figure 16-1. Snowshoes

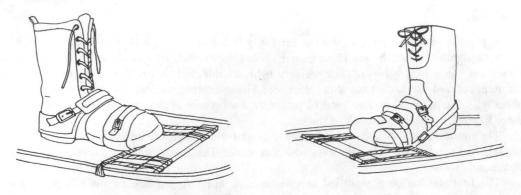

Figure 16-2. Bindings

Try a variety of snowshoes before making a final decision. Most dealers will provide some demonstration models. Take a careful look at the areas where you will be going—the snow conditions, the terrain, and the frequency with which you will be using the snowshoes. The maintenance factor should also be given considerable attention. Many prefer a snowshoe that requires little or no maintenance. Check into this before making a final decision. Prices range from $45 to $100, depending on the size, style, and materials.

Bindings

Bindings are a controversial topic in snowshoeing. The controversy lies in the fact that various bindings are reportedly better for different types of terrain. The most common styles consist of a toe piece with a heel strap and an instep strap. Variations of this style have a wider toe piece and tongue that cover the complete toe. This style is good for downhill travel. Bindings constructed of leather are good for the purist, but are not as durable as neoprene. Neoprene will stretch when wet, but when combined with buckles for closures of straps, it provides a secure and comfortable fit.

One of the most inexpensive and functional bindings can be made from old tire inner tubes. Cut a tire inner tube as shown in Figure 16-3. The dimensions provided are to fit an average foot; for a larger foot, size 12 or bigger, add one inch to each dimension. Tie-down points should be reinforced with patches and glued down with neoprene cement. This type of binding is especially good for school or recreational use.

Boots, Poles, and Ice Axe

When selecting boots for snowshoeing, you must consider two factors, fit and warmth. Improper fit will cause discomfort and blisters on downhill travel if the toe is too tight. A very tight-fitting boot will cut off circulation, resulting in cold feet. A good boot on the market today is one constructed of rubber soles and sides with a leather top with felt liners for warmth. Army-style "Mickey Mouse" boots also work exceptionally well.

Ski poles can be easily used for snowshoeing. They are good for balance and can be used in the same way as a walking stick. Beginners should use two ski poles when they are just starting to develop skill on snowshoes. Advanced snowshoers may want to carry an ice axe in order to prevent a long fall down the side of a steep slope. An ice axe can be fitted with a ski pole basket for deep snow travel. An ice axe of 85 centimeters or longer is recommended.

BASIC SKILLS

Traveling on snowshoes is almost as simple as walking. A beginner can experience success in a matter of minutes, and long training periods are not necessary. This is the beauty of snowshoeing.

The best way for a beginner to learn snowshoeing is to use a longer, narrower snowshoe such as the Maine model or a modified bearpaw, which will give greater stability. A hard-packed trail should be selected and a pair of ski poles should be used for added balance and security. The snowshoers should try to use a normal walking gait and remember to pick up each foot so that the edge of the snowshoe does not get tangled with the opposite snowshoe. The feet do not have to be extra wide apart. The normal walking gait should be emphasized. A slight pause after each step will aid the snowshoer since this allows the snow to settle after each step, making it easier to push off on the next step. Some people suggest a slight lateral shifting of weight for added balance and fluidity of movement. This is really an individual preference and will be determined by experience.

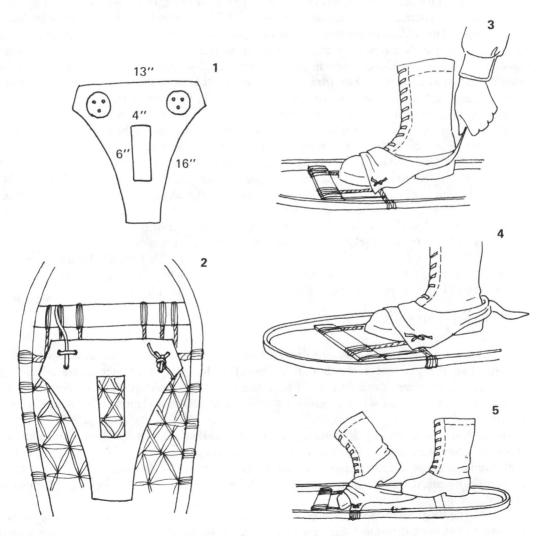

Figure 16-3. Inner tube bindings

After the beginner feels comfortable on a hard-packed track, he or she should move to the deep powdery snow and learn to break a new trail. This requires a shortened stride and a hard plant with the heel in order to keep the tips from sinking too far in the snow. Breaking a trail requires a considerable amount of strength and energy. Be sure to be aware of overdoing the trail-breaking aspect. Sore muscles may result from too much time spent trail breaking.

Turning on snowshoes can present a considerable problem for the beginner. We suggest the tip turn, the tail turn, and the kick turn. These techniques are exactly the same for snowshoes as for skis. Please refer to the explanation and diagrams in Chapter 15. Backing up is another problem that can be solved by using poles to hold the toes of the snowshoes down while moving the snowshoes backwards. Poles can also be used as an aid in getting up after a fall in the soft snow. It is important to make sure that your snowshoes are as flat as possible and are across the side of a hill before you try to get up from a fall. Trees and bushes can also be relied upon for assistance. Only as a last resort should a person take off the snowshoes and use them as an aid in standing up. Try to avoid much rolling and thrashing around. This is one reason why snowshoers should go out in groups.

For uphill travel on gentle slopes, snowshoers can use the same techniques as on flat land. As the hills get steeper, a herringbone technique may be useful. The traverse is probably the best method for steeper slopes. This technique involves making a diagonal cut across the hill, turning around, and then making another cut back across the hill. As the slope becomes very steep, the snowshoer must dig the edges of the snowshoes into the snow in order to avoid slipping sideways on the hill. Edging on snowshoes is a much more difficult task than on skis. The weight must be placed on the inside edge of the snowshoe and each step should be firm in order to hold in the snow. Obviously, this technique is much easier to learn with a narrow snowshoe such as the Maine or Alaskan models.

Moving downhill can be a problem because some bindings may cause the toe of the boot to catch beneath the snowshoe. This can be avoided by tightening the toe piece of the binding before going downhill. When traveling downhill, it is important to lean back a bit more than normal. The weight should be on the heels in order to raise up the snowshoe tips. It may be possible to slide down some specific hills with hard-packed snow. Simply slide one snowshoe ahead of the other and then kneel or sit down on the back snowshoe. Be careful that you do not get out of control and be sure to look for possible obstacles. Keep your poles behind you to prevent them from getting caught in front of you, and also use them for a brake or rudder by dragging them in the snow.

The easiest way for a group of snowshoers to travel is single file because this allows people to take turns breaking the trail, the most exhausting aspect of traveling. It is also important to give the person in front of you enough room so that you do not step on his or her snowshoes.

SAFETY PROCEDURES

Snowshoeing is subject to the same dangers that exist in other outdoor winter activities, namely, frostbite, hypothermia, and avalanches. It is important for you to become aware of the signs, symptoms, and treatment procedures for these common outdoor problems. We also mentioned that a good physical examination was a necessity for all vigorous activities. This also holds true for snowshoeing.

We also recommend that you travel in groups of no less than three or four in case someone has to go for help. Someone in the group should have an emergency kit with medical supplies, repair equipment, compass, maps, matches, and other materials (depending on the length of your expedition). Avoid long, overnight trips without someone who has experience in winter travel and is familiar with the area.

Avoid traveling on frozen bodies of water unless you are sure that they are frozen solid. Be prepared to get your snowshoes off in a hurry in case the ice should give way. Practice unfastening your bindings quickly. Be careful while crossing various ravines, valleys, and gullies because snowshoes will break. Unlike most types of skis, they were not made for covering moguls and bumps. In crossing over a fallen log, turn your snowshoes sideways and step on or over the log if possible.

If you are traveling in woods with a lot of fallen trees and bushes, remember that your snowshoes will slip on other pieces of wood. Exercising caution may prevent an unexpected injury. It is also important to remember that a broken snowshoe can cause a great deal of trouble if you are far from help. However, with some ingenuity, repairs can be made. Do not panic if you break a snowshoe.

TEACHING ACTIVITIES

Snowshoes can sometimes be obtained from army surplus stores. Dealers will sometimes provide special rates for schools and recreation groups. Check into all of the options in your area before you make a final decision. It is a good idea to build up a supply large enough so that all members of a program can have snowshoes. Inner tube bindings are inexpensive and easy to use.

Paths can be made on available grounds or in nearby woods. Access to a variety of terrains can add to the fun and excitement of the program. Once students have developed enough competency to move about on the snowshoes, a variety of sports and games can be added to the snowshoeing program. Sprint races, distance races, hurdles, relays, baseball, dodgeball, football, and orienteering activities can all be fun on snowshoes.

QUESTIONS FOR REVIEW AND DISCUSSION

1. Why are snowshoes still an important means of winter travel for some people?
2. What kinds of people make use of snowshoes?
3. What are the five most popular models of snowshoes?
4. Which model is best for the beginner?
5. Why are snowshoe bindings a controversial area among experts?
6. How can an inner tube be used as a binding?
7. What skills need to be mastered by a beginning snowshoer?
8. What safety problems may occur during a snowshoeing expedition?
9. How should a snowshoer cross a fallen log or tree?
10. What kinds of games or activities can take place while wearing snowshoes?

REFERENCES

Osgood, William, and Leslie Hurley. *The Snowshoe Book.* Brattleboro, Vt.: Stephen Greene Press, 1973.

SUGGESTED READINGS

Kjellstrom, Bjorn. *Be Expert with Map and Compass.* Harrisburg, Pa.: Stackpole Books, 1967.
Prater, Gene. *Snowshoe Hikes in the Cascades and Olympics.* Seattle: The Mountaineers, 1969.
——. *Snowshoeing.* Seattle: The Mountaineers, 1974.

seventeen

future of outdoor adventure activities

The future of virtually all types of outdoor activities is quite bright. More and more people are pursuing activities that make use of our earth's various environments—mountains, deserts, hills, rocks, lakes, rivers, streams, and snow. Current professional literature in the fields of recreation and physical education suggests that the popularity of these activities will continue to grow. For example, Max Cogan points to the popularity of the following new and innovative activities in college instructional programs: skin diving, scuba diving, mountain climbing, orienteering, camping, kayaking, hiking, canoeing, and sailing.[1]

Daryl Siedentop has said: "Perhaps the most important programmatic innovation in physical education during the past decade is the current emphasis on outdoor pursuits. Not since lifetime sports were added to the traditional offerings of gymnastics and team games has the general physical education curriculum been so radically altered."[2]

Robert Singer has pointed out the popularity of mountaineering, orienteering, rock climbing, snow skiing, ski touring, water skiing, canoeing, sailing, angling, skydiving, and deep-sea fishing in various programs across the country.[3] The February 1975 issue of the *Journal of Physical Education and Recreation* focuses on a variety of fresh ideas for physical education programs in the area of outdoor pursuits such as orienteering, cycling, canoeing, and sailing.[4] Jim Whittaker, the noted mountain climber and recreational equipment promoter, has cited the tremendous growth of backpacking, camping, and mountaineering, particularly since the mid-1960s.[5] In addition, Harvey Manning points out that more than 20 million Americans have already tried some form of backpacking.[6]

Statistics seem to indicate that many more people are making use of our national parks and forest systems in addition to the growing number of commercial campgrounds that are being used. Many campgrounds are now requiring reservations several weeks or months in advance, especially during the summer months. Hiking and camping areas that were once secluded are now crowded and overrun with people.

---

[1] Max Cogan, "Innovative Ideas in College Physical Education," *JOHPER* 44 (February 1973):28-29.

[2] Daryl Siedentop, *Physical Education—Introductory Analysis.* 2nd ed. (Dubuque, Iowa: William C. Brown Company, 1976), p. 179.

[3] Robert N. Singer, ed., *Physical Education: Foundations* (New York: Holt, Rinehart and Winston, 1976), pp. 381-388.

[4] "Fresh Ideas for College Physical Education," *JOPER* 46 (February 1975):37-44.

[5] Jim Whittaker, Foreword, in Harvey Manning, *Backpacking—One Step at a Time* (Seattle: REI Press, 1972), pp. v-vii.

[6] Harvey Manning, *Backpacking—One Step at a Time* (Seattle: REI Press, 1972).

Summer workshops, clinics, and courses are being offered in the area of outdoor pursuits. The April 1976 issue of the *Journal of Physical Education and Recreation* indicated the offering of nine workshops for the following summer at such institutions as the University of Utah, the University of California at Davis, the University of Maine at Portland-Gorham, the University of Northern Colorado, and the University of Montana.[7] Topics included a wide range of activities—cycling, canoeing, arts and crafts, trout fishing, and outdoor education curriculums. These offerings add strength to the argument that these activities are indeed gaining popularity.

Many recreation programs across the country are also incorporating outdoor activities into their programs. For example, the city recreation department in Saco, Maine recently completed an extensive ropes course, which will be available to participants in their program. These programs are offering instruction as well as participation in various outdoor activities.

SUCCESS-ORIENTED ACTIVITIES

While there are a number of reasons to explain the popularity of outdoor activities, we feel that one major reason for the popularity is that the activities tend to be success oriented. Robert Singer suggests that these activities are popular because they provide people with a certain amount of success in a relatively short time span.[8] The requirements for strength, endurance, speed, eye-hand coordination, and motor skill in general are not extensive. Students who do not possess a great deal of athletic ability will still have an excellent chance to become competent or accomplished performers in many of these pursuits.

In addition, it seems that students enjoy the idea of being able to express their individuality in various types of activities. Most adventure activities lend themselves nicely to this idea: for example, dress requirements are wide open, the activities can be performed alone, with a small or large group of people, and the requirements for specific types of behavior are few.

The competitive aspect between individuals or groups is usually reduced or eliminated in these types of activities. Participants are competing against themselves or against an element in their environment such as hills, rocks, rivers, or snow. Many people dislike activities that continually pit them against other people. In addition, these activities also lend themselves to co-ed participation since requirements for strength, endurance, and speed are minimal. Students also seem to enjoy instructional and recreational environments that are co-ed. With the nationwide implications of Title IX and co-ed participation, outdoor activities should be a valuable asset to recreation programs and physical education curriculums.

LEISURE TIME, MOBILITY, AND ECONOMICS

The concept of leisure has received growing recognition over the past few years. It is still misunderstood by many people but it is generally accepted in our society. Experts in the area of leisure pursuits point out the continued trend toward more leisure time, changes in lifestyle, more money for recreational activities, and greater mobility. Work weeks have slowly decreased to a point where Americans are averaging less than forty working hours per week. Weekends, holidays, and longer vacation periods are providing people with enormous amounts of free time. Estimates indicate that there will be 600 billion more leisure hours in the year 2000 than in 1950.

---

[7] "Summer Workshops in Outdoor Education," *JOPER* 47 (April 1976):57.
[8] Singer, pp. 386-388.

Verhoven and Vinton point out that the leisure industry accounted for $150 billion in 1971 and that this figure will continue to increase as salaries continue to grow.[9] People are going to spend additional money in the areas of recreational or leisure pursuits.

The mobility of Americans has obviously increased and will continue in this direction. People are traveling greater distances in order to pursue recreational activities. The American Automobile Association has estimated that Americans travel in excess of 225 billion miles per year to and from various recreational areas. This travel ability will provide people with access to many outdoor areas and activities in their particular geographic location.

It seems reasonable to suggest that increased leisure time, mobility, and finances will have an effect on the number of people participating in various types of outdoor activities. More people will want to become involved because of increases in these three variables.

CONCERN FOR THE ENVIRONMENT

As people have become more aware of the various problems that are having a negative effect upon our environment, many have rekindled an interest in using the environment as a means for recreational or leisure pursuits. Environmental issues that focus on wilderness permits, dams on rivers, and preservation of natural gamelands have awakened a new spirit in many, and people are realizing that the environment needs to be protected in order for all to make use of its varying terrain.

POPULATION GROWTH

The growth of our cities and urban areas will slowly reduce the amount of room or space that each person can call his or her own area. People are looking for ways to get away from the highly populated areas for at least a brief period of time. Various outdoor areas and programs are going to provide such opportunities.

RISK AND ADVENTURE

We believe that the popularity of outdoor activities will also continue because of the elements of risk and adventure inherent in them. New challenges, activities, and environments give people a variety of new and different experiences which increase the excitement and adventure in their lives. This final reason for the continuation of the growing popularity of outdoor activities may be one of the most attractive features of the program.

It seems extremely valuable for various recreation and physical education programs to develop opportunities for including these types of programs in their respective curriculums. The popularity of these programs is unquestioned. Learning the various physical skills, techniques, environmental skills, and safety factors should be done in a systematic, logical, progression and not in a trial and error fashion which could result in a personal tragedy. Consider the experience of the author in the following narrative:

> It was a bright sunny morning in the Pocono Mountains, near the Delaware Water Gap on the Pennsylvania–New Jersey border. A young faculty member and two graduate assistants from East Stroudsburg State College decided to take a climb up the side of a rock face located on the New Jersey side of the Delaware Water Gap.

---

[9] Peter J. Verhoven and Dennis A. Vinton, *Career Education: The Leisure Occupation Cluster* (Columbus: Center for Vocational and Technical Education, Ohio State University, 1973).

Two of the three individuals had a very minimal amount of rock-climbing experience; the third individual was a beginner. These three picked up a variety of gear from the college, including ropes, carabiners, bolts, chocks, ring descenders, and webbing for seats. However, they failed to pick up any protection for their heads, because the available helmets had already been checked out by another group. Helmets are a necessity for any type of rock climbing because of the possibility of falling rocks, debris, or equipment.

These climbers proceeded up the side of the rock face without any major problems. The climb was to take place in three stages, with rest stops on two ledges located on the side of the face. Trees were located on each ledge and were to be used as security points for belaying and rappelling during the climb and the descent. At the first ledge, which was about 75 feet from the ground, the beginning climber decided that he did not want to go any higher and would wait on this ledge while the others continued up the face. The other two continued up to the second ledge and on to the top of the rock face without any problems.

The descent of the face was to include a three-stage rappel with stops on each of the ledges below. The two climbers looped a rope around a tree at the top of the face, and the first person started rappelling down. As this person continued down, the rappel rope must have loosened several small and medium-sized rocks above the rappeller. One of these rocks hit the rappeller on the head and stunned him momentarily. He continued on down to the upper ledge and found out that the rock had opened a good-sized gash on his head. He immediately applied pressure on the cut and waited for the second rappeller to come down. As the second rappeller arrived, they applied pressure with a T-shirt and succeeded in stopping the bleeding. They set up the second stage of the rappel and made it down to the lower ledge where the beginning climber was waiting.

Once the final stage of the rappel had been rigged, the injured person went down first. The beginner, who was rappelling for the first time, went second and made it to the bottom, visibly shaken but unharmed. Luckily, they all made it down to the bottom of the face. The injured person was taken to the hospital, where he received about 15 stitches to close the wound. All three climbers learned a lesson the hard way even though it could have been much worse.

This experience illustrates several points. The most important focuses on the need for proper instruction in outdoor activities that involve a certain amount of risk. It is essential for people to receive the proper training in order to avoid tragic experiences. Many accidents have occurred because people have participated in various activities without an adequate amount of skill or knowledge. Recreation programs and physical education programs must make sure that they are providing experiences for people that ensure a safe and prosperous outing.

CONCLUSION

This tremendous growth in outdoor activities is going to create obvious environmental and instructional problems for various programs. Qualified teachers, leaders, and administrators will be in great demand. It seems important for college and university recreation and physical education programs to provide the necessary experiences for preparing people with this type of expertise. Specialists in outdoor activities should be able to make a valuable contribution to this particular need in American education.

People are going to need specialized training in the various techniques of preserving the environment while participating in these activities. The future of our environment and the opportunities for making use of the environment will depend upon how effective our various education programs will be in changing peoples' behavior. Recreation programs and physical education programs must be given a large responsibility in this area in order to meet the needs of the American people and to preserve the natural environment of our earth.

QUESTIONS FOR REVIEW AND DISCUSSION

1. What evidence is there to indicate that activities involving adventure and risk are gaining popularity?
2. Why do these activities provide people with some type of instant success?
3. Why are some people disenchanted with traditional physical activities?
4. Why are individualists attracted to these activities?
5. How has increased mobility facilitated the growth of these activities?
6. What services should physical education and recreation programs provide for people relative to these outdoor programs?
7. What future trends do you see for outdoor activities?

REFERENCES

Books

Manning, Harvey. *Backpacking—One Step at a Time.* Seattle: REI Press, 1972.

Siedentop, Daryl. *Physical Education—Introductory Analysis.* 2nd ed. Dubuque, Iowa: William C. Brown Company, 1976.

Singer, Robert N., ed. *Physical Education: Foundations.* New York: Holt, Rinehart and Winston, 1976.

Articles

Cogan, Max. "Innovative Ideas in College Physical Education." *JOHPER* 44 (February 1973):28-29.

"Fresh Ideas for College Physical Education." *JOPER* 46 (February 1975):37-44.

U.S. Department of the Interior, Bureau of Outdoor Recreation. *Selected Outdoor Recreation Statistics.* Washington, D.C.: U.S. Government Printing Office, 1971.

Verhoven, Peter J., and Dennis A. Vinton. *Career Education: The Leisure Occupations Cluster.* Columbus: Center for Vocational and Technical Education, Ohio State University, 1973.

appendix a

programs in outdoor adventure activities

Breckenridge Outdoor Education Center
P.O. Box 168
Breckenridge, Colorado 80424

The Breckenridge Outdoor Education Center is a nonprofit organization dedicated to the development and maintenance of an alternative adaptive program and activities research model to (1) employ experiential education to minimize the handicap of disabled persons and (2) maximize the opportunities for disabled and ablebodied persons to serve one another in reaching toward a common goal of attaining higher levels of awareness.

EMS Adventures
1041 Commonwealth Avenue
Boston, Massachusetts 02215

EMS Adventures offers personal and challenging leisure experiences on several continents. Activities include hiking, backpacking, mountaineering, river running, and photo safaris. Areas explored include the Grand Canyon, the Canadian Rockies, the North Cascades, British Columbia, Zambia, and Mexico.

Grand Canyon Youth Expeditions
Dick and Susan McCallum
R.R. 2, Box 755
Flagstaff, Arizona 86001
(602) 774-8176

Grand Canyon Youth Expeditions is an action-oriented river trip program designed for young people between the ages of 16 and 26 (with exceptions). The program stresses self-reliance, problem solving, nature, responsibility and challenge. Each river trip is limited to 20 per group. Trips are conducted on the Grand Canyon River and the Colorado River.

Homeward Bound
Allan A. Collette, Superintendent
Department of Youth Services
Commonwealth of Massachusetts
Brewster, Massachusetts 02631

The Homeward Bound Program is an alternative to institutionalization for male youth offenders between the ages of 14 and 17. Phase I is a one-week orientation period during which the boys are taught map and compass, campcraft, basics of rowing, sailing, canoeing, and kayaking, first aid, and basics of rock climbing. Phase II, modeled after the Outward Bound program, uses the lessons from Phase I in addition to the run-and-dip, 100-mile expeditions, and three-day solo experience. The major goal is to develop self-reliance, self-discipline, and self-confidence.

The Infinite Odyssey
14 Union Park Street
Boston, Massachusetts 02118
(617) 542-0060

The Infinite Odyssey is an educational, nonprofit organization whose primary purpose is to involve high school and college students in educational, experiential outdoor expeditions in North America. Emphasis is placed on group responsibility, environmental awareness and the ability to adapt to the challenges of the wilderness. The program is designed for men and women 16 years and older. Applicants must be in good health and be prepared to take part in strenuous activities. No prior experience is necessary for participation on most trips. Small groups with a maximum of 12 participants travel with two experienced leaders.

Nantahala Outdoor Center
Star Route Box 68
Bryson City, North Carolina 28713

The Nantahala Outdoor Center emphasizes the whitewater training program which includes some of the best paddlers in the country for both kayak and canoe. Scheduled programs vary in length and intensity depending upon the needs and interests of the group or individual. Other activities include raft trips, backpacking, rock climbing, and orienteering. Emphasis includes river safety, navigation, and conservation.

National Outdoor Leadership School
Box AA
Lander, Wyoming 82520
(307) 332-4381

NOLS is a private, nonprofit educational institution and licensed private school, which teaches wilderness skills and leadership year round. Courses range from two weeks to full sixteen week semesters, and operate in Kenya, Baja, Alaska, Washington, Wyoming, Montana, and Utah. Specialty courses include women's mountaineering, speleology, and fly fishing. College credit in Outdoor Education, Biology, and Geology is available for most courses.

Outward Bound
165 West Putnam Avenue
Greenwich, Connecticut 06830
(203) 661-0797

Outward Bound in the United States encompasses six schools and the Dartmouth Outward Bound Center. Courses are offered year-round and vary in content with season and terrain. Each school features a major activity focus, such as sailing, mountaineering, backpacking, skiing, canoeing, and river rafting. You can do more than you think you can. When a person is forced to deal with an environment of understandable stress, he or she comes to grips with elements that may be tapped at a later time.

Students come to a greater knowledge of themselves through a direct encounter with a wilderness setting; they learn teamwork from close involvement with others in their small patrol. Outward Bound schools provide courses for adults as well as boys and girls 16½ years and older. There are coed groups and special seminars for teachers and instructors. The standard course is three and one-half weeks long, and there are short courses (from 4 to 14 days). No special skills or training are required. The schools are:

Colorado Outward Bound School
945 Pennsylvania Avenue
Denver, Colorado 80203
(303) 837-0880

Dartmouth Outward Bound School
P.O. Box 50
Hanover, New Hampshire 03755
(603) 646-3359

Hurricane Island Outward Bound School
P.O. Box 429
Rockland, Maine 04841
(207) 594-5548

Minnesota Outward Bound School
1055 East Wayzata Boulevard
Wayzata, Minnesota 55391
(612) 473-5476

North Carolina Outward Bound School
P.O. Box 817
Morganton, North Carolina 28655
(704) 437-6112

Northwest Outward Bound School
0110 Bancroft Avenue, S.W.
Portland, Oregon 97201
(503) 243-1993

Southwest Outward Bound School
P.O. Box 2840
Santa Fe, New Mexico 87501
(505) 988-5573

Project Adventure
P.O. Box 157
Hamilton, Massachusetts 01936
Robert Levtz, Director
(617) 468-1766

Project Adventure has two major components: (1) a physical education program which incorporates initiative games, ropes course activities, and winter outdoor skills, and (2) adventure curriculum activities in swamp ecology and urban ecology, designed to develop confidence and problem-solving skills. The project also offers workshops in both physical education and adventure curriculum.

Project U.S.E.
Phillip M. Costello, Director
336 West Street
Long Branch, New Jersey 07740
(609) 877-6388

Project U.S.E. M.A.I.N.E.
Charles Reade, Director
RFD #1 Maple Ridge Road
Harrison, Maine 04040
(207) 583-2946

An adventure-based, action oriented approach to education which uses the natural and man-made environments of the Northern East Coast and New England as laboratories for self-discovery, U.S.E. conducts 1- to 30-day courses year-round for high school, junior high school, college groups and the general public. It has evolved into a consultative and direct service effort with the objective being: the development and extension of affective experiential learning environments through the use of environmental awareness and wilderness pursuit programs designed to promote personal growth and confidence, develop group skills and renewed meaning of "community" in participants, the identification of new personal inventory-skill-building techniques and the development and coordination of exploratory, "challenge" environmental awareness field trips which have relevancy for a variety of client categories.

Sea Education Association
Dick Hawkins
P.O. Box 6, Church Street
Woods Hole, Massachusetts 02543
(617) 540-3954

Sea Education Association is a nonprofit, tax-exempt education institution that teaches students about the oceans through a combination of classroom studies ashore and practical experience at sea aboard a large sailing ship engaged in oceanographic research. Activities include the following:

1. Marine science—oceanography, marine biology, data collection techniques, meterology, marine geology, etc.;
2. Nautical science—navigation, seamanship, marine engineering, etc.;
3. Marine affairs—man's relationship to the sea in law, politics, industry, exploration, etc.

A full semester of college credit is available through Boston University.

Wilderness Bound, Ltd.
R.D. 1, Box 365
Highland, New York 12528
Larry Arno, Director
(914) 691-2377

Groups of teenagers, 14-19, travel in passenger vans and camp out. Trips run a month or longer and include backpacking, canoeing, river running, mountaineering, and rock climbing. The varied itineraries include the backcountry of the National Parks and National Forests of the United States and Canada. Three guides accompany each group of 9-12 students, who select courses rated according to the challenge that they present. All courses are suited to the abilities of novices and advanced outdoors people.

Wilderness School
P.O. Box 2243
Goshen, Connecticut 06756
John S. Flood, Director

The Wilderness School is a unique learning experience consisting of an integrated program of an orientation, wilderness course, and followup. The students are between the ages of 15 and 21 and are referred from agencies within the state, such as youth service bureaus, boards of education, probation and parole boards, and community action programs. Activities include safety and first aid, whitewater canoeing, backpacking, rock climbing, map and compass skills, and environmental awareness.

Wolfcreek Wilderness
P.O. Box 596
Blainsville, Georgia 30512
Keith W. Evans, Director
(404) 745-6460

Wolfcreek Wilderness is a nonprofit educational organization open to both individuals and groups. The school conducts workshops in canoeing, caving, backpacking, and mountaineering.

appendix b

manufacturers of do-it-yourself kits for outdoor activities

Altra, Inc.
5441-Y Western Avenue
Boulder, Colorado

> Clothing, down and polyester sleeping bags, two-man tents, day packs, down and polyester booties, tote bags

Black Forest Enterprises
Box 1007
Nevada City, California

> Snowshoes

The Book Bin
16 Onyx
Larkspur, California 94939

> Canoes

Carikit Outdoor Equipment
P.O. Box 1153
Boulder, Colorado 80302

Country Ways
3500 Highway 101 South
Minnetonka, Minnesota 55343

> Polyester clothing, polyester sleeping bags, frame packs, frameless packs, day packs, stuff sacks, polyester booties, canoes, kayaks, cross-country skis and snowshoes

Eastern Mountain Sports, Inc.
1041 Commonwealth Avenue
Boston, Massachusetts 02215

> Clothing, polyester sleeping bags, tents, frame packs, frameless packs, polyester booties

Frostline Outdoor Equipment
P.O. Box 1378
Boulder, Colorado 80302

> Clothing, down and polyester sleeping bags, frame packs, frameless packs, day packs, stuff sacks, down and polyester booties, overboots, mittens, gaiters, dog pack and cycle packs

Holubar Mountaineering
P.O. Box 7
Boulder, Colorado 80302

Clothing, down sleeping bags, two-man tents, day packs, down booties, gaiters, mittens, dog pack and cycle packs

Klepper America
35 Union Square West
New York, New York 10003

Folding boats and kayaks

Mountain Adventure Kits, Co.
P.O. Box 571
Whittier, California 90608

Polyester clothing, polyester sleeping bags, two-man tents, stuff sacks, polyester booties, overboots and gaiters

appendix c

sources of information on outdoor activities

FEDERAL AGENCIES

Bureau of Outdoor Recreation
U.S. Department of the Interior
Washington, D.C. 20240

ERIC Document Reproduction Service
4936 Fairmont Avenue
Bethesda, Maryland 20014

Fish and Wildlife Service
U.S. Department of the Interior
Washington, D.C. 20240

Forest Service
U.S. Department of Agriculture
Washington, D.C. 20250

Geological Survey
U.S. Department of the Interior
Washington, D.C. 20240

National Park Service
U.S. Department of the Interior
Washington, D.C. 20240

Office of Education
U.S. Department of Health, Education and Welfare
Washington, D.C. 20202

Superintendent of Documents
U.S. Government Printing Office
Washington, D.C. 20402

NATIONAL ORGANIZATIONS

American Forest Institute
1835 K Street, NW
Washington, D.C. 20036

American Forestry Association
919 17th Street, NW
Washington, D.C. 20006

Conservation Foundation
Post Office Box 450
Madison, Wisconsin 53701

Conservation Foundation
1250 Connecticut Avenue, NW
Washington, D.C. 20036

Izaak Walton League of America
1326 Waukegan Road
Glenview, Illinois 60025

National Association of Conservation Districts
Davis Memorial Conservation Library
P.O. Box 776
League City, Texas 77573

National Audubon Society
1130 Fifth Avenue
New York, New York 10028

National Council of State Garden Clubs
4401 Magnolia Avenue
St. Louis, Missouri 63110

National Wildlife Federation
1412 16th Street, NW
Washington, D.C. 20036

Nature Conservancy
1800 North Kent Street
Suite 800
Arlington, Virginia 22209

Soil Conservation Society of America
7515 Northeast Ankeny Road
Ankeny, Iowa 50021

The Wilderness Society
729 15th Street, NW
Washington, D.C. 20005

appendix d

learning activities
with map and compass

TEACHER DEMONSTRATION NUMBER 1
LOST ACTIVITY

Introduction

In this demonstration, students will learn that:

1) A compass without a map is generally worthless, unless you know the precise direction in which you wish to travel, or, you just want to go in a straight line.

2) A map need not be a sophisticated affair; a simple sketch could prevent an individual from becoming lost.

3) Terrain features which are easily identified on a map may be difficult to find on the ground, because of the disparity between map scale and real object size.

Materials

1) Overhead projector and audio-visual marking pens.
2) Transparency (or projection facsimile) of "Lost National Forest" and "Saganaga Lake."
3) Liquid filled compass with *transparent* base (suitable for use on overhead projector).
4) Student copy (xerox) of Saganaga Lake.

Procedure

1) Turn on the overhead projector so a "square of empty light" strikes the screen. Ask students the following question: "You are hiking in this area (move hand around on the projector) and suddenly realized you are lost. Which way will you go to get home?"

Ultimately, after much discussion, students will realize that there is no way of knowing which way to go, because you don't have any idea of "what is where." In essence, you don't have a map.

Some students will suggest that you "travel north." Point out that, in Minnesota, at least, you could trudge all the way to the arctic circle without encountering civilization. *Develop the concept*

The teacher demonstration and activities 1 through 8 were written and produced by the Minnesota Department of Natural Resources, Bureau of Information and Education, St. Paul, Minnesota. Reprinted by permission of the director of the Bureau of Information and Education.

that the ability to locate and travel in a given direction is of value ONLY if some identifiable object lies in that direction.

2) Place the map of *Lost National Forest* on the projector.

3) Move a finger around on the map and close your eyes tightly so students can see you are not looking at the map. Tell students you are hiking in the forest and are not paying attention to where you are walking. Have the students tell you to stop someplace when it appears you are lost.

4) Open your eyes, and note your position on the map.

5) Show the students how, with the aid of a compass, you can return to the road and locate your car (head east to strike the road).

6) When the idea has been established that a map and compass are both important, develop the concept of *precise direction finding* by claiming that "Lost Lake has great fishing . . . but how do you find the lake?" Students should get the idea that to locate the lake, you must know *exactly* where you entered the national forest. And, you must head off in a *precise direction,*

8) Ask students to look at the *Saganaga Lake Map.* Inform them they are at a *point A.* Ask them how to get to *point B.* Next turn on the slide projector with the Saganaga Lake Slide. Develop the concept of vastness of reality by comparing *map scale* to ground (lake) scale.

ACTIVITY NUMBER 1
HOW TO HOLD THE COMPASS AND READ THE COMPASS DIAL

Time: 50 minutes

Materials

1) Orienteering style compasses—No more than two students per compass.

In This Activity Students Will Learn:

1) How to accurately read a compass dial.
2) How to properly hold a compass for finest accuracy.
3) How to determine the "bearing" or direction of an object on the horizon from a given starting point.

Directions

1) Sign out compasses to students.
2) Have students form a long line, arm's length apart, facing you.
3) Explain how to read the compass dial. Make sure students understand how to interpolate between graduation marks on the dial.

  a) Practice setting and reading the compass dial. You can check every third person in the line for accuracy and they can check the students on either side of them.
  —Stress Accurate Settings—
  b) Make sure students can precisely set and read the compass dial before preceeding to number four.

4) Explain how to hold the compass for accurate sighting using the information given below. "Call out a bearing" and have students set it on their compasses. Students should then turn in the proper direction and identify an object on the horizon which is on the given bearing. (Since students will *all* be facing in the same directional plane, you should quickly and easily be able to pick out individuals who are having difficulty).

—Spend the Remainder of the Hour Practicing This, or—
predetermine the bearings of a variety of features from different "stations" or orienting points. Place corresponding numbers on the floor and walls of a room in either paint or tape or in the dirt. "Post" a master list of the correct bearings in a convenient place so that students may check the accuracy of their readings. When you are convinced that students can accurately read and sight the compass, allow them time to practice on the known "bearing stations".

How to Hold a Compass

How to Hold an Orienteering Style Compass. Most people do not know how to hold a compass. For a compass without sights, correct holding will usually result in a high degree of accuracy.

Begin by cradling the compass in your right hand—right thumb pointing forward, away from your body. Place the compass along the direct center line of your body about half way between hips and neck. "Lock" your forearm tightly against your chest, so the compass is in a steady position next to your body so that you can merely "shift your eyes" up and down from the dial to your objective. Use your left hand to help support the instrument and to turn the dial. *It is important that you be able to shift your eyes from the needle to your objective without moving your head up and down.* Take three or more "eye shift" readings, taking care to stand perfectly still until your "average" destination has been determined. Good compasses can be read to within 1½ degrees of true bearings after practice.

How to Hold an Inexpensive Dial Compass. For those who already own a good quality dial compass, the following method of support will give accurate results. Frame the compass dial between the fingers (Figure A). Assume you wish to travel on a heading of 270 degrees.

Locate 270 between your two forefingers. Next, hold the compass tightly against your body, forearms pressed against the chest for support. Rotate your BODY (not the compass) until the north end of the magnetic needle points to North on the compass dial. You are now facing on a bearing of 270 degrees. Take three "eye shift" readings as previously explained to identify your objective.

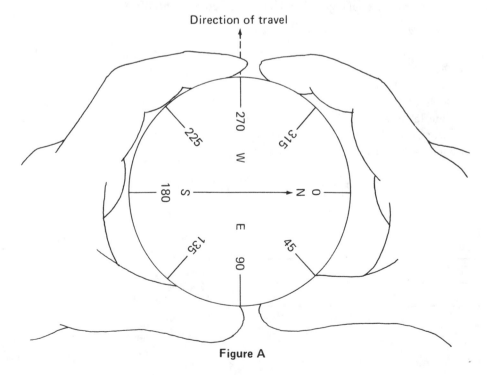

Figure A

ACTIVITY NUMBER 2

STUDENT EXERCISE #1—"PACING"
STUDENT EXERCISE #2—"RUNNING A SQUARE"
STUDENT EXERCISE #3—"LEFT LEG, RIGHT LEG"
STUDENT EXERCISE #4—"MAGNETIC INFLUENCE"

Time: 50 minutes

Materials

1) Orienteering style compasses—one per student.
2) One numbered "can lid stake" per compass.
3) One blindfold for every two students.
4) One 100-foot (or shorter) measuring tape.

Directions

1) Before beginning the activity, measure out a 100-foot distance. Place a can lid with "nail stake" or, sharpened wood stake at each end of the measured distance.
2) Provide one copy of *Student Activity Sheet Number 2* for each student.
3) Complete the activity in an outdoor setting (school yard or natural site).

In This Activity Students Will:

1) Lay out a square tract of land.
2) Determine the length of their stride or pace.
3) Learn that through the ages, people have lost their sense of direction because of non-use, and if unaided by instruments, will travel in a wide circle.
4) Learn how iron or steel objects "influence" the compass needle.

Exercise 1—"Pacing"

Directions: Count the number of steps it takes you to walk the 100 foot distance between the two stakes. Pace the distance *three times* and count every time your RIGHT foot strikes the ground. How many paces did it take you to travel 100 feet?

Be Sure to Emphasize to Students a *Natural Walk* Rather Than a Gait or Stride

Fill out the table below and compute the average length of your pace. Round off your average pace to the nearest one-half foot. In other words, four feet, four inches equals *4½ feet,* and four feet two inches equals *4 feet,* etc.

**Number of Paces
to go 100 feet**

First time	
Second time	
Third time	
Total	

$$\frac{\text{Total}}{3} =$$ Average number of
"paces" to go
100 feet

Average number of
"paces" to go
100 feet

= Length of average pace

100 feet

Exercise 2–"Running a square"

Directions: Find a spot in the area where there are no obstacles (fences, trees, etc.) for a distance of 50 feet in any direction. Put a "can lid stake" into the ground to mark your position.

Remember your stake number.

1) Determine the number of paces required in order to go 50 feet. (If your pace is five feet, then 50/5 = 10 paces, etc.)

How many of *your* paces are required to go 50 feet?_____

2) Set *any* bearing you wish on your compass.

3) Stand next to your can lid stake and travel 50 feet in the direction indicated by your compass. Be accurate.

4) At the end of 50 feet, STOP! Add 90 degrees to the reading on your compass and go 50 feet in the new direction.

5) Complete the "legs" of a square by adding 90 degrees to each compass reading after you have travelled 50 feet. (See diagram.)

6) If you have not made too great an error, you should return to your starting point.

How far were you from your starting point when you finished?_____

7) When you have successfully completed the square with 50 foot legs, complete another square with 100 foot legs.

How far were you from your starting point when you finished?

Exercise 3–"Left leg, right leg"

General Information: Most people, when lost, will travel in a circle, the radius of which is seldom over one-half mile. Thus, if you ever get lost, you will probably be within one-half mile of your starting point. Moreover, the direction of the circle (right or left) depends on the terrain and the

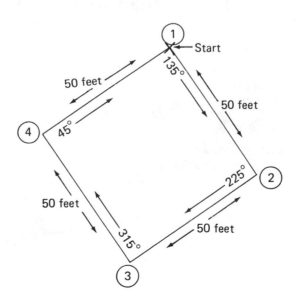

length of each leg. Did you know that nearly everyone has one leg which is very slightly longer than the other (no kidding)? On flat ground, a lost person would probably veer (turn) away from his longest leg. So, if you circle to the right on level ground, your left leg may be slightly longer than your right.

This exercise should prove conclusively that you can't travel in a straight line without using a compass.

Directions:

1) Work in pairs.

2) Find a tree or other obstacle and place your back against it. Sight towards an object on the horizon at least 100 yards away.

3) Face directly towards the object on the horizon you identified. Without disturbing the direction of your body, put on the blindfold and begin walking towards the object.

(Your partner should walk about five feet away and watch you to make sure you don't walk into any obstacles. Your partner should not influence your direction by talking to you or touching you. He or she should tell you to stop only if you are in danger of running into something.)

4) When you have walked about 100 yards, remove the blindfold and open your eyes. Sight back to your starting point.

Did you go in a straight line, or did you circle? _____ Do you think one leg is longer than the other?_____ Which one? _____

Exercise 4–"Magnetic influence"

Direction: Place your compass near a steel or iron object like a sign post or fire hydrant. How does the steel object affect the compass needle?

Place the compass near an aluminum pole. What happens? _____
Can you use a compass in an aluminum canoe? _____

ACTIVITY NUMBER 3
GOING FROM POINT TO POINT

Time: 30 minutes

Materials

1) Orienteering style compasses.
2) One copy of *activity sheet number 3* per student.

In this activity students will learn:

1) How to compute scale distance from a map.
2) How to determine the bearing of a line drawn on a map.

Directions

1) Give each student a copy of the activity sheet.
2) Explain how to convert meters into centimeters and millimeters.
3) Tell students that the bearings they compute should be accurate to within two degrees, and distances should be accurate to within one meter (m).

4) The map (Activity Sheet) should be aligned so that the North arrow coincides with magnetic North. Do this by setting the compass dial to magnetic North, move the compass so that the needle is framed by the arrow in base of dial. It now points to magnetic North. Align either of the long sides of the map sheet with the long edge of the compass base and tape it securely to a *nonmagnetic surface.* (Remember wood floors have nails, and some concrete floors have steel rods in them.) You are now ready to complete the activity.

STUDENTS SHOULD USE A SCALE OF: 1 cm ON THE MAP = 10 m ON THE GROUND
CORRECT BEARINGS AND DISTANCES

FROM POINT	TO POINT	BEARING	DISTANCE (cm)	DISTANCE (m)
A	B	57°	2.3	23.0
B	C	127°	3.2	32.0
C	D	123°	6.9	69.0
D	E	270°	7.6	76.0
E	F	169°	3.2	32.0
F	G	34°	9.1	91.0
G	H	315°	3.6	36.0
H	I	75°	2.6	26.0
I	J	196°	6.7	67.0

OPTIONAL STUDENT ACTIVITY 4
BUILDING A CHRISTMAS TREE

Time: 30 minutes

Materials

1) One orienteering style compass per student
2) Pencil
3) Graph paper

In This Activity:

Students will learn how to use their compass to convert a given bearing and distance to a map direction and scale distance. Using the information given, students will construct a diagram (see teacher KEY which follows) or simple "map". This exercise is the basis for actual map construction and should be required if you plan to do any mapping of ground features.

Directions

Give the following directions to your students—
1) Assume your piece of graph paper is a map. Where is north on the map? (Ans: at the top of the paper).
2) Place a "dot" in the center of the *southeast quadrant* of your map. This dot is the start of your map.
3) Using the bearings and distances on the "board", construct the map diagram.
4) When you have completed the diagram let them show it to you so you can check it for accuracy.

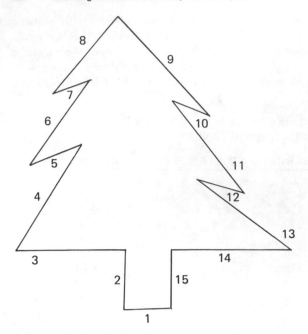

BEARING	DISTANCE (cm)
269	2.2
2	2.7
266	4.9
30	6.5
246	2.6
34	5.0
244	2.0
37	4.6
136	6.3
293	1.9
141	5.2
284	2.4
125	5.2
271	5.1
179	2.7

ACTIVITY NUMBER 5

SAGANAGA LAKE CANOE TRIP

Time: 100 minutes

Materials

1) Orienteering compass and pencil
2) Saganaga Lake map
3) Notebook paper
4) Slide projector and Saganaga Lake slide (teacher)
5) Transparent projector and Saganaga Lake transparency

In This Activity:

Students will learn how to compute a course across a large body of water and accurately locate topographic features. In addition, they will become familiar with some of the basic requirements for the use of Minnesota's most popular wilderness—the Boundary Waters Canoe Area.

Directions

1) Refer students to the Saganaga Lake map. Tell them they are located on the campsite (the little "c") just to the southwest of "Honeymoon" island in the central portion of the map (point "A"). Ask them how to get to point "B". By now, students should have sufficient background to be able to compute the bearing and distance from "A" to "B". While they are "computing", turn on the projector with the Saganaga slide as you did in Teacher demonstration number one. The "notch" just right of center *is* point "B". Ask students if they think they could have located this point without their compass. Allow time for development of this "map-ground" relationship.

2) Using the scale given on the map, students should compute the distance in miles from point "A" to point "B".

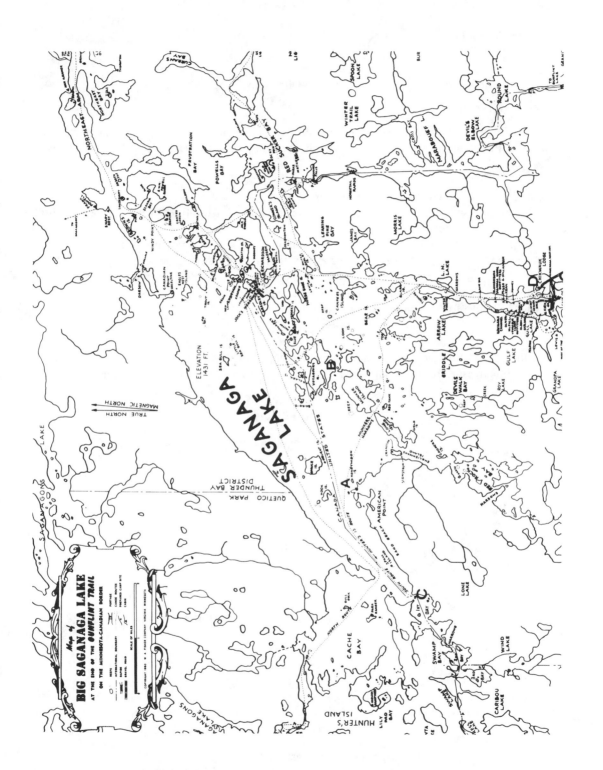

Map of
BIG SAGANAGA LAKE
AT THE END OF THE *GUNFLINT TRAIL*
ON THE MINNESOTA-CANADIAN BORDER

ACTIVITY NUMBER 6
TREASURE HUNT

Time: 40 minutes

Materials

Orienteering compass and "Buried Treasure Directions."

In This Activity:

Students will attempt to locate the "buried treasure," using the directions from an "Old Pirate Map." To stimulate interest in the activity, give away a giant chocolate bar or Coke to the winner.

Directions

1) Give each student the "Old Pirate Map."
2) Students should put a tin can stake in the ground, at least 100 feet from the nearest obstacle. This is their starting point.
3) Students attempt to locate the "buried treasure" using the "pirate map" directions.
4) When students reach the spot where they think the treasure is buried, they should "shoot a bearing" back to their starting point as they did in activity 2A (the mini-traverse).
5) The "closing" bearing and distance should be given to you.
6) The student who is most accurate wins.

Note

This activity must be done outdoors or in a gymnasium. The more alert students will realize they can find the treasure on paper alone. This should be considered cheating and students who do this

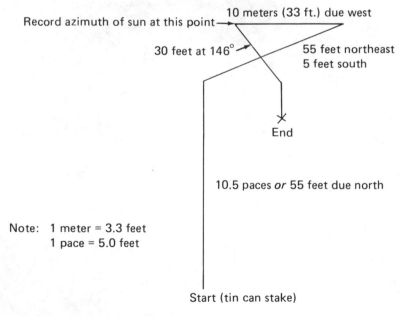

Teacher's Key

Record azimuth of sun at this point → 10 meters (33 ft.) due west

30 feet at 146° ↘

55 feet northeast
5 feet south

✗
End

10.5 paces *or* 55 feet due north

Note: 1 meter = 3.3 feet
        1 pace = 5.0 feet

Start (tin can stake)

Bearing from end to start = 213°
Distance from end to start = 58 ft. or 17.7 meters

should be disqualified. In case of a tie, the participant who finds the treasure in the shortest period of time will be the winner, or the most accurate reading of the Sun's azimuth can be used to settle ties.

Suggestions before the Treasure Hunt:

1) Show students how to convert feet to meters and meters to feet.
2) The sun will be at the following azimuths at these times:

12:00 am—360°	4:30 am—68°	9:00 am—135°	1:30 pm—203°
1:30 am—23°	6:00 am—90°	10:30 am—158°	3:00 pm—225°
3 am—45°	7:30 am—118°	12 noon—180°	4:30 pm—248°

ACTIVITY NUMBER 7
ORIENTEERING RACE

Time: 30 minutes

Materials

1) One orienteering compass per student or team.
2) One set of bearing cards per student or team.
3) Eight numbered tin can stakes.

In This Activity:

Students will put to practical use what they have learned by participating in a scaled down orienteering race. Competition may be keen, especially if a prize is awarded to the winner. The "race" may be run individually, in pairs, or as a team of four.

Directions

1) Lay out the traverse given on back side and mark each leg with a numbered tin can stake. Distances given may be shortened or lengthened as the site requires. However all distances must be shortened *proportionately* so the bearings remain the same. Bearings and distances are labelled on the traverse.

2) Reproduce the *Bearing Map* and make as many copies as you have students. Cut out each *Bearing Map* card and have students glue them onto a cardboard backing. Provide each individual or team with a *complete set* of the eight *Bearing Map* cards.

3) When teams or individuals are ready to begin, start each team at a different point on the traverse. For example:

Team one—Start on *M* (stake #1). Write this information in your notebook. Go from M to N to O to P. Stop at P. Read the number on the stake at point P and record it in your notebook. Tell me that number immediately. If you have finished on the correct stake and you have the fastest time, you will be the winner."

Team two—Start on stake *N* (stake #2). Write this information in your notebook. Go from N to O to P to Q. Stop at Q. Read the number on the stake at point Q and record it in your notebook. Tell me that number immediately. If you have finished on the correct stake and you have the fastest time, you will be the winner.

Team three—Start on Stake *O* or stake #3. Write this information . . .

4) When teams return you need only look on your Bearing Map to see if they ended where they were supposed to. You can require each team to write down the bearing, distance, and number of each stake. You can then check for errors. However, since this is a competitive event, this should not

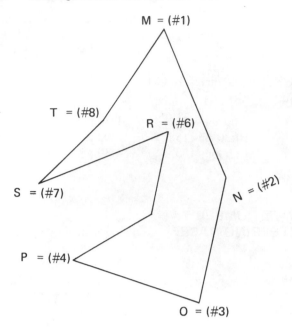

STAKE	BEARING	DISTANCE (feet)
M → N	159°	88
N → O	191°	72
O → P	290°	74
P → Q	61°	51
Q → R	14°	47
R → S	247°	85
S → T	47°	54
T → M	34°	62

be necessary. By now, students should know how to effectively use a map and compass, and any error will cost them the "prize."

5) Students will use their Bearing Map Cards to go from one stake to another, i.e., team one would use card M first, N second, O third and P fourth. From the traverse you can see that point P is stake #4, and this is where team one should end.

NOTE: Since each group starts and ends on a different stake, it is impossible to cheat. You can make out a different bearing map each year, or you can merely change the numbers of the can lid stakes each hour. About five stations are the limit for an orienteering race in a 30 minute period.

OPTIONAL STUDENT ACTIVITY NUMBER 8
TOPOGRAPHIC MAP

Introduction

The two most commonly used maps are Canoe Maps (for use in the BWCA) and Topographic Maps. Recently, many Minnesotans have discovered the advantages of topographic maps in the pursuit of their favorite outdoor activities. Reliable maps showing relief features, woods, clearings and water courses are of great value to persons interested in such life-time sports as backpacking, hiking, cross country skiing, hunting, fishing, and orienteering.

The United States Geological Survey was established in 1870 to perform the tasks of making accurate topographic and geologic maps and collection of information regarding public land use. For a better understanding of topographic maps let us turn to the U.S.G.S. for a definition: "A topographic map is a graphic representation of selected man-made and natural features of a part of the earth's surface plotted to a definite scale: The distinguishing characteristic of a topographic map is the portrayal of the shape and elevation of the terrain."

Definitions

1) *Map Scale:* expresses the size relationships between the features shown on the map, and the same features on the earth's surface. We should be familiar with three scales expressed in fractions or ratios. They are—1/24,000 or 1:24,000; 1/62,500 or 1:62,500; and 1/250,000 or 1:250,000. The numerator, usually 1, represents map distance; the denominator, a large number, represents ground distance. Thus the scale 1:24,000 states that any unit such as one inch or 1 foot on the map represents 24,000 of the same units on the ground.

Large-Scale	Medium-Scale	Small-Scale
1:24,000 scale	1:62,500 scale	1:250,000 scale
1 inch = 2000 feet	1 inch = nearly 1 mile	1 inch = nearly 4 miles

To select a map of proper scale for a particular use, remember that large-scale maps show *more detail* and small-scale maps show *less detail.*

2) *Map Symbols:* are the graphic language of maps including their shape, size, location, and color; all have special significance. Symbols for water features are printed in blue; man-made objects including roads, railroads, buildings, transmission lines, and many others are shown in black; and wooded areas are in green. Land surface—the distinguishing characteristics of topographic maps are printed in brown. We should pay special attention to:

a) *Intermediate contours*—these brown lines on topographic maps connect points of the same elevation.

b) *Index contours*—(every fifth brown line)—they are *heavy brown lines,* which have their specific elevation written on them.

c) *Depression contours*—are generally closed contours that indicate a depression in the ground i.e. lake or a basin (drained or un-drained).

When locating specific places on a topographic map, divide each Section (the numbered squares) into quarters, and if necessary, quarter each quarter as well, so that, we would say:

"A building" is located in the N.E. ¼ of the S.W. ¼ of Section 7, Township 35N, Range 16W.

COMPASS ROSE GAME

Materials. Pole or staff—5 feet long. 16 players.

Lay-out of course. Game may be played in classroom, gymnasium, or outside. The larger the circle, the more difficult the game becomes.

Playing game. Sixteen players form a circle. One person is chosen to give up his direction position in the circle. In the diagram you will note that position 14 is vacated. This is direction WNW. This person will hold the pole and start the game.

The game is started by WNW going into the middle. Note the remaining players each have a direction. They represent the balance of the cardinal and intercardinal compass points. (If the group is not too familiar with the 16 points, the instructor should name each person.)

Action. The center player calls out a direction and drops the pole. The point called must run to the center and grab the pole before it hits the floor. If the player fails to grab the pole, he then must stay in the circle—game continues.

Variation. Game is played with a compass rose game board. The game board is made of cardboard and the dimensions are 24″ × 24″. The game is played by two people challenging each other. One person has direction cards, the other person has degree bearing cards. On the signal "start," the direction cards try to beat the degree bearing cards. The competition involves placing the cards in the correct box located on the compass rose game board.

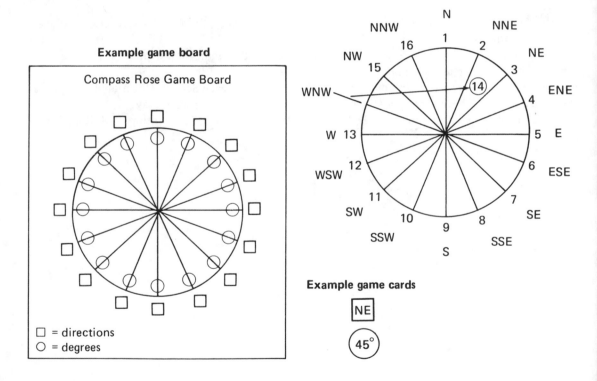

Example game board

Compass Rose Game Board

□ = directions
○ = degrees

Example game cards

NE

45°

The activities described on pages 292-303 are from John W. Horstman, "Map and Compass Games," presented at the National Conference of Outdoor Education, Duluth and Isabella, Minnesota, March 1976. Reprinted by permission of the author.

In the boxes,
write directions

Who will finish first?

In the circles,
write bearings

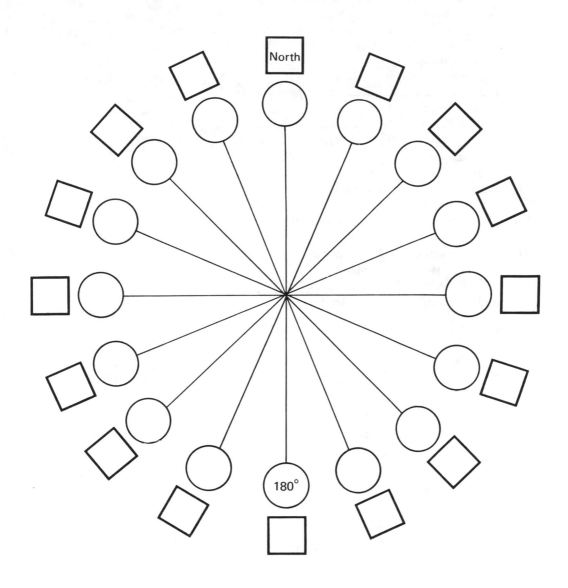

DIRECTIONS

The dotted line on the map shows how you drove from your home to Boy Scout camp. The questions that follow are about the map. Circle the best answer on this sheet.

1. When you started your trip, what direction did you go first?
   North   South   East   West
2. If you had walked west of Minneapolis, what would you have come to?
   Great Sand Desert   Ocean Lookout   Pacific Ocean
3. When you got to Highway 66, what town did you pass first?
   Mapleville   Winona   H&H Gas
4. The mission is _____ of the Pacific Ocean.
   North   South   East   West
5. The Santa Fe Railroad runs _____ and _____ .
   North   South   East   West
6. The Scout camp is _____ of H&H Gas.
   North   South   East   West
7. The oasis is _____ of Highway 6.
   North   South   East   West
8. From the ocean lookout, what direction is the Bear Tooth Mountain Range?
   North   South   East   West
9. The first town west of the Scout camp is:
   Winona   H&H Gas   Mapleville
10. In the winter the birds fly _____ .
   North   South   East   West

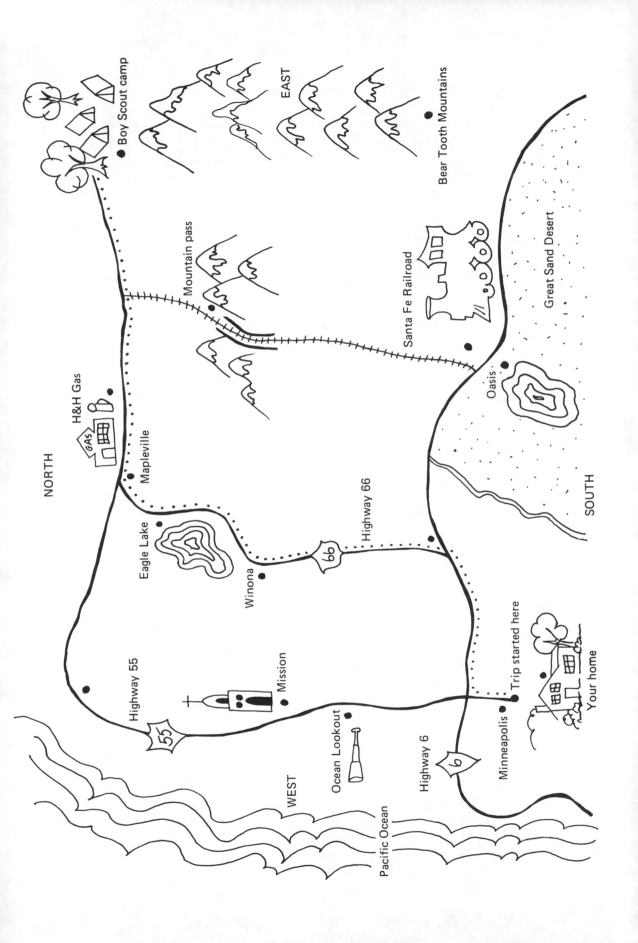

DOT-TO-DOT HIKE

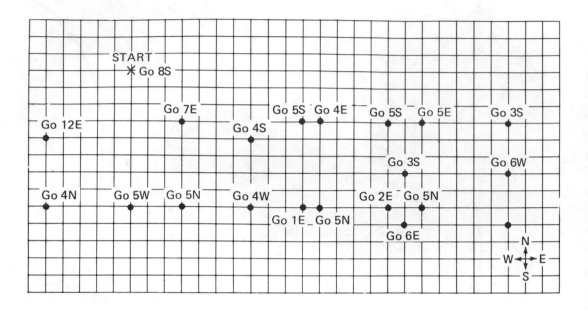

DIRECTION WALK

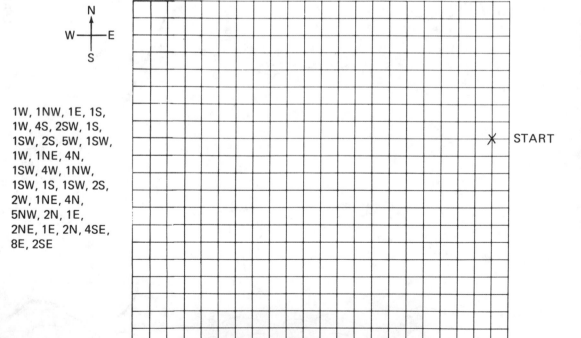

1W, 1NW, 1E, 1S,
1W, 4S, 2SW, 1S,
1SW, 2S, 5W, 1SW,
1W, 1NE, 4N,
1SW, 4W, 1NW,
1SW, 1S, 1SW, 2S,
2W, 1NE, 4N,
5NW, 2N, 1E,
2NE, 1E, 2N, 4SE,
8E, 2SE

BLUEPRINT

Here is a blueprint of a house. The address of the house is 9247 Zinnia North. You can tell a lot about the house from the blueprint. Write the answers to each question below.

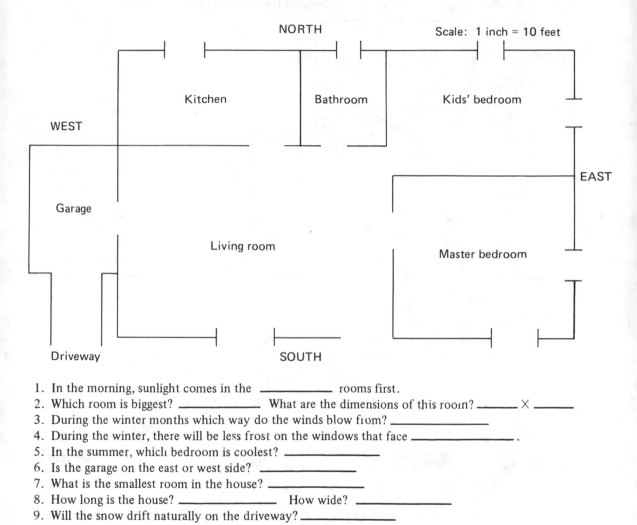

1. In the morning, sunlight comes in the _____ rooms first.
2. Which room is biggest? _____ What are the dimensions of this room? _____ X _____
3. During the winter months which way do the winds blow from? _____
4. During the winter, there will be less frost on the windows that face _____ .
5. In the summer, which bedroom is coolest? _____
6. Is the garage on the east or west side? _____
7. What is the smallest room in the house? _____
8. How long is the house? _____ How wide? _____
9. Will the snow drift naturally on the driveway? _____

NUMBERS AND NUMERALS

Equipment. Silva compass, scorecard, numbers 1-10, roman numerals I-X, pencils

Layout. Tape the numbers 1-10 around the floor so they are equally distributed. Tape the roman numerals at random around the walls.

Playing game. The game is timed with a stop watch. A player may start at any number on the floor. . . . If a player starts at number 5, he will then shoot a bearing toward roman numeral five. After this is completed he moves to the next and continues until all the numbers have been completed.

Scoring. Before the activity begins, the instructor shoots the correct bearing to each number-numeral. A player receives 10 points for each correct bearing. In case of ties, the fastest time determines the winner.

Outcomes. The game teaches how to properly hold a compass and shoot a bearing from one object to another. Care should be taken to understand the overriding concept involved.

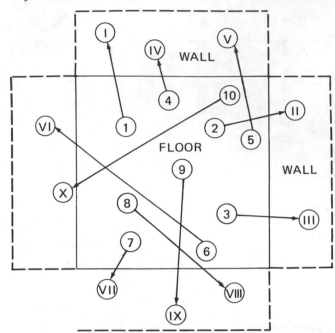

Scorecard

NUMBER	BEARING
1—I	_____
2—II	_____
3—III	_____
4—IV	_____
5—V	_____
6—VI	_____
7—VII	_____
8—VIII	_____
9—IX	_____
10—X	_____

STEP COUNTING

Pace (even terrain)

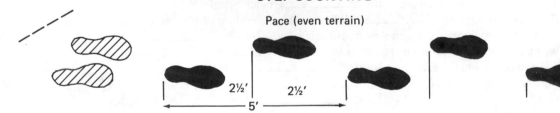

Materials. To work on step counting you should be outside. You should have several diverse areas so that one might be done on flat terrain and another in a wooded terrain. You will need a 100 foot tape measure, markers, and paper and pencil.

Working on the Activity. What is a pace? _____

Find the average number of paces in 100 feet. Repeat this exercise 3 times.

Trial 1   _____
Trial 2   _____
Trial 3   _____

TOTAL _____

Divide this total by three to find the average pace in 100 feet. To find the length of each pace divide your average into 100 feet.

Number of Paces in 100 Feet		
	Flat Ground	**Wooded**
Walking		
Trial 1	_____	_____
Trial 2	_____	_____
Trial 3	_____	_____
Average	_____	_____
Running		
Trial 1	_____	_____
Trial 2	_____	_____
Trial 3	_____	_____
Average	_____	_____

Number of Paces in Other Distances		
	Flat Ground	**Wooded**
Walking	_____	_____
100 yards	_____	_____
200 yards	_____	_____
440 yards	_____	_____
1000 feet	_____	_____
Running		
100 yards	_____	_____
200 yards	_____	_____
440 yards	_____	_____
1000 feet	_____	_____

ORIENTEERING MERIDIAN MAP AND COMPASS FUN

Materials. Silva compasses, pencils

Methods. Using the Silva compass, determine the bearings from the center circle dot to each of the letters *radiating* from the center dot. The meridian lines to determine the bearing are represented by lines similar to those found inside the compass. Note: North is indicated by the arrow within the circle.

Hints. Use the side of your compass for drawing lines from center dot to each individual letter. Make sure that the direction of travel arrow is pointing from the center dot toward the letter. Make sure that the orienteering arrow is pointed toward meridian north, which is represented in the drawing in a similar way to the orienteering arrow within the compass.

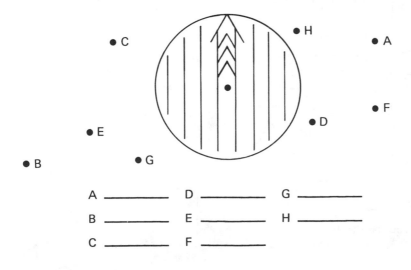

A _____   D _____   G _____

B _____   E _____   H _____

C _____   F _____

SEA ADVENTURE

Can you imagine the adventure of sailing away from home on a raft? The map of your trip is shown here. You will have to compute the bearings using your Silva compass.

_____   You start your trip from your home. On the first week of your voyage you spot the
Bearing 1   ocean liner USS Meadow Lake. What is the bearing from your home to USS Meadow Lake?

_____   The second week you are caught in a windstorm. Your second bearing is from USS
Bearing 2   Meadow Lake to the windstorm.

_____   The third week you encounter several sharks. Your third bearing is from windstorm to
Bearing 3   sharks.

_____   The fourth week you enter a soft sea breeze area. Your next bearing is from sharks to
Bearing 4   soft sea breeze area.

_____   The fifth week you spot a huge blue whale. Your next bearing is from soft sea breeze area
Bearing 5   to whale.

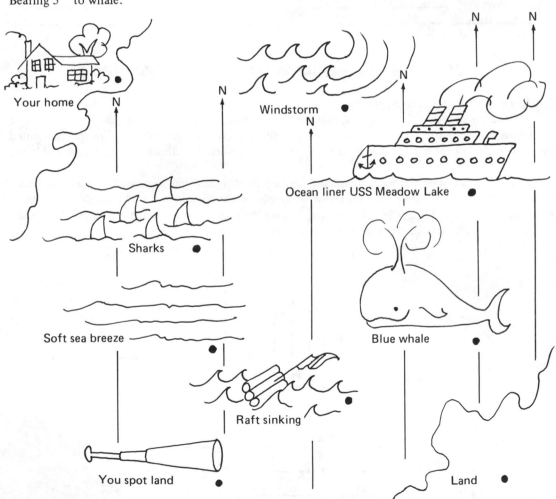

———————— The sixth week finds your raft sinking. Your next bearing is from whale to sinking raft.
Bearing 6

———————— The seventh week you spot land. Your bearing is from raft to where you spot land.
Bearing 7

———————— The eighth week your raft touches land. Your bearing is from where you spot to land.
Bearing 8

THREE-LEGGED COMPASS GAME

Equipment. Compass, three-legged compass cards, starting marker (fake silver dollars)

Layout. Any outdoor area. The game may be played in wooded or semi-wooded area. If the game is played indoors, the distances on the card should be carefully established depending on the size of the indoor room.

Playing Game. You will be given a card that will have a bearing and a distance written on it. On each card there will be three bearings and three distances. If the correct bearings and distances are walked, each contestant should start and finish at the same starting location. To establish the starting location, a fake silver dollar is placed at the location you will start from. If you finish correctly, you should arrive back at the silver dollar after the third compass bearing is shot.

Playing Game without Compass Cards

a. Set the compass at any degree under 120. Let's say that you choose 40 degrees. On each of the three legs you must walk the same distances. In the above case, let's walk 50 feet.

b. For the second leg, we always add 120 degrees to the degree chosen at the start. This would mean 40 + 120 = 160 degrees for the second leg. Again we walk 50 feet.

c. When we arrive at our second leg, we again add 120 degrees to the previous setting which in this case would give us 160 + 120 = 280 degrees. Again we walk 50 feet. This should take us back to the original spot.

d. Note: One can use any degree setting, just remember that any time in your adding that if you go beyond 360 degrees, you must subtract 360 degrees from this.

Example: 1. 225 degrees—50 feet

           2. 340 degrees—50 feet

           3. 465 degrees
              <u>-360</u>
             105 degrees—50 feet

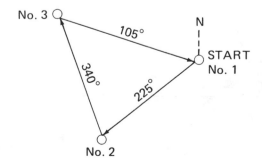

RELAY ORIENTEERING

Materials. 1 compass for each relay team, 1 master map, several control markers, scorecards and maps for each relay team.

Background. This type of orienteering is the most popular type of team competition. All of the rules of cross-country orienteering apply with one addition: Each competitor runs only one loop.

Course Layout. The relay course can be laid out over any area that has suitable maps for any other type of orienteering.

Playing Game. Each team is composed of three or four team members. The number of each team must be the same. The game starts from a centralized location. At the start, the Number 1 person from each team runs toward the master control map. When arriving, they write down the control points on the loop of the relay they are to run. Team 1 might start at Loop A—Team 2 at Loop B—Team 3 at Loop C . . . Immediately after computing the proper distances and bearings, they go out and collect the proper control markers in their loop. When they are finished, they return to the starting location and give the baton (scorecard and map) to the Number 2 member of their team. Number 2 might be assigned Loop B or whatever it has been planned beforehand. The game continues until everyone finishes.

Scoring. The scoring is based on collecting the correct control markers and time for the entire event. If the correct controls are not collected in the numerical manner, the team is disqualified.

Example relay master map

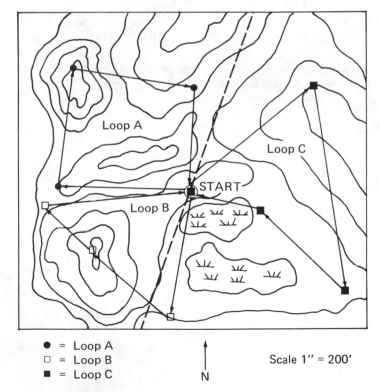

● = Loop A
□ = Loop B
■ = Loop C

N

Scale 1″ = 200′

Sample scorecard

Relay Orienteering Team _____

Runner	Loop	Controls
1 _____		□ □ □ □
2 _____		□ □ □ □
3 _____		□ □ □ □
4 _____		□ □ □ □

Start time _____
Finish time _____
Place _____

DESTINATION UNKNOWN

Material. 4 compasses, 1 control marker
Layout. Outside area, 1,000' × 1,000'

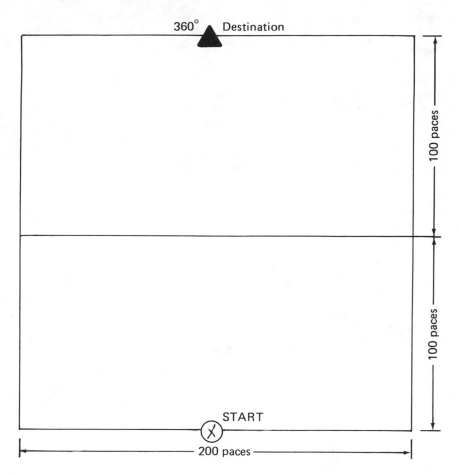

Team Bearings.

Team I		Team III	
90°–100 paces		45°–71 paces	
360°–100 paces		315°–71 paces	
270°–100 paces		45°–71 paces	
360°–100 paces		315°–71 paces	

Team II		Team IV	
360°–100 paces		315°–71 paces	
90°–100 paces		45°–71 paces	
360°–100 paces		315°–71 paces	
270°–100 paces		45°–71 paces	

Playing Game. Class is divided into 4 hiking groups. Each group follows a different compass route. If they follow correct bearing, they should end up at the same destination. Assign one member of group as the nature scribe. Many variations of game can be created. Game is truly project-oriented.

index